THE OFFICE OF LORD CHANCELLOR

The Office of Lord Chancellor

DIANA WOODHOUSE

Oxford Brookes University

·HART·
PUBLISHING

OXFORD – PORTLAND OREGON
2001

Hart Publishing
Oxford and Portland, Oregon

Published in North America (US and Canada) by
Hart Publishing c/o
International Specialized Book Services
5804 NE Hassalo Street
Portland, Oregon
97213-3644
USA

Distributed in the Netherlands, Belgium and Luxembourg by
Intersentia, Churchillaan 108
B2900 Schoten
Antwerpen
Belgium

Hart Publishing is a specialist legal publisher based in Oxford, England.
To order further copies of this book or to request a list of other
publications please write to:

Hart Publishing, Salter's Boatyard, Folly Bridge,
Abingdon Road, Oxford OX1 4LB
Telephone: +44 (0)1865 245533 or Fax: +44 (0)1865 794882
e-mail: mail@hartpub.co.uk
WEBSITE: http//www.hartpub.co.uk

British Library Cataloguing in Publication Data
Data Available
ISBN 1–84113–021–1 (cloth)

Typeset by Hope Services (Abingdon) Ltd.
Printed and bound in Great Britain on acid-free paper by
Biddles Ltd, www.biddles.co.uk

Preface

THE RESEARCH into the office of Lord Chancellor began in October 1997 with a grant from the ESRC for a project, "The Responsibilities and Accountability of the Lord Chancellor in a Market Economy". The application to the ESRC had been made early in 1997, while Lord Mackay was in office, and had been triggered by developments during his Lord Chancellorship. These included his assumption of responsibility for the magistrates' courts and his acceptance of the need for greater accountability. For the first time, the Lord Chancellor was represented in the Commons by a junior minister, he and his officials appeared before the Home Affairs Select Committee to answer for the work of his Department and the Parliamentary Commissioner for Administration was given jurisdiction over court officials. Such developments were notable in their own right. However, they did not produce the headlines which resulted from Lord Mackay's attempts to curb public spending and improve efficiency. Measures, such as the establishment of the Court Service Agency and the reform of the civil courts and legal aid, together with proposals for the reform of the legal profession, resulted in an unusually public tension between the Lord Chancellor and senior members of the judiciary and brought into question his position as both a Cabinet minister, intent on giving effect to government policies, and head of the judiciary, with responsibility for protecting judicial independence.

This was the background against which the research project was planned. However, before it had started Lord Irvine succeeded to the office of Lord Chancellor and the project had to adapt and expand to take account of a range of new issues. Under Lord Irvine the position of the Lord Chancellor, as Cabinet minister and head of the judiciary, has become even more questionable, as his role in policy making has extended beyond the administration of justice to include the Government's constitutional reforms. In addition, his location at the heart of government has resulted in his role as judge being challenged. Moreover, this challenge may be sustainable, given the incorporation of the European Convention on Human Rights through the Human Rights Act 1998 and a decision of the European Court of Human Rights in 2000. The Lord Chancellor's responsibility for judicial appointments is also under attack, many considering that a government minister should have no part in appointing judges, who with the Human Rights Act and devolution legislation, are assuming a constitutional role, and his role as Speaker, while supported by the Wakeham Commission's report on the reform of the House of Lords, may be less certain if, as Wakeham recommends, the House becomes, in part, elected.

As the research progressed, it became evident that questions have to be asked about the sustainability of the office of Lord Chancellor in the twenty-first century. This book deals with these questions. It analyses the development and current position of the Lord Chancellor as head of the judiciary, member of the Cabinet, judge and Speaker and considers his role in relation to judicial appointments. It also looks at the LCD, the development of which acts as an indicator of the change in the office of Lord Chancellor. It ends by making proposals for reform, the most far-reaching of which is the abolition of the office.

I would like to thank the ESRC for its funding and colleagues at Oxford Brookes and elsewhere, who by their questioning of seminar papers and drafts of chapters helped me to formulate my ideas. I am also grateful to those who gave me information and their views on particular issues. In addition, I owe thanks to James Naylor, who spent many hours trawling through parliamentary reports, to the librarians at Oxford Brookes and the Bodleian, and, particularly, to Richard Hart of Hart Publishing, who was so supportive of this venture.

As ever, I alone am responsible for the contents of what follows.

Diana Woodhouse
Oxford Brookes University
October 2000

Contents

1

Introduction

THE OFFICE OF Lord Chancellor is one that has frequently been questioned. Sometimes the questions posed have concerned the constitutional integrity of the role. At other times they have related to the personality and effectiveness of a particular Lord Chancellor, "Lord Chancellors and controversy hav[ing] long been close allies".[1] However, the extent and diversity of the questioning seldom attained the proportions reached in the latter part of the twentieth century, when they drew attention to the deficiencies of the position of Lord Chancellor, the inherent tensions within that position, and the incongruity of such a role in a modern democracy.

AN HISTORICAL OFFICE

R. F. V. Heuston begins his renowned work, *Lives of the Lord Chancellors*, by stating; "The Lord High Chancellor of Great Britain, to give him his full official title, occupies a position of great antiquity, much dignity and considerable importance".[2] The antiquity is evident in the distant, misty origins of the office and its dignity in the ceremony and costume attached to it. Its past importance is reflected in the Lord Chancellor's possession of two maces, symbols of royal authority, his place in the order of precedence, after the Royal Family only the Archbishop of Canterbury ranks higher than the Lord Chancellor, and the fact that the assassination of a Lord Chancellor remains an act of high treason. Its current importance lies in the range of responsibilities that it has acquired over the centuries, which the Lord Chancellor still exercises today.

The office of Lord Chancellor has been in existence nearly as long as the monarchy and longer than Parliament. It has its origins in the *cancellarius,* or official, who sat at the *cancelli* or lattice screens, which separated the court from the public, and who, at some stage, progressed to being the notary or secretary of the court.[3] The specific date at which the office of Chancellor first came into being is uncertain. John Campbell, himself Lord Chancellor for a short time in the mid-nineteenth century, claimed the position was established in the seventh century and he named St Swithin as an early holder of the office,[4] while the Lord

---

[1] M. Berlins, *A Man for All Roles,* BBC Radio 4, 9 April 1998.
[2] R.F.V. Heuston, *Lives of the Lord Chancellors 1885–1940* (Oxford, Clarendon Press,1964).
[3] Lord Elwyn-Jones, *In My Time; an Autobiography* (London, Futura, 1988) p. 264.
[4] John Campbell, *Lives of the Lord Chancellors* (5th edn., 1868).

Chancellor's Department lists the first holder of the office as Angmendus in 605 AD,[5] a date also identified by Lord Mackay as being that from which the position originated.[6] On this basis he claimed that he was the two hundred and tenth incumbent.[7]

Most constitutional historians seem to prefer the eleventh century as an official starting point. Underhill, although identifying Cnut (1016–35) as the first king likely to have had a chancellor, cites the first documentary evidence of an official with that title as dating from 1068,[8] while Anson dates the office to the reign of Edward the Confessor (1042–66).[9] The specific year in which the office was created is not particularly important. What is important, because it laid the foundations for some of his current day responsibilities, are the roles that the first chancellors assumed. The early chancellors were all clerics, with education, and hence reading and writing, being the preserve of the Church. They therefore assumed the position of senior royal chaplain, as well as supervising the scriveners and administering the royal revenues from vacant benefices. However, it was the Chancellor's administrative position as custodian of the king's seal which gave him his first "departmental" responsibility, namely responsibility for the "king's writing office".[10] The combination of functions which fell to the Chancellor made him an official of considerable importance; "As Secretary he enjoyed the King's confidence in secular matters; as Chaplain he advised the King in matters of conscience; as Keeper of the Seal he was necessary to all outward and formal expressions of the royal will".[11]

The Chancellor's administrative role, which put him at the centre of legal and political events, continued to develop such that by the beginning of the thirteenth century the Chancellor was "the head of a clerical establishment, the royal chancery".[12] The "possession of the royal seal", the use of which was required for the authorisation of writs and thus for much of government business, made his office of "first importance"[13] and, together with the demise in 1268 of the office of chief justiciar as head of the court of justice, it resulted in the Chancellor becoming the dominant minister in council and thus the king's first minister. Even the establishment of the position of Keeper of the Privy Seal,

---

[5] LCD Website: www.open.gov.uk/lcd/lc-confr.htm.

[6] "The Lord Chancellor in the 1990s" (1991) 44 *Current Legal Problems*, 241–59 at 241.

[7] Lord Irvine claimed he was the 258th. This difference is explained by the fact that Lord Mackay's figure was based on the number of individuals who have held the position, while Lord Irvine's relates to the number of times the chancellorship has changed hands, even when it reverted to a previous incumbent.

[8] N. Underhill, *The Lord Chancellor* (Lavenham, Suffolk, Terence Dalton, 1978) p. 1.

[9] Sir William Anson, *The Law and Custom of the Constitution*, Vol. II, Part 1 (4th edn., Oxford, Clarendon Press, 1935) pp. 164–70; F. W. Maitland, *The Constitutional History of England* (Cambridge, Cambridge University Press, 1965) and R. C. Mitchell, *Chronicle of English Judges, Chancellors, Attorneys General and Solicitors General* (Oswego, N. Y., W. P. Mitchell, 1937) also see the position as dating from the 11th century.

[10] N. Underhill, *The Lord Chancellor*, p. 1.

[11] Sir William Anson, *The Law and Custom of the Constitution*, pp. 164–5.

[12] F. W. Maitland, *The Constitutional History of England*, p. 69.

[13] Ibid, p. 202.

during the reign of Henry III (1216–72), did not lessen the importance of the Chancellor, despite the fact that, in matters directly affecting the king, the Privy Seal was used to give "directions to the chancellor as to the use of the great seal".[14] This "doctrine of the seals", which required each seal to be kept by a minister of the king, laid the foundation for the convention of ministerial responsibility, in that the assignation of seals in this way, meant that "for every exercise of the royal power some minister [was] answerable".[15] Thus, the origins of a convention upon which modern departmental government is based, can be traced back to the primary responsibility of the first chancellors.

The executive power of the Chancellor, which arose "almost magically" out of the "mystical significance" of the Great Seal during medieval times, continued to increase through the Tudor period, until Cardinal Wolsey was second only to the king.[16] In fact, this power was evident before Wolsey's chancellorship, with Thomas Langley (1405–7, 1417–24) running the country during the period that Henry Vth was campaigning in France and Cardinal Beaufort (1403–5; 1413–17; 1424–6) being recognised as the most powerful man in the country in the early years of Henry VIth's reign. The importance of the seal was such that a later Lord Chancellor, Lord Eldon (1800–27), was said to have slept with it under his pillow. Responsibility for its custody still lies with the Lord Chancellor and "in accordance with the Sovereign's commands he causes the Sovereign's Letters to be made Patent under the Great Seal for the creation of Peers, the appointment of Bishops, for colonial and other charters (e.g. those of new towns) and for many other purposes".[17] Moreover, because of this responsibility, the Lord Chancellor can only leave the country with the permission of the sovereign, who appoints commissioners for its custody in his absence.

The growth in the Chancellor's administrative or executive role was accompanied by a developing judicial role. By the mid-fourteenth century the Chancellor had become "an important judicial officer",[18] an inevitable development given that writs played such a central part in legal, as well as administrative, proceedings. His judicial work was conducted not only in Chancery, which was by this time an established court of law, but also in council, from whence the Court of Star Chamber eventually emerged. The Chancellor's concern for the administration of the law took a number of forms. He was required to advise the King's Council on questions relating to Roman and Canon, as well as common, law. In addition, it was his duty to draw up the writs, whereby actions were begun in the king's courts of common law, and to hear allegations that the "king has made a grant of what does not belong to him" and, if necessary, to advise the king to revoke his grant.[19] He also took increasing responsibility for

---

[14] Ibid.

[15] Ibid, p. 203.

[16] Earl of Kilmuir, *Memoirs: A Political Adventure* (London, Weidenfeld and Nicolson, 1962) p. 35.

[17] Lord Kilmuir, "Office of the Lord Chancellor" (1956) 9 *Parliamentary Affairs* 132 at 135.

[18] N. Underhill, *The Lord Chancellor*, p. 75.

[19] F. W. Maitland, *The Constitutional History of England*, p. 222.

petitions to the king from citizens, who were unable to secure an effective remedy in the common law courts and sought the king's intervention. Indeed, by the fifteenth century these petitions were being automatically referred by the Council to the Chancellor. Inevitably the practice developed whereby those who wanted civil relief addressed their petitions directly to him rather than to the king and he dealt with them without reference to the sovereign or Council. He also became involved in disputes concerning the use of trusts in relation to land, stepping in "in the name of equity and good conscience" to resolve the matter.[20] The result was that by the reign of Henry VII the Court of Chancery was established as a court of equity, a position which was to last until 1875.

The increased importance and influence of the Chancellor inevitably meant that "the office came more and more to be affected by political pressures". [21] As a consequence, the appointment of Chancellor was "liable to be influenced, or indeed dictated, by shifts in the balance of power between the king and his greater subjects".[22] The later medieval chancellors therefore fall into two categories, those who were professional administrators and, lacking political support from elsewhere, were dependent on the king for their position, and those who were imposed upon the king as "the instruments or, more rarely, the leaders of political factions".[23] During this period, the function and role of the chancellor therefore varied considerably, depending upon his power base, his relationship with the other political actors and his own personality. Cardinal Wolsey (1515–29), who, during the reign of Henry VIIIth, was "virtually Prime Minister",[24] owed his extensive powers to "the peculiar relationship between himself and King Henry VIII".[25] Because of this, the powers he amassed were "personal to him" and made him "unique among English chancellors".[26] Nevertheless, their nature demonstrated "the range of powers available to medieval chancellors and, to some extent, to their later successors",[27] even those who hold office in the twenty-first century.

Wolsey was in the traditional mould of chancellors, who, before the Reformation, were "almost always ecclesiastic",[28] and often bishops or archbishops.[29] His successor, Thomas More (1529–33), who was also a powerful chancellor, was, on the other hand, a layman. He "is conventionally represented as the first of a new breed of Lord Chancellor", the usage of this title also being established at around this time.[30] He had no strong political position but had been Speaker in the House of Commons, a position also held by his successor

---

[20] Ibid, p. 224.
[21] N. Underhill, *The Lord Chancellor*, p. 41.
[22] Ibid, p. 42.
[23] Ibid, p. 45.
[24] Lord Hailsham, *A Sparrow's Flight* (London, Collins, 1990) p. 379.
[25] N. Underhill, *The Lord Chancellor*, p. 67.
[26] Ibid.
[27] Ibid, p. 68.
[28] F. W. Maitland, *The Constitutional History of England*, p. 221.
[29] The last clergyman to hold the position was John Williams, Archbishop of York (1621–5).
[30] N. Underhill, *The Lord Chancellor*, p. 97.

Audley (1533–44) and subsequently by Lord Rich (1547–52), and their elevation to Chancellor was a sign of the increasing political importance of Parliament in the sixteenth century. A further indication was the "new significance" and "new definition" of the Lord Chancellor's role, as spokesman for the king in Parliament.[31] It became "specifically associated with the House of Lords", where the Lord Chancellor "presided over their meetings and acted as an intermediary between the House and the king".[32] In 1539 the Chancellor's pre-eminence in the Lords was given statutory recognition and "his traditional seat on the woolsack" was ordained.[33] However, while this position was important at the time, in the long term it diminished political interest in the appointment of Lord Chancellors, the gradual shift in the locus of politics from the Lords to the House of Commons making the occupant of the office of less political significance.

After the Glorious Revolution in 1688, the position of Lord Chancellor lapsed for a short period. The judicial work of the Court of Chancery, together with the administrative functions associated with the Great Seal, were carried out by Lords Commissioners, while the role of Speaker in the House of Lords passed to a senior judge. The office was resurrected in 1693 and, perhaps because of monarchical insecurity, born out of recent history, and the decline in the political importance of the position of Lord Chancellor, the Lord Chancellors of the eighteenth century "were virtually the monarch's private spies on their colleagues and constantly intrigued against them".[34] Several of the Lord Chancellors during this time served for long periods, most notably Lords Harwicke and Thurlow, who served for twenty and sixteen years, respectively, and Lord Eldon, who served from 1801–6 and then from 1807–27, a period of twenty-six years in total.

It was in the eighteenth century that the Lord Chancellor was "for the first time unquestionably recognised as the head of law – not indeed in any precise sense of ministerial responsibility, but as the most respected and influential judge in the kingdom".[35] From the inception of his office, as the keeper of the Great Seal, "it was inevitable that his office would become the center of the English Legal system and he its head and the kingpin of the constitution".[36] However, the actual recognition of his position came from the fact that he presided over the House of Lords, when it sat as a court of appeal, which meant that he was seen as "the judicial equal or superior of the Chief Justices", and from his responsibility for judicial appointments, which "clearly served to set him above, and apart from them, even if the origins of the practice were in his

---

[31] Ibid, p. 102.
[32] Ibid.
[33] Ibid.
[34] Lord Hailsham, *A Sparrow's Flight*, p. 379.
[35] Ibid.
[36] C. P. Patterson, *The Administration of Justice in Great Britain* (Austin, Texas, University of Texas, 1936) p. 28.

administrative rather than his judicial role".[37] Moreover, having sat as a member of the Star Chamber, he naturally progressed to membership of its successor, the Privy Council. Thus the legislative and judicial positions of the Lord Chancellor were established, while his administrative duties assured him of a place within a Cabinet rapidly becoming independent of the monarch.

By the end of the nineteenth century the Lord Chancellor was responsible for a government department, albeit a very small one and one that was seen as different from other Whitehall departments because of the responsibilities of the Lord Chancellor and his peculiar constitutional position. His influence in government had declined since its medieval heyday. Economic and social changes meant that the "finances of the realm came to depend more on commerce and less on the disposition of landed estates".[38] The Lord Treasurer's money raising skills thus became more important than those of the Lord Chancellor and he tended to focus more on his judicial responsibilities. Nevertheless, his government position was retained and, after the Second World War, the balance began to shift back towards his political and administrative responsibilities. This was due, initially, to changes in the sittings in the House of Lords, which made it more difficult for Lord Chancellors to sit frequently on the judicial committee,[39] and, subsequently, to the passing of the Courts Act of 1971, which made the civil court system the sole responsibility of the Lord Chancellor and resulted in a big expansion of his Department[40] and his executive role.

From this point the Lord Chancellor became a "real" departmental minister. Yet, there remains "no clear statement in statute of [his] overall functions".[41] A number of Acts impose duties and responsibilities but a "general description"[42] of what he does is missing. This may be because "the variety of functions carried out by the Lord Chancellor are difficult to encapsulate in one simple statement of functions as title",[43] or it may be that, as with the position of Prime Minister, the need has not been felt to define, and thus confine, the role. In line with the nature of the British constitution, it has therefore evolved over time, adjusting to accommodate political and constitutional changes and "the individual qualities and character of the Chancellor himself", upon which "the emphasis of the office"[44] and its influence largely depend. As history demonstrates, the role played by the Lord Chancellor is, to a considerable extent, "determined by each holder of the office"[45] and his relationship with his patron,

---

[37] F. W. Maitland, *The Constitutional History of England*, p. 170.
[38] Lord Elwyn-Jones, *In My Time*, p. 264.
[39] See Chapter Five.
[40] See Chapter Three.
[41] Lord Mackay, "The Lord Chancellor's Role within Government" (1995) 145 *New Law Journal* 6719, 1650–53 at 1650.
[42] Ibid.
[43] Ibid.
[44] Lord Elwyn-Jones, "Foreword" in N. Underhill, *The Lord Chancellor*, p. ix.
[45] Sir Francis Purchas, "The Constitution in the Market Place" (1993) 143 *New Law Journal* 6624, 1604–09 at 1606.

who, in modern times, is the Prime Minister. It owes "nothing to legal doctrine", which played no part in its development,[46] and "far more to history than it does to constitutional principle".[47] Moreover, the origins and age of the office mean that, given Britain's constitutional development, it is inevitable that the position of Lord Chancellor has retained considerable historical baggage. It is this baggage and the responsibilities contained within it, which make the position unique, such that "nowhere in the world is there a similar office".[48] They also give rise to descriptions of the office as " a heap of anomalies"[49] and of the Lord Chancellor as "the most anomalous creature in the constitution".[50]

THE OFFICE OF LORD CHANCELLOR IN THE TWENTY-FIRST CENTURY

The office of Lord Chancellor, as it exists today, combines executive, legislative, judicial, and, unusually in the British context, constitutional functions. There is little logic in the combination of responsibilities, which cut across and overlap those of the Home Secretary and the Law Officers. The holder of the office, whose position is in the gift of the Prime Minister is, by convention, a member of the Cabinet. He is therefore bound by the doctrine of collective responsibility. He is also in charge of a government department and has ministerial responsibility for "the fair, efficient and effective administration of justice". He is thus accountable to Parliament for the formulation and implementation of government policies in relation to these responsibilities. In addition, he is a member of the legislative chamber of the House of Lords, by convention accepting a peerage upon appointment, if not already entitled to sit in that House. In his legislative capacity he assumes some of the functions of the Speaker in the House of Commons, takes part in debates, speaking on behalf of the government, and votes in divisions.

As well as these executive and legislative functions, the Lord Chancellor is also a senior judge. He sits in the judicial committees of the House of Lords and Privy Council, and, on occasions when he chooses to exercise the right, presides over these courts. He is also President of the Supreme Court in England,[51] an *ex officio* judge of the Court of Appeal,[52] and President of the Chancery Division.[53] In his judicial capacity he is, of course, required to act completely impartially, and despite the fact that unlike other judges he has no security of tenure, he must take no account of his political position or allegiances.[54]

---

[46] Lord Elwyn-Jones in M. Berlins, *A Man for All Roles.*
[47] Lord Elwyn-Jones, "Foreword" in N. Underhill, *The Lord Chancellor*, p. x.
[48] Lord Woolf, H.L. Debs., 26 November 1997, col. 937.
[49] W. Bagehot, *The English Constitution* (London, Fontana Press, 1963).
[50] Viscount Hailsham, "The Duties of a Lord Chancellor"(Holdsworth Lecture 1936) in B. Harvey (ed.), *The Lawyer and Justice* (London, Sweet and Maxwell, 1978) p. 2.
[51] Supreme Court Act 1981, s.1.
[52] Ibid, s.2.
[53] Ibid, s. 5 (1) a).
[54] For further discussion, see Chapter Five.

The Lord Chancellor therefore has a dual role, which requires him to keep political and judicial functions separate. Moreover, if this were not enough, as head of the judiciary he has a constitutional role. This requires him to preserve and protect judicial independence and integrity, ensuring that it is not undermined by the other arms of government or by the actions of judges themselves. Whether this is an appropriate role for someone who is also a government minister is open to question. At the least it can produce confusion over whether the Lord Chancellor is speaking as a minister or as head of the judiciary, particularly when replying to debates in the House of Lords. In most instances he will respond as a member of the Cabinet, and thus defend the government's stance. However, in exceptional debates, which concern the role of the judiciary, his reply will be as its leader.[55] Such a chameleon-type role breaches any idea of the separation of powers, however loosely defined. Indeed, "his office illustrates the contradictions of the English political system. In a nation, which prides itself on the independence of its judiciary, the Chancellor is a partisan officer".[56]

The broad executive, legislative, judicial and constitutional functions cover a range of more detailed responsibilities which include chairing Cabinet committees, advising the government on legal and constitutional matters, deciding individual cases in a court of law, making and advising on judicial and quasi-judicial appointments, arranging the judicial business in the House of Lords and the Privy Council, making procedural rules for the Supreme Court and Crown Courts, overseeing the court system and most areas of civil law reform, and supervising legal aid and advice schemes. In addition, they carry with them indirect responsibility for the education and regulation of the legal profession and the provision of legal services, as well as responsibility for the Great Seal, the Land Registry, the Official Receiver and other miscellaneous bodies. The Lord Chancellor also has "considerable" ecclesiastical patronage, which, extending as it does to twelve canonries and nearly five hundred benefices, is "almost as much as the two archbishops together", although the patronage at his disposal is mainly confined to the "poorer benefices of the Church".[57] Such patronage is an obvious example of the way in which the responsibilities of the Lord Chancellor have arisen through accidents of history. Even relatively recent responsibilities, assumed by the Lord Chancellor, may have an historic basis, as would seem to be the case where responsibility for the preservation of public records is concerned. This was given to the Lord Chancellor by the Public Records Act 1958 and it would seem that "in his exercise of these functions a direct line can be traced from the original secretarial work of the medieval

---

[55] In a debate on the Judiciary and Public Controversy; Lord Simon assumed that the Lord Chancellor would be replying in that guise and noted that only a few weeks previously he had replied as a minister (H. L. Debs., 5 June 1996, col.1280).

[56] F. Morrison, *Courts and the Political Process* (London, Sage, 1973) p. 199.

[57] R. F. V. Heuston, *Lives of the Lord Chancellors 1940–1970* (Oxford, Clarendon Press, 1987) p. 25.

chancery".[58] Thus any logic in responsibilities lies in history not in a rationale for efficient government.

The diversity of responsibilities of the Lord Chancellor clearly requires political, administrative and judicial skills. They also need considerable dexterity in balancing the different interests concerned. It would therefore be reasonable to assume that the qualifications for the position are considerable. However, as Heuston states, "There are none. The great office can, as a matter of strict law, be conferred on any person, male or female, who is capable of swearing the oath of allegiance and the official oath".[59] Since Wolsey, the last great ecclesiastical Chancellor, it has been customary for the Lord Chancellor to be a lawyer, Lord Shaftesbury, who resigned in 1673, being the last non-lawyer to hold the position.[60] But the lack of stipulations as to professional background means "there is no requirement that the Lord Chancellor, unlike the judges whom he himself appoints, should have a professional qualification in English Law".[61] This was demonstrated by the appointment in 1987 of Lord Mackay, who came from a Scottish law background.

While there is no requirement for legal standing, during the twentieth century there was some uncertainty as to whether the position was subject to a religious disability, which prevented a Roman Catholic from becoming Lord Chancellor. This doubt "was sufficiently real" in 1943 "to stop a Prime Minister, in practice, from recommending the appointment of an otherwise suitable candidate".[62] It arose from a number of sources, one of which was the ecclesiastic functions which, because of historic associations, accrue to the Lord Chancellor and relate to the Anglican Church. Another was "the peculiar concept of the Lord Chancellor as 'keeper of the King's conscience' ".[63] There has been debate as to whether this responsibility related to the Lord Chancellor's role as religious mentor or chaplain to the sovereign, or to his equitable jurisprudence. Whatever the interpretation, two holders of the office, Lords Simon and Hailsham declared the concept meaningless in the modern context and thus as providing no grounds for questioning the religious credentials of any Lord Chancellor. However, the main source of uncertainty was the Test Act of Charles II[64] and the effect of subsequent legislation. The Test Act required that those who held office under the Crown "should not merely receive the Sacrament after the ritual of the Church of England but should take the oath abjuring the doctrine of transubstantiation".[65] The Act was a response to attempts by James II "to infiltrate the Church of England by appointing open or covert Roman Catholics to

---

[58] N. Underhill, *The Lord Chancellor*, p. 199.
[59] R. F.V. Heuston, *Lives of the Lord Chancellors 1940–1970*, p. 3.
[60] Lord Kilmuir, "Office of the Lord Chancellor" p. 133.
[61] R. F. V. Heuston , *Lives of the Lord Chancellors 1940–1970*, p. 4.
[62] Lord Simon, H.L. Debs., 11 June 1974.
[63] R. F. V. Heuston, *Lives of the Lord Chancellors 1940–1970*, p. 5.
[64] 25 Car.II, c.2.
[65] Anson, *The Law and Custom of the Constitution*, p. 169.

high office in the Church and State"[66] and would seem to have applied to Lord Chancellors. Certainly when Lord Eldon resigned in 1821, at a time when Catholic emancipation was on the agenda, George III stipulated that his successor should be anti-Catholic,[67] although his motivation was politics and prejudice rather than law.

Whatever the legal position, in 1828 the requirement regarding the taking of the sacrament was removed and a year later the Roman Catholic Relief Act[68] changed the oath in a way which was acceptable to Catholics. However, in doing so, it also provided that "neither the Chancellor of Great Britain nor the Lord Keeper, nor the Lords Commissioners of the Great Seal, should be relieved of any requirements to which they were at the time subject".[69] Moreover, while the Statute Law Revision Act 1863 wholly repealed the Test Act and the Test Abolition Act 1867 removed the requirement of the oath against transubstantiation, by "inadvertence on the part of the nineteenth century draftsman",[70] the exception included in the Catholic Relief Act appeared to prevent a Roman Catholic from assuming the position of Lord Chancellor.

It was to clarify the situation that, "in an abundance of caution",[71] the Lord Chancellor (Tenure of Office and Discharge of Ecclesiastical Functions) Act was passed in 1974. It states; "For the avoidance of doubt it is hereby declared that the Office of Lord Chancellor is and shall be tenable by an adherent of the Roman Catholic faith"[72] and it makes provision for the exercise of ecclesiastic functions should a Lord Chancellor be a Catholic, providing that in such circumstances, "it shall be lawful for Her Majesty's Council to make provision for the exercise of any or all the visitational or ecclesiastical functions normally performed by the Lord Chancellor, to be performed by the Prime Minister or any other Minister of the Crown".[73] Thus any uncertainty as to whether the Lord Chancellor can be a Catholic was removed.

The degree of doubt that had existed until 1974 about the position of Catholics had not attached to other faiths. There was "no legal incapacity attached to Jews, Moslems, Christian Scientists, Buddhists or atheists".[74] However, in 1989 the Statute Law (Repeal) Act repealed the Religious Disabilities Act, which had been passed in the 1840s, giving rise to concern by Lord Alderdice that the position of other faiths was no longer protected. He therefore sought an amendment to the 1974 Act so that it included other faiths. In this he was unsuccessful, such an amendment being seen as unnecessary as doubt about incapacity had only arisen in relation to Catholics. Yet there would

---

[66] Lord Hailsham, H.L. Debs., 11 June 1974, col. 417.
[67] J. B. Atlay, *The Victorian Chancellors*, Vol. 1 (London, Smith, Elder & Co.,1906) p. 50.
[68] 10 Geo. IV, c.7.
[69] Anson, *The Law and Custom of the Constitution*, p. 169.
[70] Lord Hailsham, H.L. Debs., 11 June 1974, col. 417.
[71] Lord Mishcon, H. L. Debs., 13 March 1998, col. 411.
[72] Section 1.
[73] Section 2.
[74] Lord Elwyn-Jones, *In My Time*, p. 280.

seem to be some merit in the position of all faiths being clearly stated in legislation.[75]

Despite the lack of formal qualifications required of a Lord Chancellor, in practice, the person appointed is always a member of the legal profession, deemed to be "adequately equipped with academic legal scholarship and practical experience".[76] Ideally, he should be a "lawyer of first-class ability, capable of evoking the respect, and even fear, of lawyers, politicians, and civil servants".[77] Moreover, as well as being a "good lawyer", he also needs to be "a good judge [and] good administrator with a sound knowledge of public affairs".[78] This does not necessarily mean that the Lord Chancellor needs to have been a politician. In the nineteenth century the special career structure for barristers in Parliament meant that there was an expectation of promotion by the Lord Chancellor from the House of Commons to the bench or to the position of law officer and from there to higher judicial office or the office of Lord Chancellor.[79] Being Attorney-General or Solicitor-General was seen as a logical first step to becoming Lord Chancellor and between 1873 and 1945 eight Attorneys General and four Solicitors General were appointed directly to the position.[80] Since 1945 this logical progression is less apparent, perhaps because of a dearth of legal talent within the House of Commons, and only Jowitt, Dilhourne, Kilmuir, Elwyn-Jones and Havers have arrived at the position of Lord Chancellor by that route, either directly or indirectly.

Indeed, with few exceptions,[81] "the Lord Chancellor's appointment has always been based on political grounds",[82] although it has not always been thought necessary to give the job to a politician. During the twentieth century, a number of those rising to the position, including Lords Sankey, Maugham, Simonds, Gardiner, Mackay and Irvine, had not sat in the House of Commons before being appointed. They were, of course, all sympathetic to the government in office and, with the exception of Gardiner, who had been chairman of the Bar Council and "a noted campaigner for law reform",[83] and Irvine, who was the head of a commercial law chambers, they were all full time judges. Indeed, Maugham (1933–9), Simonds (1951–4) and Mackay (1987–97) were already law lords.

---

[75] See H. L. Debs., 13 March 1998 for discussion of issues.

[76] Lord Hailsham, "The Office of Lord Chancellor and the Separation of Powers" (1989) *Civil Justice Quarterly* 308–18 at 317.

[77] R. F. V. Heuston, *Lives of the Lord Chancellors 1940–1970*, p. 4.

[78] M. Berlins, *A Man for All Roles*.

[79] See Chapter Six.

[80] S. H. Bailey and M. J. Gunn, *Smith and Bailey on the Modern English Legal System* (2nd edn., London, Sweet & Maxwell, 1991) p. 215.

[81] e.g. Lord Sankey, who was a Liberal, served in the Labour Government but remained in office when the government became predominately Conservative.

[82] S. Shetreet, *Judges on trial: A Study on the Appointment and Accountability of the English Judiciary* (Amsterdam, North Holland Publishing,1976) p. 50.

[83] N. Underhill, *The Lord Chancellor*, p. 201.

It is also generally seen as essential for the Lord Chancellor to carry "both professional and political weight; only thus can he protect the rule of law and the independence of the judiciary from within the Cabinet, and, conversely, keep the courts within their proper sphere".[84] He also needs to be able to handle political colleagues, not just because his responsibilities overlap with those of the Home Office and the Law Officers but also because he needs to fight for funds for his department.

A DIFFICULT POSITION TO DEFEND

However, regardless of the qualities required of Lord Chancellors and how well individual holders of the office may meet them, the position of Lord Chancellor is difficult to defend for a number of reasons. First, its cross-institutional nature does not accord with even the weakest doctrine of the separation of powers. The notion that a government minister should be head of the judiciary would seem to undermine, rather than protect, judicial independence. Secondly, the appointed nature of the position means that the Lord Chancellor lacks a democratic mandate and constituency base, as well as any body of support in the House of Commons. As a result, his relationship with the Prime Minister may be even more important than that of other ministers for, unlike them, he is totally reliant upon the Prime Minister for his power base. Thirdly, the Lord Chancellor is required to carry out executive and legislative functions of which, unless he has previously been a member of the government or sat in Parliament, he will have had little experience. Fourthly, despite the fact that his department is a spending department of some note, he is not directly accountable for it on the floor of the House of Commons, only in the less political environment of the Lords. Fifthly, although he may have received little or no training as a judge, the Lord Chancellor is expected to sit as a law lord and assume the role as head of the judiciary, a role that elevates him above those before whom he may have appeared a few weeks previously on behalf of a client.

Yet in this mix of roles, he is restrained not by constitutional law but by convention and internal rules. It is therefore little wonder that the role of Lord Chancellor is frequently questioned and that the questioning increased with the political and constitutional developments at the end of the twentieth century. The emphasis of governments since the 1980s on efficiency, value for money and reducing public expenditure has had a fundamental effect on the structure and nature of the Lord Chancellor's Department and on the position of Lord Chancellor which, on any spectrum of responsibilities, has moved even further towards the executive and political end. The Lord Chancellor has become a reformist minister, intent on giving effect to government priorities, and his policies have brought him into conflict with senior judges and tested the viability of

---

[84] N. Underhill, *The Lord Chancellor*, p. 201.

his role as head of the judiciary. Moreover, his subsequent engagement in constitutional reform further emphasises his position at the heart of government and poses questions about his position as judge. It also raises issues about how, in a new constitutional settlement, the office of Lord Chancellor can be sustained. The "multiple role" of the Lord Chancellor has always entailed "a heroic piece of stagecraft, one which requires a massive suspension of disbelief on the part of the spectator".[85] Moving into the twenty-first century, it would seem that either the stagecraft is no longer sufficiently persuasive or the audience is less trusting. Either way the position of Lord Chancellor no longer seems convincing.

The following chapters analyse the position of Lord Chancellor through his different roles or functions, that is, through his constitutional, executive, judicial and legislative roles. The nature of the office means that such distinctions are not always easy to make. The responsibilities of the Lord Chancellor do not lend themselves to being neatly compartmentalised, rather the roles tend to fade into one another. The distinctions that are made are therefore inevitably imperfect and are intended to provide a convenient mechanism for analysis rather than a definitive statement of the roles. The chapters also consider the developments in the latter part of the twentieth century. These have had a particular impact on the Lord Chancellor's Department (LCD), the modern development of which is considered in a separate chapter. Changes within the LCD, which have meant that it is no longer separate from the rest of Whitehall, have further increased the questioning of the Lord Chancellor's position.

---

[85] G. Drewry, "Judicial Independence in Britain; Challenges Real and Threats Imagined" in R. Blackburn (ed.), *Constitutional Studies* (London, Mansell, 1992) p. 156.

2

The Lord Chancellor in the Constitution

I N THE BRITISH context, where there is no legal prescription of constitutional functions, it is unusual to talk of constitutional responsibility, let alone to assign it to a particular individual. Yet the Lord Chancellor is charged with responsibility for the preservation and protection of judicial independence and integrity. This responsibility stems from his position as head of the judiciary, a position recognised in the eighteenth century, which arose from the conjunction of his judicial role as president of the House of Lords, when it sits as a court of appeal, and his executive role through which he appoints, or recommends for appointment, all judges. In the absence of a written constitution, the responsibility for judicial independence places the Lord Chancellor at the heart of Britain's constitutional arrangements. It affects the way in which he fulfils his other functions and his relationship with the different institutions of government. Moreover, at least for Lord Hailsham, it constitutes his "paramount duty".[1]

The belief that the judiciary should be separate and independent from the other arms of government, namely the legislature and the executive, is "such a familiar part of British vocabulary that . . . [i]t has melted into the landscape of political and constitutional discourse".[2] Independence is seen as essential for the protection of civil liberties and to prevent an abuse of power by an over-mighty executive. It is also crucial for the maintenance of public confidence in the court system and, more widely, in the whole system of government. It underpins the requirement of judicial neutrality, that is that a judge should "give effect to the common values of the community, rather than any sectional system of values to which he may adhere",[3] which can only be assured if judges are independent in the sense that they are free from improper external pressures and have "the capacity . . . to resist such pressures without fear of penalty".[4]

The principle of judicial independence is seen as so fundamental to our constitutional arrangements that Lord Hailsham argued that Lord Chancellors

---

[1] Lord Hailsham, "The Office of Lord Chancellor and the Separation of Powers", p. 312.
[2] G. Drewry, "Judicial Independence in Britain", p. 149.
[3] J. Bell, *Policy Arguments in Judicial Decisions* (Oxford, Clarendon Press, 1983) p. 4.
[4] G. Drewry, "Judicial Independence in Britain", p. 151.

should be measured by their success in defending and preserving it, such that; "If he does it well, he is a good Lord Chancellor whatever his other defects. If he does it ill, whatever his other qualities, he is not".[5] Such a measurement, even if desirable, is not easy to make, particularly when there is dispute as to what judicial independence encompasses, and any assessment is likely to be subjective. This does not detract from the importance of there being an independent judiciary. However, it poses questions about the viability of the Lord Chancellor's role in its preservation.

CONSTITUTIONAL JUSTIFICATIONS FOR JUDICIAL INDEPENDENCE

The need for judicial independence is supported by the rule of law and the separation of powers, concepts which are used to provide judicial independence with a theoretical underpinning and thus with constitutional authority. Indeed, talk of judicial independence is usually framed within the context of the rule of law or the separation of powers and frequently coupled with references to either or both. Thus any perceived encroachment on judicial independence is said to undermine the rule of law and to interfere with, or be contrary to, the separation of powers. The role of the Lord Chancellor in upholding judicial independence is also placed within this constitutional framework.

There is a general acceptance of the rule of law as a constitutional principle,[6] at least in the narrow sense of government within the law, and a recognition that if government is to be legally accountable to the courts for its actions, the courts need to be independent from it. Indeed, "The existence of a judiciary that operates independently of and is protected against improper pressure by the executive is universally regarded in developed democracies as a bulwark of both representative government and the rule of law".[7] Justifications for judicial independence on the basis of the rule of law are therefore sustainable. However, the rule of law does not support the need for the head of the judiciary and the guardian of its independence also to be a Cabinet minister. Indeed, such an amalgam of responsibilities may be seen as interfering with the constitutional role of the judiciary in relation to the executive and with judicial independence.

In a similar way, the position of the Lord Chancellor weakens justifications for judicial independence, which are based on the separation of powers. These justifications, in any case, have less authority because the relevance of the doctrine, either as a description of the constitution or a constitutional ideal, is disputed, the argument ranging from the view that the separation of powers has no

---

[5] Lord Hailsham, "The Office of Lord Chancellor and the Separation of Powers", p. 311.

[6] See, for instance, C. Turpin, *British Government and the Constitution* (3rd edn., London, Butterworths, 1999); J. Jowell and D. Oliver (eds.), *The Changing Constitution* (3rd edn., Oxford, Clarendon Press, 1994).

[7] G. Drewry, "Judicial Independence in Britain: Challenges Real and Threats Imagined" in P. Norton (ed.), *New Directions in British Politics* (Aldershot, Edward Elgar, 1991) p. 37.

place in the constitution[8] to the view that the British constitution "is firmly based" upon it.[9] The doctrine of separation of powers has given rise to a " substantial body of literature . . ., much of it confused and contradictory".[10] As expounded by Locke[11] and Montesquieu[12] it has three elements. The first divides government into executive, legislature, and judicial agencies; the second, designates the chief functions of government in accordance with this division, and, the third, separates government personnel, such that the functions carried out by the agencies are "in distinct hands".[13] This institutional, functional and personal separation theoretically ensures a division of power, such that, there is an automatic balance and protection against its abuse. However, even in the United States of America, where the doctrine is one of the principles upon which the Constitution is based, such a complete separation has never been realised and, as a consequence, it is necessary to allow each institution some powers of interference outside its own competence to ensure some balance of power is maintained – hence the system of checks and balances for which the United States is renowned.

In the British context, "balance" is also seen as an important attribute. Indeed, Lord Irvine echoed seventeenth century notions of the "balanced constitution" when, in support of the separation of powers, on which in 1997 he insisted "the British Constitution is firmly based",[14] he held its operation to "represent a delicate balance".[15] Such a vague description lays him open to criticism that the separation of powers is "the favourite vehicle of writers on political science and constitutional law for the conveyance of fallacious ideas".[16] These ideas include the suggestion that there is "some objective hidden hand which holds the constitution in perpetual equilibrium",[17] or that the separation of powers "has some mystical virtue as an iron law of the constitution and as a yardstick against which the merits of institutional arrangements can be measured".[18] Interestingly, two years later Lord Irvine had modified his position on the separation of powers, preferring instead to argue, "we fashion our constitutional arrangements pragmatically".[19]

---

[8] See O. Hood Phillips; "A Constitutional Myth; Separation of Powers" (1977) 93 *Law Quarterly Review* 11.

[9] Lord Diplock, *Duport Steels Ltd.* v. *Sirs* [1980] 1 WLR 142 at 157.

[10] G. Drewry, *Law, Justice and Politics* (2nd edn., Essex, Longman, 1981) p. 3.

[11] *Second Treatise of Civil Government* (1690).

[12] *Spirit of the Laws* (1748).

[13] M. J. C. Vile, *Constitutionalism and Separation of Powers* (Oxford, Oxford University Press, 1967) p. 1.

[14] *Speech to the Lord Mayor's Dinner for Her Majesty's Judges* (Mansion House, London, 23 July 1997).

[15] Lord Irvine, H. L. Debs., 5 June 1996, col. 1255.

[16] W. A. Robson, *Justice and Administrative Law* (3rd edn., London, Stevens, 1951) p. 16.

[17] J.A.G. Griffith, *The Politics of the Judiciary* (4th edn., London, Fontana Press, 1991) pp. 222–3.

[18] G. Drewry, *Law, Justice and Politics*, p. 4.

[19] H. L. Debs., 24 June 1999, cols. 1061–2.

Certainly any measurement of the institutional arrangements of British government would fall far short of the definitive version of the separation of powers. The law lords sit in the legislative chamber of the House of Lords and thus have a legislative as well as a judicial function, although this may be seen as a minor incursion and one, which is tempered by convention. Much more significant is the fusion of the legislature and the executive, whereby ministers are members of both agencies and are involved in both functions, and the fact that functions, which can most conveniently be labelled "judicial or legislative", are frequently carried out within government departments rather than by the courts. Such arrangements give effect to parliamentary government, a later constitutional development, and allow government in its twentieth century form to be conducted efficiently. However, they clearly diverge from "that antique and rickety chariot known as the separation of powers".[20]

Indeed, "Nothing underlies the atheoretical nature of the British Constitution more than the casualness with which it approaches the separation of powers".[21] This does not mean that the separation of powers is totally irrelevant in the British context. Aspects of the doctrine are considered "eminently sensible"[22] and, with some provisos, help to explain our constitutional arrangements. The categorisation of functions, while "somewhat imperfect", is "a useful shorthand way of describing a lot of things that go on in government, providing we remember that the boundaries between them are indistinct and that they are fundamentally interrelated".[23] The division of institutions is also recognised in the sense "that the Queen in Parliament is, and therefore ought to be, a different legal entity from the Queen as the source of justice, and that neither is the same entity as the executive departments headed by the Queen's ministers".[24] So in legal theory there is a recognition of separation, although it is a separation of "unequal powers"[25] and thus of uncertain balance.

Moreover, as long as it is accepted that "separation does not mean mutual exclusion" but rather "interlocking spheres of constitutional competence",[26] the notion of separation can be seen as playing "a large part in our constitutional practice and in institutional arrangements which separate executive and judicial functions".[27] It can therefore be a useful guiding principle. But it is in relation to the judiciary that the doctrine has most vibrancy. It is accepted as "probably a good idea to have a judiciary which is somewhat aloof from the rough and tum-

---

[20] W. A. Robson, *Justice and Administrative Law*, p. 16.

[21] R. Stevens, *The Independence of the Judiciary; the View from the Lord Chancellor's Office* (Oxford, Clarendon Press, 1997) *p.* 2.

[22] G. Drewry, *Law, Justice and Politics*, p. 3.

[23] Ibid, p. 4.

[24] Sir Stephen Sedley, "The Sound of Silence: Constitutional Law without a Constitution" (1994) 110 *Law Quarterly Review* 270–91 at 271.

[25] Lord Mackay, "The Lord Chancellor in the 1990s" *Current*, p. 250.

[26] Sir Stephen Sedley, "The Sound of Silence", p. 271.

[27] Lord Steyn, "The Weakest and Least Dangerous Department of Government" [1997] *Public Law* 84–95 at 87.

ble of party politics".[28] The reality of a judiciary set to one side of the party political elements of government, both in relation to the executive and Parliament, in the form of the House of Commons, therefore finds a constitutional basis, although one that may be overplayed and, at times, misused. Portrayals of the separation of powers, as providing "an essential constitutional safeguard of judicial independence" and preventing "the rise of arbitrary executive power", become less persuasive when the safeguard extends to protecting "the integrity of the administration of justice".[29] Given the breadth of the term, "administration of justice", in today's context, the assumption that it should be seen as exclusively judicial territory, and thus protected from executive or political influence, may be dubious and "less a question of one branch of government under the separation of powers; . . . more a question of . . . what role the judges themselves should play in deciding appointments and terms of service, and in running the courts".[30]

Resort to support from the separation of powers thus has a territorial ring to it and perhaps this best explains its use. It is concerned with demarcation lines and with preserving constitutional boundaries, and with power and status. Lord Irvine may have been right when he said; "The public know, or sense, what the separation of powers is about. They are unhappy if the Government is attacking the judiciary and the judiciary is seen to be hitting back in return. They then feel that all is not well with the nation".[31] The problem is that the boundaries have become imprecise and what is "judicial" and what is "executive" is not always agreed. As a consequence, both sides perceive incursions into their territory and judges, concerned to preserve their power base and their status, resort to appeals to the separation of powers and judicial independence. Constitutional principle is therefore used to protect vested interests, thereby confirming that "in England, without any clear separation of powers, the status of judges has become the core of the discussion of the independence of the judiciary".[32]

THE LORD CHANCELLOR: DEFENDER OF JUDICIAL INDEPENDENCE

In a similar way, justifications of the position of Lord Chancellor in terms of the separation of powers have a hollow ring and suggest the use of constitutional mythology to sustain the unsustainable. Indeed, the Lord Chancellor is "the most anomalous creature in the constitution because his very existence contradicts what at least used to be generally regarded as the essential characteristic of our English system, namely, the separation between the legislature, executive

[28] G. Drewry, *Law, Justice and Politics*, p. 4.
[29] Lord Steyn, "The Weakest and Least Dangerous Department of Government", p. 87.
[30] R. Stevens, *The Independence of the Judiciary*, p. 7.
[31] *Speech to the Lord Mayor's Dinner for Her Majesty's Judges*.
[32] R. Stevens, *The Independence of the Judiciary*, p. 183.

and judicial powers".[33] Arguments that suggest that the Lord Chancellor is "there to protect the separation of powers, not to overturn it"[34] or that his function is to ensure that "within the separation of powers the separation works"[35] have little theoretical merit. Similarly descriptions of the Lord Chancellor as being at "a critical cusp"[36] of the doctrine or as sitting "somewhere near the apex of the constitutional pyramid, armed with a long barge pole to keep off marauding craft from any quarter",[37] may provide provocative images, but constitutionally defy the very doctrine they are meant to support. The truth is that within the office of Lord Chancellor "there is a fundamental congruence of executive and judicial functions".[38] This may not amount to a fusion of power in the sense that judicial and executive roles are confused,[39] but it does allow one role to dominate and thus upset the balance between the judicial and the executive. The position is therefore unsustainable on the basis of the separation of powers and, constitutionally, "seems prima facie undesirable".[40]

The constitutionally peculiar position of Lord Chancellor is traditionally justified on the grounds that the Lord Chancellor acts as a "hinge", joining the executive and judiciary, or as "a necessary link between Parliament and the executive on the one hand and the judges on the other".[41] Indeed, Lord Hailsham argued that the preservation of judicial independence and its separation from the other arms of government is only possible if the Lord Chancellor holds the balance between the executive, judiciary and legislature and "retains the confidence of all three elements in the equation".[42] More specifically, he is described as acting as a constitutional buffer or fortification, a role in which he protects the judiciary from executive interference, and as a bridge, whereby he enables the two arms of government to communicate without compromising judicial independence. Lord Hailsham, who described himself as "the private representative" of judges in Whitehall, saw his role as communicator as being concerned with fighting within the government to meet the legitimate demands of those he was representing.[43]

Lords Mackay and Irvine took a broader view of their communications role, seeing it as a two-way process. Lord Mackay suggested that, on the one hand, the Lord Chancellor provides "a voice for the judges whilst at the same time

---

[33] Viscount Hailsham, "The Duties of a Lord Chancellor", p. 2.
[34] Sir Nicholas Lyell, ex Attorney-General, H. C. Debs., 6 December 1997, col. 410.
[35] Lord Irvine in M. Berlins, *A Man for All Roles*, BBC Radio 4.
[36] Ibid.
[37] Lord Hailsham, "Problems of a Lord Chancellor" (Holdsworth Lecture 1972) in B. Harvey (ed.), *The Lawyer and Justice*, p. 5.
[38] Lord Steyn, "The Weakest and Least Dangerous Department of Government, p. 89.
[39] Vile argues that this does not necessarily contravene the separation of powers, because there is "no fusion of power here", in the sense of a confusion between judicial and executive roles (M. J. C. Vile, *Constitutionalism and Separation of Powers*, p. 342).
[40] Lord Steyn, "The Weakest and Least Dangerous Department of Government", p. 90.
[41] Lord Mackay, "The Lord Chancellor in the 1990s", p. 250.
[42] Lord Hailsham, *A Sparrow's Flight*, p. 422.
[43] Ibid, p. 312.

ensuring that they are not placed in a direct and probably inappropriate relationship with the executive", and, on the other, provides "the judiciary with an understanding of the constraints and imperatives within which members of the Government will be working".[44] Lord Irvine reflected the two-way communication when he stated that the Lord Chancellor is "the primary medium for [the] interchange between the judges and the executive",[45] acting as "the representative of the judiciary in the Cabinet and the representative of the Cabinet in the judiciary".[46] He also stressed the awesome responsibility of the Lord Chancellor, arguing that the "confidence in the free flow of information in both directions so as to create mutual understanding between the judiciary and the Executive could not take place – unless through a single individual who commanded the confidence of the professional judiciary at the same time as the confidence of his Cabinet colleagues".[47]

The role of the Lord Chancellor as a constitutional mechanism, through which the judiciary and executive communicate, raises a number of important issues. First, it suggests that the effectiveness of communications depends largely upon the individual Lord Chancellor, his ability to represent both sides and his standing with the judiciary and with his political colleagues. Secondly, it gives the Lord Chancellor considerable power. He can set the agenda and, should he so wish, play one side off against the other for his own ends. Thirdly, and most important, because of the secrecy endemic in the process, it may create suspicions of judicial/executive collusion, thereby undermining judicial independence, which is better served by conversations between the executive and the judiciary being in the public domain rather than behind closed doors.[48]

The need for the Lord Chancellor to act as a link, however this is manifested, arises from the concern that, without him doing so, "the judiciary and the executive are likely enough to drift asunder to the point of a violent separation, followed by a still more violent and disastrous collision".[49] Lord Mackay warned; "the office of Lord Chancellor provides a link, which our long history of gradual development had produced, between the judiciary, the executive and the legislature that is broken at our peril".[50] In Britain therefore the separation of powers is compromised and blurred for fear of the consequences of total judicial detachment. The position of Lord Chancellor is central to that compromise. However, during the 1990s it was evident that the compromise was not working as senior judges utilised the concept of the separation of powers, as it supports judicial independence, to oppose government policies for the reform of the legal system put forward by the Lord Chancellor.[51] This suggested that if the

---

[44] Lord Mackay, "The Lord Chancellor in the 1990s", p. 251.
[45] M. Berlins, *A Man for All Roles*.
[46] Ibid.
[47] Lord Irvine, H. L. Debs., 25 November 1997, col. 945.
[48] Lord Steyn, "The Weakest and Least Dangerous Department of Government" p. 90.
[49] Viscount Birkenhead, *Points of View* (London, 1922) p. 92.
[50] "The Lord Chancellor in the 1990s", p. 259.
[51] See Chapter Four.

constitutional position of the Lord Chancellor is as a "buffer" or "hinge", "the buffer may have broken, . . . [and] the hinge badly needs oiling".[52] It also suggested that the "flexible and effective" means of communication between the executive and the judiciary, which the Lord Chancellor was required to provide, was failing to function as it should.[53]

Most justifications for the "special and peculiar position" of the Lord Chancellor are "intimately connected with the independence of the Judges".[54] Indeed, the Lord Chancellor's Department suggests; "Over the past hundred years or so the office of Lord Chancellor has evolved to become the answer to the problem of maintaining judicial independence in a Constitution which concentrates supreme power in a democratically elected legislature dominated by party politics".[55] However, this explanation of the office, which brings democracy into the equation, would seem to have dubious foundations and be a poor justification for the multi-functioning role of the Lord Chancellor.

Lord Mackay also placed the Lord Chancellor in a democratic framework, arguing that it is "extremely important for the working of our democratic institutions that there should be in the cabinet a person who represents in a particular way the system of justice . . . it is also helpful that there should be, at the head of the judiciary, someone who can be accountable to Parliament . . . it is also convenient that it should be linked with the speakership of the House of Lords because of the very special nature of that House and the fact that I may act as Speaker and still participate in debates".[56] However, rather than supporting "our democratic institutions", the position of Lord Chancellor would seem to break all the rules of a modern democracy. Not only is its occupant unelected and unaccountable to an elected body, but it would seem "undemocratic and monarchical for one person to exercise so much control over the judiciary".[57] Arguments that "the Chancellor is the symbol of popular control exercised by the public through the party in power"[58] are unconvincing. Occupants of the position come and go with changes of government and also as a result of the removal of prime ministerial patronage. Lords Simonds and Kilmuir were, for instance, "dismissed with peremptory abruptness for reasons which seemed good to the Prime Minister of the day".[59] In this way there is a tentative link with public opinion but the amount of power accumulated in the hands of a non-elected minister and the dubious mechanisms for accountability detracts from the notion of " a symbol of popular control".

---

[52] G. Drewry, "Judicial Independence in Britain; Challenges Real and Threats Imagined", p. 155.

[53] Sir Nicolas Browne-Wilkinson, "The Independence of the Judiciary in the 1980s" [1988] *Public Law* 44–57.

[54] Lord Hewart, *The New Despotism* (New York, Cosmopolitan Book Corp., 1929) p. 109.

[55] LCD website.

[56] Home Affairs Committee, *The Work of the Lord Chancellor's Department* (1991–92) HC 214, Minutes of Evidence, Q.1.

[57] C. P. Patterson, *The Administration of Justice in Great Britain*, p. 180.

[58] Ibid.

[59] R. F. V. Heuston, *Lives of the Lord Chancellors 1940–1970*, p. 4.

Similarly, justifications on the basis of party politics are likewise unsatisfactory. Lord Hailsham argued that because the executive and legislature have become "almost inextricably intertwined as a result of the development of cabinet government and of the party system",[60] the judicial branch has become the weakest of the three institutions and needs the protection provided by the Lord Chancellor. This is a view similarly put forward by Lord Irvine who suggested "that as the executive becomes much, much more important in Parliament and the judiciary commensurately weaker, there is a huge value in having a Lord Chancellor who can mediate effectively and communicate the views of the Government to the judges and the judges to the Government".[61] This seems a strange proposition, when the Lord Chancellor is part of the legislative/executive axis from which the judges need protection. In any case, judges should be able to stand up to the executive "without the protective cushion (or 'buffer') of a minister, himself a judge, dedicated to protecting them from harm".[62]

Justifications based on pragmatic rather then constitutional grounds seem more honest. Lord Schuster, "the most powerful of the Permanent Secretaries of the Lord Chancellor's Office"[63] defended the role of the Lord Chancellor on the basis that; "The advantages which accrue to the Cabinet from the presence of a colleague who is not only of high judicial reputation but also can represent to them the views of the judiciary; to the legislature from the presence in it of one who is both a Judge and a Minister; and to the judiciary from the fact that its President is in close touch with current political affairs, are enormous".[64] This "benefit" analysis, which ignores cost, was supported by Lord Mackay, who argued that the position of Lord Chancellor is of considerable benefit to judges, in that, unlike their counterparts in America, they do not have to "argue for money" for the administration of justice, rather the Lord Chancellor, "a senior minister of the Crown . . . can compete on equal terms with other spending departments for a proper share of the public money".[65] Thus the multi-functioned, judicial-political role of the Lord Chancellor has practical advantages. However, it is still difficult to see it as necessary for judicial independence. Indeed, arguably, the dual role undermines the independence it is meant to preserve, for while a "Lord Chancellor gives the appearance to the public of speaking as the head of the judiciary with the neutrality and impartiality so involved. The truth is different. Under governments of all complexions the Lord Chancellor is always a spokesman for the government in the furtherance of its party political agenda".[66]

[60] *A Sparrow's Flight*, p. 422.
[61] Home Affairs Committee, *The Work of the Lord Chancellor's Department* (1998–99) HC 882, Minutes of Evidence, Q. 107.
[62] G. Drewry, "Justice and Public Administration; Some Constitutional Tensions" (1992) 42 *Current Legal Problems* 2 187–212 at 209.
[63] R. Stevens, *The Independence of the Judiciary*, p. 3.
[64] Memo 1943 cited in R. Stevens (Ibid).
[65] G. Drewry, "Justice and Public Administration; Some Constitutional Tensions", p. 251.
[66] Lord Steyn. "The Weakest and Least Dangerous Department of Government, pp. 90–1.

Yet the phrase "judicial independence" is frequently used to protect the Lord Chancellor's position and to retain the status quo. It has been "used as a red herring drawn across the path of those seeking a better disposition of ministerial responsibility for the law",[67] the less than convincing argument being that direct accountability to the House of Commons by the Lord Chancellor would threaten judicial independence.[68] It has also been used repeatedly not only to support the current arrangements but also as a reason not to reform the office of Lord Chancellor, any reform being said to interfere with judicial independence. However, "such a use of the concept of judicial independence is spurious"[69] and suggests, once again, that it is code for "vested interests", which judges see best protected by the combination of a judge/minister rather than the separation of these functions. This is supported by the use of "judicial independence" to preserve professional interests and to protect the legal profession from executive interference, the argument being, first, that because judges are recruited solely from the ranks of legal practitioners, "[t]he independence of the Judiciary depends more upon the independence of the legal profession than any other single factor",[70] and, secondly, that, because "in this country . . . the Judiciary rely upon the integrity of advocates in presenting their cases and the duty upon them to make available all relevant legal authorities. . . . the independence of the judges cannot be sensibly considered separately from the professions, which form the infra-structure upon which the judges rely".[71]

Such arguments were employed in opposition to the Government's proposals to remove the Bar's advocacy monopoly in the higher courts. The plan to introduce a new system for licensing advocates, which would be administered by an advisory committee responsible to the Lord Chancellor with whom final decisions would reside,[72] was greeted by senior judges and leading members of the Bar with accusations that it was a gross threat to judicial independence, a move towards executive control of the judiciary and the executive occupation of judicial territory.[73] On this occasion, opposition to the proposals resulted in the subsequent Courts and Legal Services Act 1990 including the provision that, where rights of advocacy were concerned, the four most senior judges must give their approval before the Lord Chancellor could make any alterations. However, the regulation of the legal profession remained an issue and was taken up again in 1998 by Lord Irvine, who with the Access to Justice Bill,[74] sought, first, to replace the veto the senior judges had been given over rights of audience and professional rule changes with a requirement of consultation and, secondly, to give rights of audience to all qualified lawyers. Once again, the proposal was

---

[67] R. Brazier, "Government and the Law" [1989] *Public Law* 64 at 74.
[68] For consideration of accountability, see Chapter Seven.
[69] R. Brazier, "Government and the Law", p. 74.
[70] Lord Hailsham, H. L. Debs, 7 April 1989, col. 1333.
[71] Sir Francis Purchas, "The Constitution in the Market Place", p. 1605.
[72] *The Work and Organisation of the Legal Profession* (1989) Cm. 570.
[73] H. L. Debs, 15 March 1989, col. 1331–70.
[74] Access to Justice Act 1999.

opposed on the basis of judicial independence, Lord Steyn, a senior law lord, was expressing the views of many senior judges, when he stated; "To entrust to a Cabinet minister the power to control the legal profession would be an exorbitant inroad on the constitutional principle of the separation of powers".[75] He insisted that his objection was not to the reform of the machinery for determining advocacy rights nor to allowing qualified solicitors to take Crown Court cases, but was one of constitutional principle, namely the need for an independent Bar both to support the judiciary and "place a brake on the executive".[76] This view was echoed by Lord Lane, who saw the power as making "grave inroads into the long-standing independence of the judiciary and the Bar".[77]

Talk of a threat to judicial independence was no doubt over-stated, if relevant at all, and would seem to be an example of the judges protecting the interests of their own kind, that is of barristers from whose ranks they come and of whose club they remain a member, and the use of judicial independence in this manner would seem to devalue the concept. There is also an illogicality in the contention that "the protection of the independence of the judiciary and the integrity of the profession depends on the skills and courage of a single man . . ."[78] and the argument that this "single man" is interfering with judicial independence if he assumes a regulatory function of the legal profession. More convincing would be an argument that the Lord Chancellor should have neither role.

SAFEGUARDS FOR JUDICIAL INDEPENDENCE

In practical terms the establishment of an independent judiciary was a response to the settlement of 1688 and the need to ensure the legal sovereignty of Parliament. A move towards the separation of judicial and executive functions was made as early as the thirteenth century with the extinction of the post of chief justiciarship, which meant that the head of the court of justice was no longer the king's first minister. However, this development did not mean that judges enjoyed "any great degree of independence; they [were] still the King's servants; they [held] their offices for centuries to come during the King's good pleasure, and occasions on which the royal will [was] allowed to interfere with the course of royal justice [were] but too frequent".[79] It was not until after the Revolution that monarchical power over the judges was curtailed for fear that it would be used to influence judges in their interpretation of the laws passed by Parliament and thus undermine parliamentary supremacy. The Act of

[75] H. L Debs., 14 October 1998, col. 1174.
[76] Ibid, col. 1176.
[77] Ibid, col. 1174.
[78] Lord Hailsham, "The Office of Lord Chancellor and the Separation of Powers", p. 312.
[79] F. W. Maitland, *The Constitutional History of England* pp. 133–4. Once such example was the dismissal in the early seventeenth century of Chief Justice Coke, who, in a number of cases, including the Case of Prohibitions (1607) and the Case of Proclamations (1611), sought to limit the powers of the king.

Settlement of 1701 removed the power of dismissal from the Crown and "established . . . the independence of the judiciary who were given security of tenure and thenceforward appointed not, as before . . . at will but under good behaviour".[80]

The provision by which independence began to be established was a practical manifestation of the recognition that the judiciary should at least be independent from the executive, in the sense that judges should not be reliant upon the goodwill of the political arm of government to remain in office, and "should not be removed from office unfairly or without reason".[81] A logical development from this was the subsequent legislative provision, which protects judicial salaries from reduction by the executive and makes them a charge on the Consolidated Fund and so not subject to an annual vote in Parliament.[82]

Thus, "the maintenance of a strong and independent judiciary . . . [was], by the wisdom of our ancestors, . . . secured in two ways; tenure and absence of financial worries".[83] However, these provisions, while providing the core requirements for judicial independence, are not in themselves sufficient. Other safeguards are required if judicial independence is to be assured. These include the requirement that appointments to the judiciary, and promotion thereafter, should be made on the basis of merit, rather than political affiliation or the candidate's record in cases that have concerned the government, and that they should not depend on "uncontrolled ministerial patronage".[84] Moreover, once appointed, a judge should not be subjected to improper attempts by politicians to influence his or her decision and "no man should give him orders as to the manner in which he is to perform his work".[85] Indeed, a judge should have complete discretion in his or her court in the hearing of a case, being only accountable to a superior court (through appeal or judicial review) and not to politicians or officials.

Thus if the role of the Lord Chancellor is to protect judicial independence, it follows that he should ensure that these safeguards are not infringed. In fact, in the British context, these safeguards have a number of shortcomings. First, the appointments process,[86] which has long been criticised, not least for its secrecy, provides that all judicial and Queen's Counsel positions are in the direct, or indirect, gift of the Lord Chancellor. It therefore not only offends against principles of accountable and democratic government, which support openness and decry unbridled patronage, particularly when exercised by a minister, who himself is appointed rather than elected, but also against the notion that the judiciary should be completely independent from the executive. Moreover, the

---

[80] Lord Hailsham, "The Office of Lord Chancellor and the Separation of Powers", p. 309.
[81] R. Brazier, "Government and the Law", p. 74.
[82] Applied to judges appointed after 1786.
[83] LCD Memorandum of 1952 cited in Stevens, *The Independence of the Judiciary*, p. 127.
[84] R. Brazier, "Government and the Law", p. 74.
[85] W. A. Robson, *Justice and Administrative Law*, p. 44.
[86] Fully discussed in Chapter Six.

related power of the Lord Chancellor to control or discipline judges may also be seen as a threat to independence, not because judges should not be subject to control but because control by a single, unelected minister may be regarded as inappropriate, particularly when it takes the form of a "quiet word". Such a system of control carries with it the possibility of abuse, or at least the perception by members of the public that it can be abused. The combination of secrecy and considerable ministerial power detracts from the principle that judges are totally independent of government, for there is uncertainty as to what happens behind the scenes. More appropriate from a public confidence viewpoint would be the establishment of a formal complaints machinery,[87] in which the Lord Chancellor could perhaps play a part but not a sole role. Without this, it would be preferable for the chastisement of a judge by the Lord Chancellor to be a matter of public record. This would ensure that control mechanisms were being used appropriately.

Secondly, the requirement that judges should have tenure of office, one of the core protections of judicial independence, is by no means absolute. Indeed, as far as part-time judges are concerned, it "is conspicuously weak".[88] Lay magistrates may be removed at any time by the Lord Chancellor,[89] acting stipendaries may be stood down after an initial term of eighteen months and assistant recorders, whose performance is subject to regular review, may find that, rather than being promoted after three to five years, their services are no longer required. Recorders, who are appointed for a period of three years and whose performance is similarly subject to review, can be dismissed for incapacity or misbehaviour.[90]

This lack of tenure may be contrary to the European Convention on Human Rights,[91] Article 6(1) of which provides the right to a hearing before an independent and impartial tribunal. Independence, according to the European Court of Human Rights, is determined by, *inter alia*, the manner of appointment and terms of office[92] and, following a decision of the Scottish Court in 1999, the position of assistant recorders, acting stipendary magistrates, and even recorders, may be vulnerable. The case concerned temporary sheriffs, who were recruited by the Lord Advocate and whose appointments were subject to annual renewal. The Court held that such a judge was not independent within the meaning of Article 6. The fact that the position would end after a short fixed

---

[87] Such as a judicial commission suggested by JUSTICE in its Report, *The Judiciary* (1972). It concluded that informal controls on the behaviour of judges were ineffectual.

[88] R. Brazier, "Government and the Law", p. 77.

[89] Justice of the Peace Act 1979, s. 8(2).

[90] Courts Act 1971 s. 21(6); between 1981–7 twenty-seven recorders were not renewed, at least seven because they did not satisfy the Lord Chancellor; see H.C. Debs., 16 December 1986, col. 431, WA and H.C. Debs., 21 January 1987, col. 574, WA. In 1998/99 of the 302 recorders whose appointments were considered for extension, two had extensions of less than the normal three years for reasons other than their age and four appointments were not extended, likewise for non-age related reasons.

[91] As given effect in national law through the Human Rights Act 1998.

[92] *Bryan* v. *UK* (1995) 21 EHRR 342, para. 37.

period of time, but that renewal was possible at the discretion of the executive, was seen as liable to compromise the judge's independence. Moreover, it was exacerbated by the Lord Advocate's ability to remove a sheriff from office at any time.[93] The situation is somewhat different in England and Wales. Assistant recorders are not temporary in the sense of having short fixed term contracts. Nevertheless, their need to satisfy the Lord Chancellor, if they are to continue in office, raises questions about the compatibility of these positions with the European Convention and hence the Human Rights Act.[94]

As far as district and circuit judges are concerned, there is no regular review but they can be dismissed at any time for incapacity or misbehaviour.[95] Lord Denning insisted that, in practice, members of the lower judiciary were only dismissed for misconduct[96] and his assertion is given some credence by Lord Hailsham's failure to dismiss Judge Pickles, a circuit judge, despite complaints from the presiding judge about "lapses in taste" and the failure of Pickles to obtain the permission of the Lord Chancellor before writing articles for the national press. Hailsham, it seems, was inhibited from taking action against Pickles because of press support for the judge and, more importantly, because it seemed likely that Pickles would seek judicial review. He was uncertain as to whether Pickles' misdemeanours were sufficiently connected with his office of circuit judge for dismissal of the judge to withstand a legal challenge.[97] He did not have the same concerns in 1983 over the removal of an Old Bailey circuit judge, who had been fined two thousand pounds for smuggling whisky.[98] This was an obvious case of misbehaviour, which, if the judge were allowed to continue sitting, would bring the judiciary into disrepute. However, the problem of what constitutes grounds for dismissal remains, as does the question of whether it is acceptable for a government minister to determine when such grounds exist.

In a letter to the Lord Chief Justice, copied to all judges, Lord Mackay sought to provide a definition of the grounds, which he considered could result in dismissal. He was motivated, it seems, by notions of fairness, his belief being that it could be unfair to ask a judge to relinquish office, if, given the vagueness of the concepts of misbehaviour, incapacity and inability, he was unaware that his behaviour constituted a dismissable offence. However, his good intentions caused unease among some members of the judiciary, who felt his mode of communication, by registered mail, to be somewhat heavy handed, particularly as those, who for various reasons were not available to sign for the post, subsequently received a letter asking them to inform the Lord Chancellor when they

---

[93] *Starrs* v. *Procurator Fiscal Linlithglow* [1999] *The Times*, 17 November 1999.
[94] Deputy High Court judges, who are appointed a year at a time, may also be vulnerable.
[95] Courts Act 1971 ss. 17(4).
[96] Lord Denning, *The Road to Justice* (London, 1955), p. 17.
[97] See G. Lewis, *Lord Hailsham: A Life* (London, Pimlico, 1998) p. 271 and see Chapter Seven. Pickles was subsequently publicly rebuked by Lord Mackay for holding a press conference in a public house and referring to the Lord Chief Justice as a "dinosaur". (S. H. Bailey and M. J. Gunn, *Smith and Bailey on the Modern English Legal System*).
[98] J.A.G. Griffith, *The Politics of the Judiciary*, p. 24.

could do so. Moreover, presumably in error, High Court judges also received the offence list, despite the fact that their tenure of office is not dependent upon the Lord Chancellor.[99] While Lord Mackay sought to clarify the grounds for dismissal, Lord Irvine specified the basis on which a Lord Chancellor satisfies himself that the grounds have been met, stating that the appropriate burden of proof was the civil burden.[100] The appropriateness of a government minister applying it is another matter.

Judges in the Supreme Court and Lords of Appeal in Ordinary are legally better protected as far as tenure is concerned, holding office "during good behaviour",[101] subject to an address of both Houses of Parliament. These provisions date from the Act of Settlement 1700 and ensure that, providing they do not breach the requirements of "good behaviour" or cause Parliament, for whatever reason, to seek their dismissal, senior judges are secure. Moreover, while the relevant statutes suggest that these two "offences" are separate and thus a judicial career can be terminated on either account, today "it is likely that the address procedure would be used in any case where a judge was to be removed, and, further, that is would only be done in a case of misbehaviour".[102] Given that the address procedure has not been used since 1830, when Sir Jonah Barrington, a judge of the High Court of Admiralty in Ireland, was removed for embezzling money paid into court, the tenure of office of senior judges rates highly on any scale of security.

However, the legal protection afforded to judges does not stop informal pressure being brought to bear upon individuals and there have been at least fifteen instances in the last hundred years where judges in the superior courts "have been the subject of strong pressures or inducements to resign, ostensibly on the grounds of ill-health".[103] Pressure was, for instance, brought to bear on Lord Atkinson to resign as law lord in 1928, after a decision of the Privy Council had been heavily criticised in Canada,[104] and, after the Court of Appeal had criticised Mr Justice Hallett, the Lord Chancellor, Lord Kilmuir, agreed with him that "he should continue to sit for a little while and then resign. That he did at the end of the summer term".[105]

Until 1959 High Court judges and above could stay in office indefinitely, an unsatisfactory position which, in instances of obvious ill-health or senility, encouraged the use of "informal pressure" to precipitate retirement. Who should apply this pressure was disputed in 1980, when Lord Widgery, the Lord Chief Justice, was suffering from the onset of Parkinson's disease. Lord

[99] Confidential source.

[100] In response to a Parliamentary Question on a circuit judge, Judge Gee (H. L. Debs., 13 July 1999, col.WA31).

[101] Supreme Court Act 1981, s. 11(3) and Appellate Jurisdiction Act, s.6, as amended.

[102] S. H. Bailey and M. J. Gunn, *Smith and Bailey on the Modern English Legal System*, p. 221.

[103] A. Paterson and St John Bates, *The Legal System in Scotland* (2nd edn., Edinburgh, Green, 1986) p. 172.

[104] R. F. V. Heuston, *Lives of the Lord Chancellors 1885–1940*, pp.303–4.

[105] Lord Denning, *The Due Process of Law* (London, Butterworths, 1980) p. 62.

Hailsham was urged to act by the law lords but argued that for the Lord Chancellor, a member of the Cabinet, to seek the resignation of the Lord Chief Justice would undermine judicial independence. In the end, Lord Denning spoke to Lord Widgery but many judges thought that Hailsham "was shirking a painful obligation",[106] rather than protecting judicial independence.

The position of judges in the High Court was changed by the Judicial Pensions Act 1959, which set the retirement age at seventy-five, an age that was further reduced to seventy for all members of the judiciary by the Judicial Pensions and Retirement Act 1993, which came into effect in April 1995. The introduction, and subsequent reduction, of the retirement age was accepted, if not welcomed by most judges. Less acceptable was a provision included in the Bill which gave the "appropriate minister" power to extend a judge's tenure of office on an annual basis up to seventy-five, if he considered this to be in the public interest. The continuation in office of able judges, beyond the official retirement date, was not in question. This is beneficial to the development of the law and to the Treasury, the number of judges available to sit being increased without all the costs associated with the employment of additional full time judges. What was questioned was the location of the power in a minister to determine who should continue in office, for such a power might be used to keep judges in office who were sympathetic to government policies or to notions of executive sovereignty, or to put pressure, or appear to do so, on a judge hearing a case. As Lord Taylor, the Lord Chief Justice noted; "Senior judges not infrequently have to hear applications for judicial review of ministerial decisions. On occasion they may concern the Lord Chancellor himself. It would be unfortunate if extension of a judge's tenure were under consideration by the appropriate Minister at or about the time the judge was deciding such a case".[107] The perceived danger was that the power, no matter how scrupulously used by the Lord Chancellor, would be seen as a mechanism by which the government could keep in office the judges it favoured. This is hardly in the interests of judicial independence and, not surprisingly, the measure was strongly opposed in the Lords as "objectionable constitutionally and as a matter of principle".[108]

A third shortcoming relates to judicial salaries. While such salaries are legally protected to prevent a government from reducing the amount paid to individual judges or classes of judges, in the interwar years there was judicial concern at the government's failure to increase them. A particular issue was the plight of county court judges, who, in real terms, faced a reduced standard of living.[109] There was also considerable judicial opposition to the imposition of a pay cut through the National Economy Act 1931 and a related Order in Council. The salary reduction applied to "persons in Her Majesty's Service" and was resisted on the grounds of principle, namely, that it interfered with judicial indepen-

---

[106] G. Lewis, *Lord Hailsham*, p. 273.
[107] H. L. Debs., 16 June 1992, col. 140.
[108] Lord Donaldson, Ibid, col. 148.
[109] For details see R. Stevens, *The Independence of the Judiciary*, pp. 45–9.

dence. Despite the national emergency, judges, it seems, believed they should be above economic requirements and should not be treated in the same way as others in public service.[110] Moreover, although argued largely in terms of judicial independence, the issue of status was again not far from the surface.

For most of the post-War period, in fact until the 1990s, judicial salaries were not contentious. They were high enough to prevent potential judges from being faced with "an unacceptable cut in income if they were to accept appointment" and to maintain the status and "dignity of judicial office".[111] They were also structured to "reflect the promotional stages between various ranks" and regular reviews ensured that they "ke[pt] pace with other professional incomes and with inflation".[112] However, in 1992 the remuneration of judges was back on the political agenda when the Conservative Government of John Major rejected the advice of the Committee on Top Salaries to raise judicial salaries by twenty per cent and, instead, awarded judges a four per cent increase. The committee, established in 1971, makes recommendations on judicial pay awards to the Lord Chancellor, who, with the approval of the Prime Minister, has the discretion to raise, but not reduce, salaries.[113] The position of the committee means that, in effect, it has become "the protector of judicial salaries – and thus of independence",[114] although in making its recommendations the preservation of judicial independence would not seem to be its main consideration. More important is ensuring that the salary is at a level to attract barristers of the right calibre to the bench and that the status of judges in the community is maintained.[115] Thus the benchmarks that the committee uses are the salaries of civil servants and of those practising at the Bar.

The decision of the Government not to follow the committee's recommendation in this instance "repoliticised"[116] the issue of judicial salaries. Moreover, it confirmed the link between status and independence, the Lord Chief Justice and other senior judges arguing that the rise was inadequate, failed to reward judges in relation to what they would have earned at the Bar, and that the Government, by demeaning the position of judges, was interfering with judicial independence. Similar arguments were made when legislation was passed, which, on the one hand, increased the qualifying period for pensions from fifteen to twenty years, and, on the other, reduced the age of retirement for judges.[117] Its introduction by the Lord Chancellor led to the comment by Sir Francis Purchas that "[o]ne might be excused the thought that this was a strange thing for the person charged with protecting . . . [judicial] independence and integrity to do".[118]

---

[110] Ibid, pp. 56–63.
[111] R. Brazier, *Constitutional Practice* (Oxford, Clarendon Press, 1990) p. 232.
[112] Ibid.
[113] Supreme Court Act 1981, s. 12.
[114] R. Stevens, *The Independence of the Judiciary*, pp. 135–6.
[115] S. H. Bailey and M. J. Gunn, *Smith and Bailey on the Modern English Legal System*, p. 226.
[116] R. Stevens, *The Independence of the Judiciary*, p. 138.
[117] Judicial Pensions and Retirement Act 1993.
[118] "The Constitution in the Market Place", p. 1608.

Thus while the protection of salaries by law is an important safeguard to judicial independence, it is not absolute and the failure to increase remuneration adequately may be seen as a cut in real terms and thus as a threat to status and hence independence. This, of course, raises the question of who should decide what is adequate – judges or the executive, and what is the position of the Lord Chancellor in such a situation. Does he, as head of the judiciary, assert the views of the judges or does he, as a government minister, support the government in its view of what the country can afford? Given that his responsibility for judicial salaries arises from his executive role, he is bound to follow the government line but clearly this may conflict with his constitutional responsibility.

The fourth area, where safeguards to judicial independence have been found wanting, concerns the requirement that politicians should not attempt to influence the legal process and the principle that a judge has complete discretion in his or her own court. In 1947 Lord Jowitt, then Lord Chancellor, wrote to Lord Goddard, the Lord Chief Justice, expressing the hope that " 'the judges will not be lenient on those bandits [who] carry arms [to] shoot at the police' ".[119] How much influence this had is not known, although as Stevens comments, given "what is now known about Lord Goddard, there was little danger of this urging falling on deaf ears".[120] In any event, two years later Derek Bentley was sentenced to death by Lord Goddard. In a similar way, Mrs Thatcher, when Prime Minister, is reputed to have expressed the wish that "an appropriately severe member of the judiciary would be on hand"[121] to hear the case against Clive Ponting, the civil servant on trial under the Official Secrets Act for leaking secret information on the sinking of the Argentinian cruiser, the General Belgrano, during the Falklands campaign. Whether or not coincidentally, her wish would seem to have been granted, as was evident in the way in which the trial judge equated the "public interest" with "government interest", thereby attempting, unsuccessfully as it happened, to reduce the effectiveness of Ponting's defence. During the miners' strike of 1984, the Attorney-General, Sir Michael Havers, was also accused of trying to influence the court when he predicted that the National Union of Mineworkers would be "brought to heel" by the High Court.[122] Again, the outcome of a number of cases suggested that the Home Secretary's words had been heeded, although, of course, the result would no doubt have been the same.

These apparent attempts to influence the courts were controversial. However, none gave rise to the degree of concern provoked by the action of the Lord Chancellor, Lord Mackay, in 1994, when he sought to persuade the President of the Employment Appeals Tribunal, Mr Justice Wood, to review the appeal procedure he had adopted for reasons of efficiency and cost effectiveness. In the resulting debate in the House of Lords considerable anxiety was expressed that

[119] LCO 2/3830, quoted in R. Stevens, *The Independence of the Judiciary*, p. 95.
[120] Ibid.
[121] *The Times*, 14 September 1984.
[122] See D. Oliver, "Politicians and the Courts" (1988) 41 *Parliamentary Affairs* 1, at 24.

the principle that a judge has complete discretion in his own court was being eroded, thereby posing a threat to judicial independence.[123] Moreover, the anxiety was heightened by the fact that the threat came from the person charged with protecting that independence and it appeared to arise from a conflict between his executive and constitutional roles.

A major concern in any apparent attempt to influence the judges is how such an attempt is perceived. Judicial independence is not just an end in itself. It is also a means to an end, the end being public confidence in the system of justice. Judges must therefore not only be independent of the executive, but "be seen and well understood by the public at large to be independent".[124] The use of judges to chair royal commissions, departmental committees, or to undertake other inquiries into matters of public concern, is controversial for this reason, for while they give an aura of independence to the process, there is a danger that the process itself will be seen as political and that the judges will be perceived as instruments of the executive, thereby casting doubt on their independence.[125] This was evident in 1963–4 when Harold Wilson, the Opposition leader, made derogatory remarks about the use of Lords Radcliffe and Denning in the Vassall Tribunal and the Profumo investigation, both of which concerned alleged breaches of national security. They were defended by Lord Dilhorne, the Lord Chancellor, who called Wilson's remarks, "A Libel on the Judges".[126] In 1996 a different problem presented itself, when Sir Richard Scott reported on his inquiry into the Matrix Churchill affair.[127] His report was highly critical of some officials and ministers and was subject to a whispering campaign in Whitehall and Westminster, which sought to undermine its findings and Scott's integrity and to distort its conclusions. Moreover, when Sir Richard defended his report, he was accused of being "anti-government" and thus, by implication, of not retaining the independence and objectivity required.

The requirement that judges should be seen as independent is also traditionally given form through the convention which requires that they do not speak on party political matters or engage in public debate on matters of government policy. Indeed, until 1987 the Kilmuir Rules required members of the lower judiciary to secure the permission of the Lord Chancellor before giving interviews, publishing or speaking in public. During his first term in office as Lord Chancellor, Lord Hailsham considered relaxing the rules but felt that "since only a small number of Judges would prove to be satisfactory performers on television or radio, if any change were to be made, he should keep control in his

---

[123] See Chapter Four.

[124] Sir John Donaldson, MR, "Address to the Law Society" (12 April 1987) reported in *The Times* (13 April 1987).

[125] Stevens notes that during the period 1945–69 over one third of royal commissions and departmental committees were chaired by judges (R. Stevens, *The Independence of the Judiciary*, p. 98).

[126] *The Times*, 25 September 1963, cited in B. Abel Smith and R. Stevens, *Lawyers and the Courts* (London, Heineman, 1967) p. 310.

[127] Sir Richard Scott, *Report of the Inquiry into the Export of Defence Equipment and Dual-Use Goods to Iraq and Related Prosecutions* (1995–96) HC 115, HMSO.

hand".[128] In any case the Heads of Division were "resolutely against any relaxation", so the rules stayed in place. This caused Lord Denning to assert, in typical style, "Judges are independent and not in any way subject to any kind of discipline by the Lord Chancellor".[129] The requirement imposed by the rules was finally dispensed with in 1989 by Lord Mackay, who felt that while the spirit of the rules should continue to be observed, judges should exercise their own discretion in such matters. However, he stressed that because of the nature of their office, judges should be "very cautious about their exposure to the media", and if they have "any serious doubts about the wisdom of participating" they should not do so. More specifically he wrote; "they must avoid public statements either on general issues or particular cases which might cast doubt on their complete impartiality. Above all they should avoid any involvement, either direct or indirect, in issues which are or might become politically controversial".

Senior members of the judiciary have always had discretion, regarding what they should say in public, but this has not prevented them from being chastised by the Lord Chancellor when he considers they have exercised their discretion unwisely. Thus Lord Simonds wrote to Mr Justice Lloyd-Jacob over a letter to *The Times* on the use of atomic energy; "A judge ought not to express his views in public on matters which are either political or controversial, and the subject-matter of your letter is both. In my opinion it was a breach of your duty, as a judge to write the letter, and I am deeply sorry that you wrote it".[130] In more general terms Lord Irvine, prior to becoming Lord Chancellor, suggested that senior judges were "unwise" to make "observations off the Bench . . . that the courts had reacted to the increase of powers claimed by government by being more active themselves . . . It suggests to ordinary people a judicial invasion of the legislature's turf".[131] He also argued in a speech in Hong Kong that the courts should "exercise self-restraint" in judicial review cases, citing the Pergau Dam case, in which the Court of Appeal had held that the payment of aid from the Overseas Development Fund for the building of a dam in Malaysia was unlawful,[132] as a "type of judicial activism which begins to blur the boundary between appeal and review, thereby undermining the constitutional foundations on which the courts' supervisory jurisdiction rests".[133] He subsequently stated that he would not have offered such a view had he been Lord Chancellor at the time. However, it is questionable whether a shadow Lord Chancellor,

---

[128] G. Lewis, *Lord Hailsham*, p. 274.

[129] A. W. Bradley, "Judges and the Media – the Kilmuir Rules [1986] *Public Law* 384.

[130] 18 May 1954, quoted in R. Stevens, *The Independence of the Judiciary*, p. 90.

[131] H. L. Debs, 5 June 1996, col. 1255.

[132] The Court held that the project was not economically "sound" and thus did not accord with the Overseas Development and Co-operation Act 1980 which confers power on the Foreign Secretary to grant assistance to overseas countries, "for the purpose of promoting the economy" of the country (R v. *Secretary of State for Foreign and Commonwealth Affairs, ex parte World Development Movement* [1995] 1 WLR 386; [1995] 1 All ER 611).

[133] Hargreaves, *Sunday Independent*, 11 October 1998.

whose party seems likely to win the next election, should offer such a view either. By doing so, he had given an indication of "how his powers might be used to put pressure on the judges".[134]

In a further attempt to prevent any suggestions of a political judiciary, the law lords are also expected to be careful in the contributions they make to debates in the House of Lords and to limit themselves to matters in which they have a special and specialist interest and which are non-political, in the party-political sense. Traditionally, they have spoken in debates relating to the constitution and to the administration of justice and the legal system, which have generally been non-controversial. However, this rule was not strong enough to prevent some law lords taking part in debates in the 1920s on the Irish Free State Bill. Moreover, "In debates upon proposed legislation having a bearing upon moral issues", such as the abolition of the death penalty, and "upon Bills believed to authorise executive intrusion into the province of the courts, the interventions of the Law Lords has sometimes been quite heated".[135] So, for instance, the law lords were "almost unanimously opposed" to a clause, subsequently dropped, in the Rating and Valuation Bill 1928, which provided for the courts' opinions on questions of law to be submitted to the Minister of Health.[136] They also spoke against the Bill which reversed retroactively the Burmah Oil decision,[137] on the grounds that it interfered with the administration of justice, and against the War Crimes Bill.[138] This was subsequently passed using the provision of the Parliament Act 1949, which allows Bills to bypass the House of Lords after a year's delay. The law lords were also critical of the Courts Bill,[139] Lord Denning, in particular, criticising clauses which he saw as giving the Lord Chancellor too much power over the judges, and, during the 1990s, they were hostile to legislation which gave effect to government policies on sentencing, the legal profession, the civil court system and legal aid. The judges claimed that these were concerned with the administration of justice, about which it was legitimate for judges to express their views. The government claimed they were political.[140]

Such confrontation inevitably raised questions about judicial independence and the viability of the Lord Chancellor's position as both a government minister, responsible for many of the reform policies, and head of the judiciary, charged with protecting judicial independence. In such circumstances, it would seem impossible for him to do both.

---

[134] Ibid.

[135] S. Shetreet, *Judges on Trial; A Study on the Appointment and Accountability of the English Judiciary*, p. 346. See, for instance, Lord Goddard's opposition to the abolition of the death penalty.

[136] Ibid.

[137] *Burmah Oil* v. *Lord Advocate* [1965] AC 75.

[138] War Crimes Act 1993.

[139] Courts Act 1971.

[140] See D. Woodhouse, "Politicians and the Judges; a Conflict of Interest" (1996) 49 *Parliamentary Affairs* 3, at 423–41.

CONCLUSION

The constitutional role of the Lord Chancellor, which requires him to protect judicial independence, can neither be justified with reference to the separation of powers nor on the basis that it provides practical safeguards. His position undermines the separation that exists between the judges and the other arms of government and, in many respects, infringes the safeguards established to protect them. In truth, at the beginning of the twenty-first century, the Lord Chancellor is above all else a government minister, and, as such, is likely to hold different views from the judges on the administration of justice. However, even more fundamental is the divergence of opinion over the meaning of judicial independence itself; the concept that the Lord Chancellor is charged with protecting.

Lord Mackay, when Lord Chancellor, took a minimalist view. He considered; "The essence of judicial independence is that the judge trying the case is free to decide it according to his judgment in the light of the existing law. This applies to the individual case and that is the essence of judicial independence".[141] While conceding that "to preserve their independence the judges must have some control or influence over the administrative penumbria immediately surrounding the judicial process",[142] by which he meant the listing of cases, he insisted that its impact on efficiency meant that it was also an aspect of his responsibility as a government minister. Lord Irvine, even before becoming Lord Chancellor, took a similar narrow view; "The duty of the judges is to apply the law as determined by Parliament; and what judicial independence means, properly understood, is their right not to be subject to any interference with their independence in carrying out that task".[143]

However, as far as many judges are concerned, to limit judicial independence, such that it "is infringed only if an attempt is made to dictate or influence the decision in a particular case",[144] is too restrictive and is evidence of a failure "properly to understand, and therefore properly to protect, judicial independence – a vital ingredient in our system of justice".[145] They see "the independence of the judiciary as a collective body, as opposed to the independence of each judge as an individual; a threat to the independence of the legal system, as opposed to the judges who operate it".[146] It is therefore "not sufficient merely to have independence in the . . . actual trial of the case and the immediate listing perumbra . . . the Judiciary must be allowed a significant role in the administration of the courts".[147]

---

[141] H.L. Debs., 5 June 1996, col. 1308.
[142] Lord Mackay, "The Lord Chancellor in the 1990s", p. 247.
[143] H. L. Debs., 5 June 1996, col. 1258.
[144] H. L. Debs., 27 April 1994, col. 779.
[145] H. L. Debs. 5 June 1996, col. 1285.
[146] Sir Nicolas Browne-Wilkinson, "The Independence of the Judiciary in the 1980s", p. 44.
[147] Sir Francis Purchas, "The Constitution in the Market Place" p. 1605.

Such arguments have been used to oppose reform to the civil court system, to object to the failure of government to appoint additional High Court judges and to resist increasing Treasury control over the court system, all of which were portrayed as interfering with judicial independence.[148] Regardless of the merit of such opposition, there is again the danger that arguments based on judicial independence create uncertainty as to whether the judges are really protecting their constitutional position or their own interests. They also suggest that judges equate "independence" with "non-interference", which makes them, and the system in which they are involved, immune from change and reform. However, most important, as far as the position of Lord Chancellor is concerned, is that public disagreement about who should run the courts seriously weakens his constitutional role, as a bulwark or buffer between the judiciary and the executive, and casts doubt over his position as head of the judiciary.[149]

In many respects therefore, the office of Lord Chancellor seems not to be fulfilling its constitutional role. Indeed, given its nature and its range of responsibilities it would seem ill-equipped to do so. Writing in 1988, Sir Nicolas Browne-Wilkinson, subsequently to become the senior law lord, wrote; "The Lord Chancellor's own position, representing as he does simultaneously both the independent judiciary and the interests of government, is becoming more and more difficult, since the price to be paid for obtaining funds for the administration of justice is dependent on satisfying the Treasury that any particular course represents in their terms, value for money. The practical manifestation of this change is the increasing stress arising in the relationship between the judiciary and the Lord Chancellor's Department".[150] It is this relationship, and the changes which have affected it, that is considered in the next chapter.

---

[148] See Chapter Four.
[149] See I. R. Scott, "The Council of Judges in the Supreme Court of England and Wales" [1989] *Public Law* 379–88 at 379.
[150] Sir Nicolas Browne-Wilkinson, "The Independence of the Judiciary in the 1980s", p. 50.

3

The Lord Chancellor's Department[1]

T HE "ESSENTIAL FUNCTION" of the Lord Chancellor's Department (LCD) is
"to promote the fair, efficient and effective administration of justice in
England and Wales",[2] the key elements of which are appointing, or advising on
the appointment of, judges, administering the court system and a number of tribunals, overseeing the provision of legal aid and legal services, and promoting
law reform and the revision of English civil law. In 1997 its stated aim was; "to
ensure that people can uphold their rights and fulfil their obligations, in particular through efficient and affordable courts and legal services, and by developing the civil law to meet society's needs".[3] In 2000 the aim was more simply
expressed as "justice",[4] the priority of the LCD being "to contribute to the
Government's commitment to fairness, growth and opportunity by introducing
a programme of reforms to provide a modern, fair and efficient system of justice
which operates in the public interest and ensures value for money for the taxpayer".[5] Thus, like all other government departments, the LCD is concerned
with giving effect to the objectives of the government of the day and is required
to take account of changes in substance and emphasis.

The LCD has a staff of approximately twelve thousand of whom more than
ten thousand work in the Court Service at courts and tribunals. To this can be
added over nine thousand staff working in the Public Records Office, the Land
Registry and the Northern Ireland Court Service, all also the responsibility of
the Lord Chancellor. It has a budget of over two and a half million pounds,
more than half of which is for legal aid,[6] and consists of headquarters and two
executive agencies, the Court Service, which "exists to carry out the administrative and support tasks necessary to enable criminal cases to be heard; civil
disputes to be adjudicated; family proceedings to be decided; and judgements
to be enforced",[7] and the Public Trust Office, whose responsibility is the

---

[1] In dealing with the LCD, this chapter is concerned only with the core responsibilities of the
Lord Chancellor. It does not consider the Public Records Office, Land Registry or ecclesiastical
patronage etc.
[2] LCD's website:www.open.gov.uk/lcd/.
[3] LCD, *Strategic Plan 1996/97–1998/99*.
[4] LCD, *Annual Report 2000–2002*.
[5] Ibid.
[6] For the year 2000–01 legal aid accounted for £1,672,000 of the total Department budget of
£2,635,000 (HM Treasury, *Spending Review 2000*, Chapter 11).
[7] LCD, *Strategic Plan 1996/97–1998/99*.

"management of private assets and financial affairs entrusted to its care by the courts by, or on behalf of, people unable or unwilling to manage these matters themselves".[8] There are also a number of non-departmental public bodies and associated offices, which, because of the Lord Chancellor's responsibility for them, come within the remit of the LCD,[9] as do the Official Solicitor, Judge Advocate of the Fleet, Judge Advocate General, the Magistrates' Court Service Inspectorate and the Advisory Committees on Justices of the Peace in England and Wales.

The headquarters is structured around an administrative and policy-making core of about two thousand staff, which receives advice, legal and otherwise, from separately managed groups within the Department and from outside bodies. As well as setting the strategic direction for the whole of the Department, headquarters provides advice and support to the Lord Chancellor in his supervision of the two agencies and the Legal Services Commission and "on policy concerning access to justice, legal aid and legal services".[10] It also assists him in the appointment of "virtually all the professional and lay judiciary, Queen's Counsel [and] some lay tribunal members" and "ensures that policy on the role, structure and procedure of the courts is developed to promote their efficient and effective operation".[11] Where the criminal courts are concerned, it works in consultation with the judiciary and "in partnership with the Home Office, the Crown Prosecution Service, the Serious Fraud Office, other prosecutors and with other organisations with a relevant interest".[12] This partnership has become increasingly important with the targeting of the criminal justice system under a joined-up government initiative, and the LCD reported in 2000 that, together with the Home Office and the Crown Prosecution Service, it was "working to reduce delays in the criminal courts, improving the service to victims and increasing the effectiveness of enforcement".[13]

The extent and diversity of responsibilities of the LCD reflect the mix of roles of the Lord Chancellor and the way in which they have developed since the establishment of the Department. They also indicate the pivotal role in the Government's programme, played by the LCD at the beginning of the new millennium, such that it "extends beyond the two core historical businesses of running the courts and dealing with the judiciary and judicial appointments".[14] It now has a strategic "vision" based on "theories of social justice, rights and

---

[8] LCD, *Strategic Plan 1996/97–1998/99*.

[9] They include the Legal Services Commission, the Law Commission, the Judicial Studies Board, the Legal Services Ombudsman, the Advisory Committee on Legal Education and Conduct, the Court Rules Committee, the Council on Tribunals, and the Civil Justice Council.

[10] *Strategic Plan 1996/97–1998/99*. It further advises him on "the protection and development of the rights of the family and individuals", ensuring that "these rights are supported, where appropriate, by effective law reform process, conducted in partnership with the Law Commission".

[11] Ibid.

[12] Ibid.

[13] *Annual Report, 2000–2002* and see Home Affairs Committee, *Lord Chancellor's Department, Crown Prosecution Service, Home Office: Criminal Justice; Working Together* (1999–00) HC 29.

[14] Ibid.

responsibilities and the law as an instrument of economic strength"[15] and it is concerned with "changing the existing justice system from one based on traditions, practices and procedures, designed to suit administrators and lawyers, to one focused on consumers". This is a far cry from the nineteenth century Office of the Lord Chancellor and its changed focus and central place in government challenges the position of the minister at its head.

DEVELOPMENT OF THE LCD

The Lord Chancellor's Department, or Office as it was initially titled, was established in 1885 with the creation of the post of permanent secretary. Until this time, the Lord Chancellor had been a "minister without a ministry",[16] who "transacted his multifarious functions without the aid of a permanent staff, and hence without any guiding framework of administrative continuity".[17] Thus while the position of Lord Chancellor is more than one thousand years old and there have been two hundred and fifty-eight holders of the office,[18] that of permanent secretary is considerably more recent and boasts only nine office holders.[19] The first permanent secretary was Sir Kenneth Muir Mackenzie. He had been appointed in 1880 personally by the Lord Chancellor, Lord Selbourne, as Clerk of the Crown in Chancery, "an office of great dignity and antiquity",[20] which supports the Lord Chancellor in his responsibility as custodian of the Great Seal. The position involved, and continues to involve, its occupant in "many important acts of State" and in 1892 it was suggested that its holder "may claim to be 'the first esquire and first clerk of England' ".[21]

Mackenzie also acted as principal secretary to the Lord Chancellor, one of three secretaryships within his office, the others being Secretary of Commissions, who dealt with the appointment of magistrates, and Secretary of Presentations, who was concerned with ecclesiastical patronage.[22] All three positions were regarded as personal secretaries to the Lord Chancellor and the principal secretary, in particular, was engaged in political as well as legal duties. Mackenzie would therefore have been expected to leave office along with his patron, Lord Selbourne, had not the Treasury accepted the need for the Office of Lord Chancellor to have a permanent staff "on whose experience each successive Lord Chancellor may rely".[23] Thus Mackenzie assumed the title of

---

[15] Ibid.
[16] N. Underhill, *The Lord Chancellor*, p. 188.
[17] G. Drewry, "Lord Haldane's Ministry of Justice; Stillborn or Strangled at Birth?" (1983) 61 *Public Administration* 396–414 at 398.
[18] Lord Irvine claimed to be the 258th.
[19] Sir Hayden Phillips, appointed in 1998, being the ninth holder.
[20] Anson, *The Law and Custom of the Constitution*, p. 168.
[21] Anson quoting from Crown Office MS, Ibid, p. 168.
[22] R. F. V. Heuston, *Lives of the Lord Chancellors 1885–1940*, p. xx.
[23] R. Stevens, *The Independence of the Judiciary*, p. 9.

permanent secretary. His political duties were devolved to a private secretary and he was left with largely legal responsibilities.

The establishment of the Lord Chancellor's Office in the latter part of the nineteenth century was a response to the increased responsibilities and hence administrative workload of the Lord Chancellor, which had arisen, in part, from the reorganisation of the superior courts under the Supreme Court of Judicature Acts 1873–5.[24] The obvious and logical development would have been for these responsibilities either to transfer to a ministry of justice, established along the same lines as other departments, or to a minister within the Home Office, where responsibility for running the Quarter Sessions and the magistrates courts was located. Either alternative would have resulted in the courts being administered by professional civil servants, and both options had political support. However, the judges were suspicious of "the new fangled Northcote-Trevelyan vision of life [which] did not sit well with the judicial self-image",[25] and preferred administrative responsibility to reside with the Lord Chancellor, who was, after all, one of them. Their view prevailed and responsibility therefore passed to the Lord Chancellor. Moreover, when the Treasury subsequently accepted the need for a permanent department, it was persuaded that rather than it being staffed by civil servants, who had been selected on merit through competitive examination, the department should be staffed by lawyers and its permanent secretary should be a barrister of at least seven years' standing, who was exempt from the Civil Service entry regulations.[26] Thus the unique position of the LCO at the "constitutional boundary between law and politics"[27] was confirmed and "[i]n a system of government characterized by 'generalism', its permanent head was to be a senior lawyer".[28]

Given the responsibilities of the Office at that time and the fact that it had a staff of only five officials, the exceptional requirement for the permanent secretary was perhaps justified. Many of his duties were of a legal nature for which professional training was necessary. However, the basis on which the LCO was founded meant that, despite the growth in its administrative duties, for much of the twentieth century it was staffed exclusively by lawyers. As a consequence, it remained largely unfettered by Civil Service rules and regulations, although it still lay claim to "the political anonymity of the Civil Service" as well as to the "political asexuality of the legal profession".[29] In addition, because of its professional affiliations, it saw its role "not as one primarily of managing the areas for which it was responsible but rather as that of a lobbyist for quasi-independent

[24] This replaced the various superior courts with a Supreme Court of Judicature which comprised the High Court, of which there were five divisions, and the Court of Appeal.

[25] R. Stevens, *The Independence of the Judiciary*, p. 8.

[26] An Order of June 4 1870 provided the general rule of competitive examination but authorised the Civil Service Commissioners to depart from it in cases for which qualifications wholly or in part professional and not ordinarily to be acquired in the Civil Service, were required.

[27] G. Drewry, "Lord Haldane's Ministry of Justice", p. 411.

[28] Ibid.

[29] R. Stevens, *The Independence of the Judiciary*, p. 7.

activities, like the judges or the courts".[30] The capture of the Department by its user groups was therefore well advanced and says much for the power of the judges and the legal profession, who "were insulated from effective management by their own version of the Civil Service – the Lord Chancellor's Office".[31]

The LCO was therefore allowed to develop outside the Whitehall mould in a way which would not have been countenanced in other areas of government. As Stevens notes, the idea that "the Ministry of Defence . . . would be solely run by regular officers or the Ministry of Health solely run by health professionals would be regarded as risible".[32] The LCO's semi-autonomy had much to do with the "amorphous" concept of judicial independence (discussed in the previous chapter) and the status of judges as "Great Officers of State, above mere politicians and certainly above the bourgeois meritocrats in the Civil Service".[33] They were also seen as the embodiment of the law rather than as public servants. Thus the notion that it would be inappropriate for those who had dealings with them to be other than members of the legal profession was easily sold, and the LCO came to have a disproportionate number of senior posts to accommodate those of a suitable legal standing.

The position of the LCO as apart from the rest of Whitehall also related to the "unusual" position of the permanent secretary[34] who retained, and continues to do so, the position of Clerk of the Crown in Chancery, an officer of Parliament. This is a distinct office, appointment to which is by the Prime Minister, and although its relationship with that of permanent secretary is one of administrative convenience only, since 1885 the two positions have gone together. Further factors which separated the LCO from Whitehall were the location of the Office in the House of Lords, where the Lord Chancellor continues to have a residence, and its size and functions, which suggested still a private office rather than a department of state. The LCO has, of course, subsequently been relocated and transformed into a modern department, even equipped with its own gymnasium.[35] However, compared with other departments, its transformation was slow and belated.

In 1912, the year that Lord Haldane assumed the role of Lord Chancellor, the office was described as, "not far removed from being an interesting little museum",[36] which provided little administrative support to the Lord Chancellor. Moreover, while there was improvement to the structure and functioning of the LCO, throughout the period 1915–72 the Office remained notably small with little change to its responsibilities. At the beginning of the Second

[30] Ibid, p. 9.
[31] Ibid, p. 163.
[32] Ibid, p. 7.
[33] Ibid, p. 21.
[34] LCD website.
[35] Opened December 1997; Press reports stated that staff were to pay £14.00 a month to be members.
[36] R. M. Jackson, *The Machinery of Justice in England* (7th edn., Cambridge, Cambridge University Press, 1977) p. 583.

World War it was much the same as it had been in 1885 and by 1960 there were still only thirteen officials, all of them lawyers, and some clerks and typists. Even in 1972 "in size terms alone it is only dimly identifiable as the remote ancestor of the large department existing today".[37] Indeed, in many respects it still had the appearance of a private office.

Yet despite limitations of size, "its power was awesome".[38] Having survived proposals of change to a Ministry of Justice made in the Haldane Report of 1918,[39] it "succeeded in installing itself almost unchallenged in a position of power and prestige".[40] Much of its power arose from its involvement in the appointment process, which increased as the practice of appointing judges for their political connections declined and appointments became based on success at the Bar. Moreover, while some Lord Chancellors were active in appointing, "it fell heavily to the Permanent Secretary to take soundings with Bench and Bar, to make recommendations to the Lord Chancellor . . . and to humour judges who were uncomfortable with the decisions".[41] Such a role "put a powerful weapon in the hands of the Civil Service",[42] how powerful depending on the character of the permanent secretary, for just as the role of Lord Chancellor has, to a large extent, depended on the incumbent, so has that of the permanent secretary.[43]

Although there were periods, notably when Lords Jowitt and Gardiner were in office (1945–51 and 1964–70, respectively), when law reform was a priority, until 1972 the LCO's major concern was patronage. There was a "gradual conversion" from control by judges of "a motley collection of almost independent fiefs in which patronage was controlled by the judges" into "a branch of the civil service . . . under the supervision of the LCO and within the control of the Treasury".[44] However, the fragmentation of court administration, which "it seems to have been subconsciously accepted . . . was the price which society paid for an independent judiciary",[45] meant that the ability of the Lord Chancellor and his Office to interfere in the administration of justice, other than through judicial appointments, was very limited. Responsibility resided elsewhere. The Lord Chief Justice determined the judges to be sent on assize, and the assize courts were organised by their own staff, who provided the clerk to the court and allocated cases. Quarter Sessions were organised by the clerk of the court, responsible to the relevant county council or local borough, which ran the court, and in all cases juries were summoned by the Under-Sheriff.

[37] G. Drewry, "Lord Haldane's Ministry of Justice", p. 400.
[38] R. Stevens, *Independence of the Judiciary*, p. 10.
[39] Cd. 9280; See Chapter Eight for details.
[40] P. Polden, *Guide to the Records of the Lord Chancellor's Department*, (London, HMSO, 1988) p. 38.
[41] Ibid, p. 40.
[42] Ibid.
[43] Thus, Stevens suggests that Schulster (1915–44) and Coldstream (1954–68) were both very influential with Napier (1944–54) being less so. (R. Stevens, *The Independence of the Judiciary*).
[44] P. Polden, *Guide to the Records of the Lord Chancellor's Department*, p. 51.
[45] R. J. S Baker, "The New Courts Administration: A Case for a Systems Theory Approach" (1974) 52 *Public Administration* 285–302 at 286.

In 1972, as a result of the Courts Act 1971, all this changed. The Act was a response to the Beeching Report 1969, itself the product of a royal commission set up in 1966, and it established a unified court service, the running of which was the ultimate responsibility of the Lord Chancellor. Under the Act the Lord Chancellor was given the power to "appoint such officers and other staff for the Supreme Court and county courts as appear to him appropriate for . . . maintaining an administrative court service; discharging any functions in those courts by or under this or any other Act on officers so appointed; and generally carrying out the administrative work of those courts".[46] Thus non-judicial support staff, such as those of the Royal Courts of Justice, who had been responsible to the judges, were now transferred to the Court Service and became responsible to senior civil servants within, what was now, the Lord Chancellor's Department. The Act also established a new superior court of criminal jurisdiction, the Crown Court, and provided for the country to be divided into circuits, managed by circuit administrators, who again were responsible to their superiors within the LCD.

The result of the changes was a shift in responsibilities such that; "The Lord Chancellor as before appoints Judges of all ranks but his Department now also organises all the old Assize Courts and all the old Quarter Sessions. . . . It also summons all juries. Thus the Department now decides who shall form a jury, where a case shall be heard, who shall try it, and who shall be the Clerk of the Court".[47] The changes were not uncontested. There was judicial concern that responsibility for the administration of justice was passing from judges to officials and that the control judges had over their own courts would be eroded. Such concerns were not new. Since the establishment of the LCO there had, at various times, been tension over who ran the courts, the executive or the judiciary. In 1943, Lord Chief Justice Hewart denounced officials at the LCO "as a sort of Quisling army determined to abuse themselves before political pressure or the financial demands of colleagues".[48]

A certain level of constructive friction is inevitable and healthy, given the constitutional requirement that judges should be independent of the executive arm of government. Indeed, a relationship between judges and officials, which was without some tension, might be cause for alarm. However, the ambiguity in the Act over the extent to which administrators in the newly created circuits worked under the direction of judges, heightened friction between officials and judges beyond what might be seen as "constructive". Lord Hailsham, whose task it had been to implement the Beeching recommendations, believed that the appointment of presiding judges, who, acting in parallel with the circuit administrators, had responsibility for the proper discharge of judicial duties within the circuits,

---

[46] Section 27; this was required to be "with the concurrence of the Minister for the Civil Service (now the Treasury) as to numbers and salaries".

[47] F. H. Alsop, "A Ministry of Justice" (1975) *Law Society Gazette*, 29 January.

[48] Lord Hailsham, *A Sparrow's Flight*, p. 422.

addressed judicial concerns.[49] This proved not to be the case, and uncertainty about the relationship between circuit administrators and presiding judges continued. Who had the dominant role seemed to depend on the strengths of the personalities involved[50] and senior judges continued to express strong views about the effect of the reforms and the way in which officials interpreted the Act. Sir Nicolas (now Lord) Browne-Wilkinson noted, "there appear to be those in the Lord Chancellor's Department who perceive its role as being far wider than is consistent with any concept of the independence of the judiciary; . . . it is clear that there is a profound difference of view as to where administration ends and where a judicial function begins".[51] Similarly, Sir Francis Purchas believed that "from 1973, the presiding judges were striving to perform their duties as they saw the position in the light of the Beeching Report and the 1971 Act, while the circuit administrators backed by the Lord Chancellor's Department were flexing their newly acquired administrative muscles. This created an on-going position of confrontation".[52] Certainly the reorganisation of the court system "produced a very substantial shift in the control of the administration of the courts from judges to civil servants in the Lord Chancellor's Department".[53]

Thus rather than the LCD being seen by the judges as protecting their interests and their power base, it was now seen as acting to undermine and even compete with them. Moreover, there were other developments, some also as a result of the Courts Act, which contributed to the heightened tension. One such development was the post-war increase in judicial numbers. In 1940 there were thirty-nine Supreme Court judges. By 1960 this number had increased to fifty-four, by the early 1980s to nearly one hundred and by the end of the century to one hundred and forty. In addition, the 1971 Courts Act resulted in an expansion of the county court judiciary as well as a modernisation of the court system and between then and 1990 the number of professional judges quadrupled. The result was that judicial administration could no longer be conducted "on quite the same intimate basis".[54] Inevitably it became "more formalised", providing "the fascinating sight of a judiciary being run by a government department".[55]

The Courts Act, which "was the most important reorganisation of the administration of justice since the civil courts had been re-ordered in 1875, and the most far reaching change in the criminal jurisdiction since the twelfth century",[56] transformed the LCO overnight from a small office to a large, high-spending department, making it "one of the major 'empire building' concerns of the Civil Service".[57] Moreover, the development of the LCD did not end there.

---

[49] See G. Lewis, *Lord Hailsham*.
[50] S. H. Bailey and M. J. Gunn, *Smith and Bailey on the Modern English Legal System*, p. 76.
[51] Sir Nicolas Browne-Wilkinson, "The Independence of the Judiciary in the 1980s", pp. 46–7.
[52] Sir Francis Purchas, "The Constitution in the Market Place", p. 1606.
[53] Sir Nicolas Browne-Wilkinson, "The Independence of the Judiciary in the 1980s", p. 46.
[54] R. Stevens, *The Independence of the Judiciary*, p. 79.
[55] Ibid.
[56] G. Lewis, *Lord Hailsham*, p. 307.
[57] F. H. Alsop, "A Ministry of Justice".

In 1989 responsibility for administering criminal legal aid passed from the Law Society to the Legal Aid Board (now the Legal Services Commission), thus coming within the Lord Chancellor's remit, as civil legal aid had done in 1948, and the LCD's budget increased beyond all recognition to cope with its demands. In addition, in 1993 the responsibility for the funding and organisation of the magistrates' courts, along with some fifty civil servants, was transferred to the LCD from the Home Office. Thus, although the running of the magistrates' courts remained a local level responsibility, in organisational terms the LCD now had responsibility for the whole court system. It was therefore no longer "a tiny office, concerned with judicial and ecclesiastical patronage" but "a large and organisationally complex government department with a huge budget".[58] This inevitably changed the nature of the Department, not least because, in recognition of its greater administrative and managerial role, the composition of staff changed, with more senior positions being filled by administrators, recruited through the Civil Service Commission, than by lawyers.

There was also a change in focus, away from the judges – their appointment, their interests and requirements, and the protection of their independence – and towards the administration of the courts. This raised questions as to whether the LCD could adequately sustain the Lord Chancellor in his constitutional role, as well as in his executive one. Ironically, the increased and changed responsibilities of the Lord Chancellor provided a catalyst for change in the LCD and that change worked to undermine his position. Moreover, doubt as to the LCD's ability to sustain the Lord Chancellor's constitutional role was compounded, during the 1980s and 1990s, by the imposition of efficiency and new public management regimes.

THE CHANGE TO A MANAGEMENT CULTURE

The growth in the size and responsibilities of the Lord Chancellor's Department was "successfully camouflaged", at least from the public and Parliament, by Lord Chancellors, particularly Lord Hailsham, until the late 1980s.[59] It was not until Lord Mackay was appointed and the Department became more open that there was general awareness of the change. However, such change had not been hidden from the Treasury. The new spending requirements of the LCD inevitably meant a different relationship with the holder of the public purse and a more important revenue seeking role for the Lord Chancellor. They also meant that the LCD became subject to the same budgetary discipline and procedures as the rest of Whitehall and, subsequently, during the 1980s, to the Financial Management Initiative and efficiency and monitoring regimes.

By the 1990s the new public management had reached the LCD and with it the Treasury driven requirements for cost cutting and value for money, expressed

[58] G. Drewry, "Judicial Appointments" [1998] *Public Law* 1–7 at 4.
[59] G. Drewry, "Ministers, Politicians and the Courts" (1992) 142 *New Law Journal* 6535 at 50.

in terms of efficiency, effectiveness and economy. Since then, like all other Whitehall departments, the LCD has been required to produce strategic plans, objectives and performance targets. Initially, as with all departments, the emphasis was on presentation rather than content. Indeed, of the forty pages, which made up the Department's 1994 Strategic Plan, "no less than nine of them, excluding the five pages of tables, contain[ed] less than 150 words . . .[and] there [was] a total of 67 page inches of totally blank space".[60] Such a profligate waste of space "invited questioning about value for money".[61] More disturbing, however, was the fact that the plan contained "worthless platitudes" and wrapped up "political objectives", for example, reducing costs in both civil and criminal business areas, in "apparently impartial statements, as objectives, targets and priorities".[62] The constitutional issues raised by changes to the administration of justice were thus side-stepped. It seemed that "managerialism [had], by stealth, and unnoticed tak[en] over from constitutionalism".[63]

It was apparent that the LCD was no longer an office or department which retained a detachment, even independence, from the executive and political arms of government. This compounded judicial concerns about the power that had been given to the LCD by the Courts Act, particularly in relation to the circuits. Moreover, these concerns increased as administrators were required to implement efficiency strategies or suffer budgetary constraints, which some judges considered interfered with the interests of justice[64] and which meant that judicial requests for additional facilities were not always met. As finance became more of an issue and the role of the Treasury increased, officials more obviously danced to the tune of the executive. Inevitably, this affected their relationship with the judiciary, reaffirming suspicions held by the judges that "departmental officials are lawyers who have failed in their profession, are consequently jealous of the judges, and seek to manipulate the Lord Chancellor",[65] and fuelling the resentment of officials who believed that "judges make little attempt to understand the realities of political life".[66]

In a stringent attack of what was happening, the Vice-Chancellor, Sir Nicolas Browne-Wilkinson, argued that the LCD's relationship with the judiciary gave it a special status, which meant that it should not be treated in the same way as other departments. He objected to the LCD being required "to formulate policy and make determinations as to 'value for money', according to financial yardsticks and without, for the most part, even consulting the judges",[67] and he insisted that the policy objectives of the court were not for the executive to

---

[60] Roger Smith (Legal Action Group), "Strategy, Management and Politics" (1994) 144 *New Law Journal* 6648 at 670.
[61] Ibid.
[62] Ibid.
[63] D. Oliver, "The Lord Chancellor's Department [1994] *Public Law* 163.
[64] See Chapter Four.
[65] G. Lewis, *Lord Hailsham*, pp. 264–5.
[66] Ibid.
[67] "The Independence of the Judiciary in the 1980s", p. 49.

decide alone. Moreover, he argued that the LCD was "being forced by the demands for financial economy to move more and more into areas which the judges consider to be their exclusive concern",[68] the consequence of which was that "judges are sitting in an environment wholly determined by executive decisions in the Lord Chancellor's Department, which in turn is operating under the financial constraints and pressures imposed by the Treasury".[69] This, according to Sir Nicolas, made the Lord Chancellor's position "more and more difficult, since the price to be paid for obtaining funds for the administration of justice is dependent on satisfying the Treasury that any particular course represents, in their terms, value for money".[70] It also resulted in "increasing stress arising in the relationship between the judiciary and the Lord Chancellor's Department as to their respective responsibilities",[71] which was heightened by judicial suspicions of "a civil service conspiracy designed to erode the independence of the judiciary and their powers" and the belief of officials that "the judges are incorrigibly concerned only with their personal status and privileges rather than the administration of justice".[72]

It was not only the nature of the LCD that changed under the new public management regime, so did its mode of operation and the parameters under which it operated. It had been the practice for judges, particularly the Master of the Rolls, to make recommendations about staffing and administrative arrangements. Such arrangements included "assessing the needs of the courts and securing resources, organising the internal structures of the courts so that they can best deal with the caseloads arising, laying down pre-trial procedures, managing the case-flow, measuring and monitoring court performance, managing court records, and planning necessary reforms to court structures and processes",[73] and while judges "did not always get all the changes they wanted . . . theirs was the initiative; and it was usually successful".[74]

The requirements of efficiency and the change to a new public management culture seemed to preclude this type of judicial input and, despite the reinstatement of the Judges Council of the Supreme Court by the Lord Chief Justice in 1988, which enables the judiciary "to put a common view to the Lord Chancellor about the needs for resources and about priorities for some needs",[75] the initiative passed to the Department and the relationship between officials and judges changed. The need "to work in partnership with the judges" was repeatedly stressed.[76] However, this was not intended to imply a relationship between officials and judges in which judges had an equal input into policies

---

[68] Ibid, p. 50.
[69] Ibid.
[70] Ibid.
[71] Ibid.
[72] Ibid, pp. 50–1.
[73] J. A. G. Griffith, *The Politics of the Judiciary*, p. 64.
[74] Ibid.
[75] Ibid, p. 65.
[76] LCD, *Stategic Plan (1994/5–1996/7)*.

affecting the courts, but rather a business arrangement, in which the judges were only one of the stakeholders.

The advice given by Lord Hailsham in 1989 to members of the judiciary therefore had a hollow ring to it. He had told them that if they felt their needs were being neglected, they should "go to the Lord Chancellor personally and tell him what they want, and why they want it, and you may be absolutely certain that he or his officials will fight to the last man and the last rounds with the councils of government to meet their legitimate demands".[77] The problem lies in what is "legitimate" and whether judicial demands fall inside the parameters within which the LCD is required to work. In times of financial restraint, value for money and improved efficiency, those in the LCD needed to have "one eye on the tricky area of 'access to justice' and the other on the Treasury".[78] Thus the Department's "fundamental aim" of ensuring "the efficient and effective administration of justice" was qualified, under a Conservative government, by the requirement that it was "at an affordable price"[79] and under Labour by the need for it to provide "value for money for the taxpayer".[80] Similarly, in support of both governments' objective of controlling public expenditure, the LCD's "strategic priority" under the Conservatives was "to control legal aid costs and contain expenditure on court services, while maintaining proper standards of service by means consistent with this priority",[81] and under Labour "to facilitate the fair, speedy and effective resolution of disputes, ensuring that costs and procedures are proportionate to the issues at stake" and "to ensure the availability of cost-effective, quality-assured legal services to those who need them, within the resources available".[82]

Whether it is possible to maintain proper standards and quality on such a basis is debatable. In addition, it begs the question of what the standard should be, and, significant in the judicial/administrative context, who decides. In times past, the LCD may have sought to advance judicial views on such matters. However, in the changed climate of the late 1980s and early 1990s, the views of management consultants seemed to be more persuasive than those of the judges, who considered themselves unrepresented in the councils of government. If this was the case, the LCD and the Lord Chancellor were no longer fulfilling their constitutional function of acting as a channel of communication between the judiciary and the executive.

This problem may subsequently have eased but the relationship between the judges and officials continues to be affected by the change in the Department's orientation, such that it sees its function as serving the court user rather than the abstract concept of "the law" or the interests of the judges and the profession,

---

[77] Lord Hailsham, "The Office of the Lord Chancellor and the Separation of Powers", p. 313.
[78] Editorial, "Inside the LCD: Mixed appeal of the controlling body" (1995) 9 *The Lawyer* 40.
[79] LCD website.
[80] LCD, *Annual Report* 2000–2002.
[81] LCD website.
[82] LCD, *Annual Report* 2000–2002.

which had sometimes previously seemed the case. Moreover, many of the commitments given by the Department, "in pursuit of its aim", are those that support the values of the new public management rather than the legal profession. They centre on value for money, efficiency and the customer or consumer and are therefore no different from those of other spending departments. The only commitment in its Strategic Plan, which set it apart, is that which concerns the safeguarding of judicial independence and the judicial process,[83] an affirmation, in theory, of its constitutional function, but one which, in practice, may no longer be either possible or appropriate.

Indeed, during the 1990s it was apparent that, as far as many judges were concerned, "the Lord Chancellor's Department [had] ceased to act as an intermediary or 'hinge' between themselves and the executive Government and [had] become as much a part of the governmental machinery as any other Department of State. Judges [felt] that in this process they [had]lost a privileged position, which also helped to preserve their independence".[84] The developments in the LCD therefore confirmed the dominance of the Lord Chancellor's executive rather than judicial or constitutional responsibilities and indicated that, like the rest of Whitehall, his Department was being driven by value for money and new public management strategies. This was evident in the language and content of its Stategic Plans, which attested to its involvement in "building structures and mechanisms, within planned levels of resources, to enable the Department to meet its Key Challenges", none of which made reference to its judicial responsibilities. It was apparent also in the production of efficiency plans, senior management reviews, which "identified streamlined management structures to maximise the Department's efficiency and flexibility"[85] and its pay and grading reviews. There was also the requirement for the Department to move, like the rest of Whitehall, from accrual to resource accounting and to produce a personnel strategy.[86]

Again like the rest of Whitehall, the Department has been required to engage in market testing exercises, contracting out, the development of IT and the use of Private Finance Initiatives (PFI), which are intended to improve quality and cost-effectiveness through a partnership of public and private investment and the exploitation of private sector management skills.[87] There are a number of PFI contracts in the LCD, particularly relating to IT systems and court building

---

[83] LCD, *Strategic Plan (1994/5–1996/7)*.

[84] J. A. G. Griffith, *The Politics of the Judiciary*, p. 65.

[85] LCD, *Strategic Plan (1994/5–1996/7)*.

[86] LCD, *Strategic Plan (1996/7–1998/9)*.

[87] Private contractors are encouraged "to come up with innovative solutions to business problems". (Home Affairs Committee, *Lord Chancellor's Department Annual Report* (1995–96), HC 596) To this end, departments are required to present their requirements in business terms, without stipulating the method of delivery or imposing unnecessary constraints. PFI agreements must, of course, represent value for money and they must also involve a "genuine risk" for the private contractor. They therefore differ from straightforward "contracting out".

projects[88] with the ARAMIS project (A Resource and Management Information Service), which was signed in February 1998, being heralded as the biggest yet and "the first of its type awarded by a government department for accounting and corporate services".[89] In 1998/99 the LCD, like the rest of Whitehall, also became subject to Public Service Agreements, which set targets and measure progress against objectives, some of which, such as improving the level of public confidence in the criminal justice system, apply jointly to the LCD, the Home Office and the law officers.[90]

The LCD is therefore now in the mainstream of government administration, no longer sitting to one side and only tangentially affected by developments in policy and public administration, and it is its similarity to other departments, as much as its differences, that now characterise the Department. Nowhere is this more evident than in the development of the Court Service, which in the new public management culture may be seen as a model for other public service providers. It also demonstrates how far the position of the LCD and the Lord Chancellor have shifted on the judicial-executive axis, away from concern for the protection of judicial interests towards concern for court users, efficiency and cost savings. A brief diversion to consider the developments in the Court Service is therefore relevant to the argument that the LCD no longer supports the constitutional role of the Lord Chancellor.

THE COURT SERVICE

The Court Service was created in 1972 and, in many respects, while still overseen by departmental officials, it has operated as a separate entity within the LCD from that time.[91] It is responsible for administrating all the courts in England and Wales, with the exception of the House of Lords, the magistrates' courts, and those tribunals within the responsibility of the Lord Chancellor.[92] During the 1980s and 1990s, it, in line with LCD headquarters, was subjected to new public management principles, value for money regimes and cost saving

---

[88] For example, computer support to the courts, improved legal aid management information for the Crown Court, a parking and fixed penalty system for the magistrates' court;. In addition, some court building projects, such as a Sheffield Family Hearing centre and extra accommodation for East Anglian Crown Courts, were operating under PFI and PFI solutions were being considered in respect of a number of magistrates' court building projects and IT support for magistrates' courts. (Ibid).

[89] LCD Press Notice, 30/98, 6 February 1998. The contract, which is for £130 million and runs for nine years, is for the development and operation of resource accounting and the provision of an extensive range of corporate and IT services.

[90] HM Treasury, *Spending Review 2000*.

[91] The Courts and Legal Services Act 1990, s. 1(12) required that its annual report should be laid before Parliament.

[92] That is, the Immigration Appellate Authorities, the Lands Tribunal, the Pensions Appeal Tribunals, the Social Security and Child Support Commissioners, the Value Added Tax and Duties Tribunals, the Transport Tribunal, the Banking Appeal Tribunal, and the Building Societies Appeal Tribunal.

measures. Accordingly, its 1994 "challenges" included "ensur[ing] access to justice while reducing its cost to the taxpayer" and "sustain[ing] improvements in the quality, efficiency and effectiveness of court services".[93]

On 3 April 1995 the Court Service received agency status, and its head at that time, Michael Huebner, became chief executive.[94] He was replaced in September 1998[95] through open competition by Ian Magee, who came from being chief executive of the Information Technology Services Agency, a confirmation that the emphasis within the LCD is now on management skills rather than legal experience. The move to agency status was said by the Lord Chancellor, at that time Lord Mackay, to reinforce the Department's commitment to improve both the management and quality of public services and to be vital for efficiency. There was concern that becoming an agency would "reduce morale in the system still further and erode its public service ethos".[96] In addition, the separation of court administration from policy was seen as "a move away from the integrated approach to providing access to justice that the LCD desperately needs".[97] More generally, there was a feeling that saving money for the Treasury was the agenda, particularly given the court closure programme that accompanied the change in status of the Court Service.

Concerns about the erosion of the public service ethos and civil service moral and reservations about the division between policy and operations are not confined to the Court Service Agency, but are common across Whitehall.[98] They arise from the shift from public administration to management, the attendant changes this has brought and the difficulties sometimes experienced in making a clear distinction between policy and operations or administration and, therefore, in determining responsibility. Moreover, agencies are undoubtedly supported by the Treasury as a mechanism for improving efficiency and thus reducing costs. The Court Service is no exception. However, the court closure programme would have been implemented anyway. The creation of the agency was therefore not in response to this but rather an indication that the LCD was catching up with the rest of Whitehall which, after the Next Steps publication in 1988,[99] had moved steadily down the agency line.

---

[93] LCD, *Strategic Plan, A Programme for the Future* (April 1994) in Lord Chancellor's Department, *Court Service Annual Report* (1994–95) HC 579.

[94] With the stipulation that, in line with practice elsewhere in Whitehall, the post would be subject to open competition once the agency had bedded in. This was to be no later than April 1997 (*Court Service Annual Report* (1994–95) HC 579).

[95] He became head of the judicial appointments group within the LCD.

[96] Paul Boateng, Labour's legal affairs spokesperson, *The Times*, April 1995.

[97] Ibid.

[98] See, for instance, Treasury and Civil Service Committee, *The Civil Service Management Reforms: The Next Steps* (1988–89) HC 494; *Developments in the Next Steps Programme* (1988–89) HC 348; *Progress in the Next Steps Initiative* (1989–90) HC 481 and Public Service Committee, Second Report *Ministerial Accountability and Responsibility* (1995–96) HC 313.

[99] Efficiency Unit, *Improving Management in Government: The Next Steps* (Report to the Prime Minister) (London, HMSO, 1988).

Under the Framework Document of the Court Service Agency, the chief executive is responsible for the day to day management of the Court Service but his role is not exclusively operational, for he also contributes to "policy development by the department both as a member of the Lord Chancellor's senior management team and by proposing policies and/or providing advice and information on the operational impact of current and proposed policies". The increased responsibility and operational autonomy of the head of the Court Service is recognised by the fact that he is directly accountable to the Lord Chancellor, rather than through the permanent secretary, for the "effective, efficient and economic management of the Court Service", a management in which the Lord Chancellor will "not normally" interfere. The permanent secretary is not, however, excluded from the arrangement, as he is responsible for advising the Lord Chancellor on the Court Service's corporate and business plans, proposed key targets and performance.

Lord Mackay was insistent that the change to agency status would not affect judicial independence and he confirmed the continuing role of judges within the agency structure. He noted "in particular, listing of cases for hearings in the civil and criminal courts is a responsibility of the judiciary although, in practice, it is undertaken by court officers on judicial directions. These arrangements will continue after the creation of the agency. The development of the agency will not alter the basis of my or my Department's partnership with the judiciary. The judiciary will continue to have access to me as they have in the past".[100] Thus while the administration of the court system was separated from LCD Headquarters, judges were not likewise to be distanced.

Moreover, Lord Mackay set out his requirements for consultation with the judges in a letter to the chief executive, which was published in the Framework Document. They included working "closely with the Lord Chief Justice and the Heads of Division, the Senior Presiding Judge, Presiding Judges and representatives of the Circuit and District Benches and other judicial officers, as appropriate, to ensure that all parties are enabled to carry out their responsibilities in the management and the administration of justice".[101] He also required "adequate mechanisms" for consultation to be established, such that, prior to submissions being made to him, there were discussions between the chief executive and members of the judiciary on the content of the Agency's Corporate and Annual Business Plans and any "major in-year change in resource allocation which may materially affect the performance of the Court Service". In addition, consultation was required about court closures and any changes to the number or boundaries of circuit administrative areas, the chief executive having to include in his submission to the Lord Chancellor "an account of the views of the appropriate members of the judiciary".

---

[100] Court Service Agency, *Framework Document* (1995), Foreword.
[101] Ibid, Annex 4.

Judicial involvement in the administration of the courts is therefore for-malised through consultation procedures. These give judges the opportunities to express their views, even if the need of the agency and chief executive to meet their targets might suggest that these views take second place to considerations of "how much" and "how many". The time when judges had a significant input into decisions about the size of the budget that should be available for the administration of justice is long past. However, they do still have a say about how the budget is used, the Court Service reporting; "in particular, the Resources Sub-Committee of the Judges' Council, which includes representa-tives of all levels of the judiciary, holds regular meetings with the Chief Executive and his senior colleagues at which the allocation of resources and other aspects of management of the Court Service are discussed".[102] Moreover, judicial involvement in court administration extends beyond discussion, judges and officials working together at all levels, to promote "the impartial and effi-cient operation of the courts".[103] Looked at positively, the arrangements sup-port the notion of "a constructive partnership",[104] although it is likely that administrators "exercise the leading influence".[105] Looked at negatively, they are "potentially dangerous",[106] confusing administrative and judicial responsi-bilities and undermining judicial independence.

The change to agency status was accompanied by the first ever review of the management structure of the Court Service,[107] which had become bureaucratic and unwieldy. There were, for instance, four layers of management involved in the administration of the county courts, such that "local court staff are answer-able to a wholly deracinated central administration which is organised on a regional basis and is in turn answerable to a higher layer at circuit level. And then all these tiers are answerable to the Lord Chancellor's Department in Westminster".[108] The review recommended the devolution of authority to local

[102] Home Affairs Committee, *The Court Service, Annual Report* (1996–97) HC 73.

[103] LCD Annual Report (2000–2002). In the circuits presiding judges have "a general responsi-bility for the judicial administration of the criminal and ordinary civil work of the circuit". This includes "ensuring that the Crown Service officers conduct the listing of cases efficiently, taking action to prevent delays in hearings, and seeing to the well-being of the judges on the circuit". In Crown Court centres this responsibility is exercised by resident circuit judges, acting as representa-tives of presiding judges, while the Heads of Division of the Supreme Court "are in regular contact with the Lord Chancellor and his senior officials about administrative matters", "the Presiding Judges and the Circuit Administrators work together at circuit level, and the Resident and Designated Judges work together with the Group Managers and the Managers of the court centres". (The Court Service, *Annual Report* (1996–97) HC 73).

[104] Lord Mackay in evidence to Home Affairs Committee, *The Work of the Lord Chancellor's Department* (1992–92) HC 214-I, Q.11.

[105] D.Oliver, "Politicians and the Courts".

[106] Donaldson, MR, *Address to Law Society* (12 April 1987) reported in *The Times* (13 April 1987).

[107] The review was part of the Lord Chancellor's response to the Civil Service White Paper, *Continuity and Change,* and was the first that had been undertaken within the Court Service (Court Service, *Annual Report* (1996–97) HC 73).

[108] H. Wilson, "The County Courts in Limbo" (1994) 144 *New Law Journal* 1453.

level, the streamlining of regional tiers of management, and the provision of support services, which were more consistent and more customer focused.[109]

The resulting new structure was implemented during 1996/97 and was intended to help the Agency meet its objectives, "in particular, to improve customer service and maximise efficiency" and to "increase the capacity of the Court Service to plan strategically and to work with other agencies in the justice system".[110] To this end it "reduce[d] bureaucracy" and paved the way "for speedier management decisions taken at the right level and in direct response to local needs". Thus court-based staff and management were freed from "superfluous tasks, better done elsewhere by specialists", and each layer of management was given "a separate, and genuinely valuable, role".[111] In addition, senior managers were better able to focus on the Agency's "strategic direction",[112] planning was improved, co-operation with other agencies in the justice process was enabled and internal and external communications were more effective.[113]

The aim of the Court Service Agency, as original expressed, was "to serve the public by providing a prompt and accurate service [and by] increasing the efficiency and improving the economy with which resources are used to deliver that service". This was translated into quantifiable objectives, namely, "to improve the quality of the service provided to the public in the courts, in particular reducing the waiting time for trial or hearing",[114] and "to counter the increasing shortfall between the expenditure on civil business and income from that business in the form of courts fees".[115] Such objectives corresponded with the responsibility of the chief executive for the effective, efficient and economic management of the Court Service but seemed less satisfactory in terms of "serving the public", who may not see their interests served by the rise in court fees, necessary to reduce expenditure on civil business,[116] or by equating a reduction in waiting times with an improvement in the quality of service.

However, they were in line with new public management thinking, as was the measurement by performance indicators of the Agency's success in meeting them.[117] More recently, in the Court Service Plan 1998–01, the Agency

---

[109] Court Service, *Annual Report* (1995–96) HC 492.
[110] Ibid.
[111] Court Service, *Annual Report* (1996–97) HC 73.
[112] Ibid.
[113] Under the new structure the chief executive remains directly accountable to the Lord Chancellor and is supported by a number of directors (for civil and family operations, criminal operations, resources and support services, the Supreme Court Group and, in addition, the Registrar of Criminal Appeals and Master of the Crown Court). For operational purposes the Agency is divided into eight commands, each of which is overseen by a circuit administrator who is expected to concentrate on corporate decision-making and to "have a more outward facing role, developing relations with the judiciary and other partners in the administration of justice". Circuit administrators are also members of the board, as are the directors and, of course, the chief executive.
[114] Court Service, *Annual Report* (1996–97) HC 73.
[115] LCD, *Strategic Plan 1996/97–1998/99*.
[116] See Chapter Four.
[117] These indicators included the percentage of the administrative process dealt with within target time, the percentage of defendants in the Crown Court whose trial begins within the waiting time

expressed its overall aim more simply to be "to provide a good quality service in a cost effective way". Thus notions of quality have been introduced in response to criticisms that these had previously been missing. However, the concern remains that the need to express quality in quantifiable terms may introduce "distorted incentives into the system"[118] and, in so doing, undermine the service provided. It may also shift the focus to value for money rather than the ability of the system to be fair, impartial and just, for such concepts are "not capable of being measured out by an accountant's computer".[119] It also encourages the manipulation of figures, so that, for instance, time targets for answering correspondence are satisfied by sending holding letters, and it may divert energies from other tasks, which are not measured. Moreover, measuring the quality of service in terms of how long it takes to answer a letter or phone call or waiting times at court, although clearly important, is in danger of trivialising the functions of the court and their more important, but less easily measured, requirements. Thus while performance indicators have a part to play in ensuring that services are delivered efficiently, they are not necessarily appropriate as a measure of effectiveness, for while this may include a consideration of cost, in its wider interpretation it embodies "for the citizen a variety of claims, entitlements and expectations", including "considerations of equity, fair treatment and reasonableness, the duty of care and attention and the proper exercise of discretion".[120]

All courts share one performance indicator, that is, meeting the standards set out in the Charter for Court Users. Commitments in the charter are frequently linked to performance targets. Thus defendants in the Crown Court are informed that the court aims "to start criminal trials within sixteen weeks of the transfer from magistrates court", the target time against which the Court Service is measured, and that, if the trial does not begin within this time, "you can ask us to explain why". Witnesses are advised that if they have to wait longer than the target two hours, they will be told the reason and how long the

target, the number of warrants paid in the county courts as a percentage of the directed warrants with which the courts have dealt, the unit cost of a productive courtroom hour in the Crown Court and of an hour of administrative work in the county court, and the percentage of costs of the civil courts recovered. Each indicator is an amalgam of targets set in the different areas. Thus, for instance, in the county courts there is a time target of five days for a range of administrative functions, including issuing default summonses and divorce petitions, entering judgments, drawing family and civil orders, responding to correspondence, and setting cases down in the list. The objective is to meet the time target in a stipulated ninety-two per cent of cases (LCD, *Business Plan 1996/97*). Other targets which relate to cost are more complex. For example, the unit cost of a productive hour in the Crown Court is measured by dividing the total Crown Court expenditure by the number of courtroom hours sat (with a judge presiding) and targets are set for the average length of a courtroom day – in 1996/97 this was 4.37 hours – and for other variables, such as the number of days that jurors sit as a percentage of attendance days.

[118] R. Bellamy and J. Greenaway, "New Right Conception of Citizenship" (1995) 30 *Government and Opposition* 4 at.483.

[119] Lord Lester, H. L. Debs., 27 April 1994, col. 758.

[120] N. Johnson, Memorandum to Treasury and Civil Service Committee, *Role of the Civil Service* (1993–94) HC 27-III.

wait may be. All courts are required to provide customer service notice boards in public areas which display information on "local performance against the standards of service of this Charter" and "details that will allow you to compare the service in the court you use with the service provided in other courts or offices". Thus the element of competition is introduced, even though, of course, court users are unable to vote with their feet. Competition is fundamental to new public management thinking, which is based on the premise that there is compatibility between the public and private sectors and that the use of the market, as a regulatory mechanism, is appropriate to both. Critics, however, see such a notion as misguided because the markets "tends to respond only to those wants that are either most easily satisfied or affect most people".[121] The consequence might therefore be that those needs that are difficult or expensive to fulfil or that affect a minority of society may be sidelined.

Closely linked with the assumption that private and public are compatible is the emphasis upon "customer" or "user" satisfaction, evident in the Court User's Charter. On the positive side, the introduction of the charter has made those who administer the courts look outwards and focus more on users of the service. However, "the stress on customers might lead to a lack of appreciation of the extent to which public services . . . [are] concerned with more than the services to individual customers", with a consequential neglect of the wider public interest.[122] This is so even if the term "user" is substituted for "customer". The administration of justice is still individualised and this could undermine its public service value and the recognition that it is in the interests of society as a whole, not just those using the courts, that the service operates efficiently and in the interests of justice, in its widest sense. Moreover, it might result in those engaged in the process expecting "customer" satisfaction from the judge, in terms of a decision in their favour. This was a concern expressed by senior judges in relation to the inclusion of judicial salaries within the costs of civil justice and the requirement that these should be met by court fees. Thus those who used the courts would, in effect, be paying the judge's salary and the independence of the judge, within his court, might be "in jeopardy".[123] The argument suggests an extreme scenario, but it is, nevertheless, indicative of the anxiety of judges that the Lord Chancellor and his Department no longer have judicial independence as their first priority.

THE POSITION OF THE PERMANENT SECRETARY IN THE LCD

It is evident that the LCD has changed fundamentally since the first permanent secretary was appointed and that these changes relate not only to its size and

---

[121] R. Bellamy and J. Greenaway, "New Right Conception of Citizenship", p. 485.
[122] Treasury and Civil Service Committee, *The Role of the Civil Service: Interim Report* (1992–93) HC 390-I, para. 14.3.
[123] LJ Saville, Reported in *The Times*, 2 December 1996.

responsibilities, but also to its structure, culture and the way in which it operates. Inevitably this means that the job description of the permanent secretary has changed, and that although the occupant of the position still holds the office of Clerk of the Crown in Chancery and is an officer of the Supreme Court,[124] in other respects "the position and responsibilities are similar to those of the Permanent secretaries of other Government Departments".[125] He must therefore "have the ability, experience and all the qualities required of the official head of a major department of state".[126] For a new appointment in the 1990s this meant; "Proven experience and ability in management of strategic policy development and implementation", "a successful track record of leadership and management at the head of a large organisation" and "familiarity with, and perhaps, preferably, direct experience of, the processes of government at the highest level".[127]

In 1997 the imminent retirement of Sir Thomas Legg, who had held the position of permanent secretary for eight years, raised the question of whether a replacement could be found who met these requirements. In the climate of open competition, the convention, whereby the outgoing permanent secretary normally nominated his deputy as his successor,[128] was clearly inappropriate, even if the deputy had the relevant experience. The problem for the Lord Chancellor, Lord Irvine, was the stipulation, contained in the Supreme Court Act 1981, that the permanent secretary of the LCD must be a barrister or solicitor of at least ten years' standing or, since the Courts and Legal Services Act 1990, a civil servant with at least five years' experience within the Department. This severely restricted the field of prospective candidates. Indeed, Lord Irvine told the House of Lords that in his Department, "there is only one official of the requisite experience who also meets the existing statutory criteria" and "over the whole senior Civil Service, only one other candidate has so far been identified who is similarly eligible for the appointment".[129]

The Lord Chancellor's answer to the problem was to remove the statutory requirement, and to this effect the Supreme Court (Offices) Bill was presented to Parliament. Lord Irvine argued that the developments in the Department since 1971 meant that it was no longer the case that a small number of legally qualified staff undertook all duties, whether legal or administrative. Rather, the Department was now structured around an administrative and policy making core, which received advice from a separately managed group of legal qualified civil servants, headed by a legal adviser who answered directly to the permanent secretary. Thus the permanent secretary did not himself need a professional qualification, particularly given that, the legal advice group aside, there was still

[124] By virtue of the Supreme Court Act 1981, as amended by the Supreme Court (Offices) Act 1997.
[125] LCD website.
[126] Lord Irvine, H.L. Debs., 25 November 1997, col. 933.
[127] Ibid.
[128] R. Stevens, *The Independence of the Judiciary*, p. 7.
[129] H.L. Debs., 25 November 1997, col. 932.

a strong representation of lawyers within the LCD, with five of the seven positions answering directly to the permanent secretary being held by qualified lawyers.

The removal of the statutory qualifications for the position of permanent secretary was yet another sign of the dominance of the Lord Chancellor's executive role. Moreover, it suggested that if the LCD was no longer different from the rest of Whitehall, then the Lord Chancellor was little different from other government ministers. The Bill therefore had constitutional implications, raising questions about the nature of the office of Lord Chancellor and whether his position was sustainable. Yet it was introduced in Parliament as if it were a minor piece of legislation, simply giving effect to an administrative practice in government. Despite the fact that the Lord Chancellor was the sponsoring minister, the Bill started in the House of Commons. Moreover, the Minister for the LCD, Mr Geoff Hoon, requested that all the stages of the Bill be taken in one go. This drew protest from Mr Dominic Grieve that the House "had had no prior notice" of the Bill and that his inquiries showed "that no consultation has taken place with any of the legal bodies . . . or with the Union for senior civil servants. In effect the Bill has no history, and no ministerial statement proceeded it".[130] The Bill, nevertheless, made the progress required. It was necessary for the Bill to go through the Commons first, and with some speed, so that the position of permanent secretary, as redefined without the statutory requirements, could be advertised in the national press, the convention being that advertisements, whose contents rely on a change in the law, can be placed at this stage.

When the Bill subsequently reached the Lords, concern was expressed by, among others, the Master of the Rolls, Lord Woolf. He considered that the statutory restrictions on the person who could be permanent secretary had supported the distinction between the Lord Chancellor and other ministers, a distinction which needed to be "meticulously observed" if the position of Lord Chancellor was to be sustained.[131] The implication was that its removal weakened the position of Lord Chancellor. He also stressed that the removal of the restriction did not alter the fact that the position of permanent secretary to the Lord Chancellor was "exceptional", in that, unlike other permanent secretaries, he or she was required to advise the Lord Chancellor on matters affecting the relationship between the executive and the judiciary, and "to tell the Lord Chancellor – discreetly of course – that he should remember which of his many hats he is wearing at any particular time".[132] To fulfil these functions Lord Woolf believed that "the desirability of that person having appropriate experience . . . is of great importance".[133] Moreover, while he accepted that "with time, a high-flying civil servant could certainly acquire the requisite experience", he thought it a "disadvantage to have to acquire the experience in office rather

[130] H. C. Debs, 6 November 1997, col. 424.
[131] H. L. Debs., 25 November 1997, col. 937.
[132] Ibid, col. 938.
[133] Ibid.

than before taking up office". He also asserted that because of the position of the Lord Chancellor as head of the judiciary, "the judiciary have a real interest in who is to hold the office".[134]

While Lord Woolf expressed his confidence that the current Lord Chancellor would ensure that a person with the appropriate experience was appointed, he was concerned for the future and for the situation arising where, without the "constitutional safeguard" provided by the statuory restriction, "a Lord Chancellor is without the benefit of an experienced permanent secretary with the necessary qualifications to give the appropriate advice" with "serious implications for the sensitive relationship between the judiciary and the executive".[135] With this concern in mind, he informed the House that he was "opening a file", which contained "the words that I have uttered today" and "the views expressed by the Lord Chancellor", with the hope that it would "be passed to my successors in office and that they will take the interest in the appointment to this very high office of state that I believe all members of the judiciary should take".[136]

For his part, Lord Hooson supported the view that it was no longer necessary for the permanent secretary to be a lawyer but continued; "we may later reach a stage, with the great expansion of the LCD, when it may be argued that the Lord Chancellor himself need not be an eminent legal figure. Therefore the time is rapidly approaching when we may have to rationalise the relationship between the two hats, as it were, which the Lord Chancellor wears; that which he wears as a head of an important and rapidly expanding department, and that which he wears as head of the judiciary, and as the conduit between government and the whole judicial system".[137]

In both the House of Commons and the Lords the main concern was the possibility of the Lord Chancellor losing a vital link with the judiciary and the legal profession which had been maintained by the permanent secretary's professional background, and of there being, in the future, a situation where no senior position was occupied by a lawyer. It was in respect of this that Sir Nicholas Lyell, who had been Attorney-General in the previous Conservative administration, proposed an amendment to the Bill which provided that if the permanent secretary were not a lawyer, his deputy should be. He argued that such an appointment would "assist the Lord Chancellor in maintaining his close relations with the judiciary" and "provide feedback to the Lord Chancellor from the legal profession . . . The vital duties of permanent secretary to the Lord Chancellor in these aspects of his work will then be fulfilled thoroughly and carefully by someone who is competent to do so".[138] His amendment was not accepted by the Government.

---

[134]   Ibid, col. 939.
[135]   Ibid, col. 938.
[136]   Ibid, col. 939.
[137]   Ibid, cols. 941–2.
[138]   H.C. Debs., 6 November 1997, col. 413.

As well as the Bill bringing the permanent secretary at the LCD into line with the rest of Whitehall in terms of appointment, it also did so with regard to tenure of office, reducing the retirement age to sixty in line with other permanent secretaries. The Lord Chancellor considered; "There is nothing inherent in the post of Permanent Secretary to the Lord Chancellor . . . which justifies its holder being given, by statute, a later retirement age than any other permanent secretary".[139] This view was contested by some law lords on the basis that the permanent secretary has to deal with judges who do not retire until they are seventy, although, given that other permanent secretaries may have to deal with ministers and members of non-departmental bodies who are also beyond the Civil Service retiring age, this seems a dubious argument.

The position of permanent secretary was advertised in 1998 under the established procedure for open competition and selection on merit. In accordance with published practice for posts of this kind, the Lord Chancellor approved the specification of the post and the qualities required but thereafter played no part in the process. This was overseen by the First Civil Service Commissioner and resulted in advice to the Prime Minister with the Lord Chancellor, as responsible minister, being involved in the final decision. Thus to allay fears about the appointment, he told the House, "in the last resort, I could refuse to accept the lead candidate" and thereby "ensure that my future Permanent Secretary will have the qualities and attributes that are so essential to this important post".[140] However, he obviously felt this was unlikely to be necessary as he could not believe "that the first Civil Service Commissioner himself will do anything other than pay close regard to our debate and the important statements which we have made in it about the appreciation of the constitutional significance of my office and the attendant constitutional importance of the office of Permanent Secretary to the Lord Chancellor".[141] He also believed that "it would be imprudent and highly unlikely if all those who aspire to be appointed permanent secretary were to do anything other than pay close attention to this debate and the strong statements that have been made in it in support of the values which must be adhered to by any candidate who is to succeed".[142] On such does the British constitution depend; a candidate's reading of debates in the House of Lords.

In April 1998 Sir Hayden Phillips became the first non-lawyer to hold the position of permanent secretary at the LCD. As has been the case with all previous permanent secretaries, he was also appointed Clerk of the Crown in Chancery, the first non-lawyer to hold this position since the office was recorded in 1332. In this capacity he is head of the permanent staff of the Crown Office and supports the Lord Chancellor in his capacity as Keeper of the Great Seal. He is thus involved in the issuing of writs to returning officers for the election of Members of the House of Commons following the dissolution of Parliament, certifying

---

[139] H. L. Debs., 25 November 1997, col. 936.
[140] Ibid, col. 935.
[141] Ibid.
[142] Ibid.

royal assents and issuing Royal Commissions, Proclamations and Letters Patent, and authenticating the use of the Great Seal, his name at the end of documents to which it is affixed confirming that the "sealing has taken place on due warrant".[143]

Sir Hayden came from being permanent secretary at the Department for Culture, Media and Sport and his appointment was somewhat ironic given Mr Eric Forth's interjection during the debate in the House of Commons, in which he asked; "Do we want to lump the Lord Chancellor's Department in with the department for youth, sport and ballet dancing, or whatever it is called these days? There is no need for restrictions on the appointments in the Department for Culture, Media and Sport".[144] Presumably, however, Sir Hayden has the necessary "high intellect, combined with integrity, judgement and independence and the energy and enthusiasm to participate in the challenges that lie ahead"[145] and met the other essential criteria listed in the advertisement for the position. This included, "an outstanding track record of leadership at, or near, the head of a large public or private sector organisation", "familiarity with the process of Government and constitutional issues", "political awareness and sensitivities", and "an awareness of the significance of the office of the Lord Chancellor at a critical interface in the separation of powers, between the judiciary and the executive, and of the duty of the Lord Chancellor to uphold judicial independence".

The role of the permanent secretary in relation to the judiciary would therefore appear to remain an integral and important part of the job. Indeed, according to Lord Irvine, "the Permanent Secretary to the Lord Chancellor has a major role in maintaining contact between the Lord Chancellor and the judiciary".[146] However, although Sir Hayden has insisted that his relationship with the judiciary benefits, rather than suffers, from his layman's background, it may not always be easy for a permanent secretary, without previous experience in the LCD and without the common ground of membership of the legal profession, to maintain the contact in the way that his predecessors did. This is not to suggest there should be a return to the statutory requirements for permanent secretaries, but rather that there should be a rethink of the relationship between the LCD and the judges and of how, at the beginning of the twenty-first century, judicial independence can best be protected.

Despite the attention paid by Lord Irvine to the judicial and constitutional functions of the permanent secretary, the appointment of Sir Hayden Phillips reflected not only the change in the LCD but the change in the role of the Lord Chancellor. There was no doubt that the executive element of the job was uppermost and that the permanent secretary was primarily engaged in

---

[143] This is required by The Great Seal Act 1884, 47 & 48 Vict. c. 29; but see modern enactments re use of Great Seal.

[144] H. C. Debs., 6 November 1997, col. 423.

[145] National press advertisement, December 1997.

[146] H. L. Debs., 25 November 1997, col. 935.

managing a department, the ministerial head of which was first, and foremost, a politician. Indeed, Lord Irvine's pivotal role in constitutional reform put the LCD at the "crossroads of Whitehall business".[147] This was illustrated by the appointment of a special adviser and an additional parliamentary private secretary in 1997, an additional parliamentary secretary in 1999 and a junior minister to sit alongside Lord Irvine in the House of Lords in 2000. These appointments concerned the political office of the Lord Chancellor, and thus were not directly relevant to the LCD. However, they illustrated the shift towards the executive functions of the Department.

The creation of a new position of director of communications in April 1998 was similarly illuminating as to the needs of the Lord Chancellor. The post was created after Lord Irvine's first year in office had been accompanied by critical press coverage, which focused on his personal qualities and the refurbishment of his official residence, rather than on policy initiatives, such as legal aid, civil justice reform and the Human Rights Bill, although this was not the reason given by the Lord Chancellor for an upgraded position within the department. He insisted that he had "a very good Information Officer, an absolutely excellent Information Officer, but because of my enhanced responsibilities in Government and because of a reappraisal by my officials of the Department and its responsibilities and its strengths and weaknesses and its priorities and allocation of resources and everything else, the view was taken because I had a much higher profile than my predecessor . . . that it would be right that the office of Information Officer should be upgraded".[148] Allan Percival, deputy press secretary in the Prime Minister's Office, was appointed to the position, above the existing head of information, Sheila Thompson who resigned her position. The shift in responsibilities of the Lord Chancellor meant that the LCD was now required to be more active in news management to ensure the press gave prominence to the right stories. Yet another reminder that it was like the rest of Whitehall.

CONCLUSION

Thus while the LCD may still have its own character born out of the constitutional responsibilities of the Lord Chancellor, "it is no longer . . . wholly different from other departments".[149] Its overriding concern is no longer administering the judicial system and responsibility for judicial appointments; "It is now an increasingly politicised ministry dealing with fundamental and high profile changes to the law".[150] For some the LCD had "been slow to react

[147] Francis Gibbs, *The Times*, 27 June 1998.
[148] Public Administration Committee, Third Report, *Your Right to Know: The Government's Proposals for a Freedom of Information Act* (1997–98) HC 398–v, Q.365.
[149] G. Drewry, "Ministers, Politicians and the Courts", p. 50.
[150] Ibid.

to its new incarnation".[151] Its integration into Whitehall was therefore overdue. However, for others "developments which make it little different from its Whitehall counterparts are seen as undermining its status and thus the status of judges, for whom it remains the mirror image",[152] and as threatening its position as "a Department with real independence and independent thinking [which is] an important safeguard to our democracy".[153]

Whichever view is taken of the integration of the LCD into Whitehall and its transformation into a political, resource-hungry department, the constitutional implications cannot be denied. The Department can no longer stand to one side of the political fray and, as a consequence, its function as a buffer or hinge between judges and the executive must be questioned. This is evident in relation to the administration of the courts, where the will of the executive dominates. Moreover, the notion of the permanent secretary, Sir Hayden Phillips, that the Department can look two ways, both upholding judicial independence and representing the views of the judges while, at the same time, ensuring that the views of "customers" are taken into account, would seem difficult to sustain.[154] Similarly, the role of the LCD in the appointment of judges and senior members of the legal profession must be questioned. Its operation as an executive arm of government means that such appointments are in danger of being tainted by accusations of political influence. This suggests that the development of the LCD is not yet complete. Its permanent secretary believes that law and justice underpin all government policy and that, as a consequence, the LCD should "reach out into departments as a real engine of social and economic policy".[155] By so doing, it would become "the glue of Whitehall".[156] Such a vision makes it imperative for there to be a proper separation between judicial and administrative functions and an acceptance that it is no longer appropriate for a department of state, which, to all intents and purposes, is like any other, to be charged with the constitutional duty of protecting judicial independence. The changing role of the Lord Chancellor was, in part, responsible for the changing face of the LCD. It would now seem that the changes in the LCD challenge his position.

---

[151] C. Philipsborn, "Closed Whitehall Cynicism Must Shift" (1996) 10 *The Lawyer* 18 p. 9.
[152] R. Stevens, *The Independence of the Judiciary*, p. 183.
[153] Mr Humfrey Malins, MP, H.C. Debs., 6 November 1997, col. 419.
[154] Interview with Francis Gibb, *The Times* (11 April 2000).
[155] Ibid.
[156] Ibid.

4

The Executive Role

INTRODUCTION

T HE EXECUTIVE ROLE of the Lord Chancellor has received considerably less attention than either his judicial or constitutional roles, as evident from Lord Mackay's comment, made when he was Lord Chancellor, that he was "not aware that there had been a great deal of analysis of the role".[1] Yet, since the 1970s, the Lord Chancellor's responsibility as a member of government "has greatly expanded",[2] such that his duties as minister and Speaker occupy "much of his time".[3] These duties are varied and complex and have been subject to change from Lord Chancellor to Lord Chancellor and over time. In the final decades of the twentieth century, they appeared to be the dominant responsibilities, giving rise to doubts about the viability of the office of Lord Chancellor, as traditionally understood.

In his executive role the Lord Chancellor, as a matter of convention, always sits in Cabinet and is usually one of its most senior members, ranking after the Prime Minister and, when there is one, the Deputy Prime Minister, although on ceremonial occasions he takes precedence over all members of the government. His position in Cabinet is hardly surprising, given his historical role as one of the sovereign's closest advisers and his custodianship of the Great Seal, which meant "he could hardly be omitted from the deliberations concerning its use which touched the whole policy, national and foreign of the realm".[4] Moreover, there were other reasons for ensuring his membership of the Inner Privy Council. He was the mouthpiece of the sovereign to Parliament and directed the commissioners on royal policy, which on circuit they spread through the country. He was also responsible for the appointment of the justice of the peace, which meant he had control, along with the lieutenants, of local government.

Membership of the Cabinet ensures the Lord Chancellor's political importance, even in periods when the emphasis of his office is on its legal functions, and also serves to remind that, whatever his aptitude as a lawyer, he owes his position to his allegiance to the party in power. As Lord Schuster observed; "No one could hold that office unless he were in close sympathy with the government

---

[1] "The Lord Chancellor's Role within Government" (1995) 145 *New Law Journal* 6719, pp. 1650–3 at 1650.

[2] Geff Hoon, H. C. Debs., 6 November 1997, col. 409.

[3] Home Affairs Committee, *The Work of the Lord Chancellor's Department* (1991–92) HC 214, para. 2.

[4] Earl of Kilmuir, *Political Adventure,* p. 134.

of the day, for he must sit in Cabinet, and, in the many problems which concern that body, while he no doubt brings to the discussion occurring at their meeting that influence which arises from his long familiarity with legal and constitutional questions, he must also concern himself with political issues".[5]

Writing of the Lord Chancellor's position in Cabinet at the beginning of the twentieth century, Maitland, the constitutional historian, noted; "It is curious that one who is the highest of judges is a member of the cabinet, a politician actively engaged in party warfare, who 'goes in and out with the ministery'. It is curious; it is a reminder that in the past judicial and governmental functions have been much blended".[6] The curiosity factor has not lessened during the twentieth century, although rather than the office of Lord Chancellor being viewed as a constitutional idiocynracy, it has increasingly been seen as an anachronism which is inappropriate in a modern democracy. Much of this change in attitude relates to the elevation of the executive and political side of the office.

The low political profile of Victorian Lord Chancellors meant the executive role was seldom seen as compromising the judicial function. Moreover, as the political domination of the House of Commons increased, the confinement of the Lord Chancellor to the House of Lords not only isolated him from the cut and thrust of party politics, it also made the position unattractive to those with political ambitions. Accepting the position of Lord Chancellor was likely to end any chance of "securing the biggest prize of prime minister".[7] Lord Chancellors were therefore not generally political heavyweights and only Lydhurst (1827–30, 1833–6, 1841–6) and Cairns (1868,1874–80) seem to have been of sufficient political standing to hold a position in Cabinet other than as Lord Chancellor.[8] Such judgments are, of course, difficult to make, but the political weight, experience and ambition of a Lord Chancellor will have a bearing on the way in which he fulfils his executive role and the extent to which he chooses to engage in political decision making. His character and style, the extent to which he feels in accord with the government's programme and ideology, and his relationship with other members of the Cabinet, particularly the Prime Minister, are also factors which determine the part he plays in Cabinet.

EXECUTIVE RESPONSIBILITIES

As a member of the executive government, the Lord Chancellor is "responsible to Parliament for the Lord Chancellor's Department and all other Departments in respect of which he is minister".[9] This includes answering questions on a day

---

[5] "The Office of Lord Chancellor" [1949] *CLJ* 175 at 177.
[6] F. W. Maitland, *The Constitutional History of England*, p. 413.
[7] Ibid.
[8] Ibid.
[9] Lord Mackay, "The Lord Chancellor's Role within Government", p. 1652.

to day basis, explaining his policies and accounting for the way in which money granted by Parliament is spent.[10] This requirement for political accountability is used to counter any suggestion that judges themselves should be responsible for the administration of the courts and, somewhat unconvincingly, to bolster arguments which support the position of the Lord Chancellor in Cabinet as well as in the courtroom and at the head of the judiciary. As far as the political duties of the Lord Chancellor in the House of Lords are concerned, these "are clearly subordinate to his political duties as a member of the Cabinet. He is a recognised spokesman for the incumbent government. Thus his role in the House is relatively narrow and stereotyped. He must present the government view on legislation, while at the same time observing norms of fairness in presiding over debates. No one expects an independent statement of his personal views; he is a government spokesman"[11] and he may be required to take through controversial Bills with which he has little sympathy. In doing so he is, of course, bound by the requirements of collective responsibility and thus his responsibility, even in relation to the administration of justice, is to further the party political agenda.[12] He is, in the executive context, partisan.

The "primary role" of the Lord Chancellor in Cabinet is, according to Lord Mackay, "to represent the vital place of the law in the affairs of Government and to participate in the formulation particularly of legal policy".[13] The Lord Chancellor is also the vehicle through which the views of the judiciary are transmitted to the government of the day. His position is described as "unique", which, in the executive context, means that "he has a more independent role than any other member of the Government. He . . . has a role in ensuring respect within government for the rule of law".[14] Unlike other ministers, he therefore has a Cabinet role, which cuts across departments. However, his main responsibilities, at least since the 1970s, have been determined by his position as head of a government department. They are therefore "largely concerned with the administration of justice in the courts and with the civil law and statute law generally".[15] In respect of these, he must obtain the agreement of colleagues for his policies and secure sufficient resources for their implementation. Moreover, in matters which "affect the resources to be raised from the taxpayer or the disbursement of these resources, it is clear that the Lord Chancellor must act as part of the Government as a whole".[16] As Lord Mackay noted, "The Lord Chancellor is not in a position, neither should he be, of being able to increase these resources at his own hand".[17] He, like the ministers of other spending departments, "is required to bid for a share of the total levy which the

---

[10] This issue is discussed further in Chapter Seven.
[11] F. Morrison, *Courts and the Political Process in England* (London, Sage, 1973) p. 205.
[12] See Lord Steyn, "The Weakest and Least Dangerous Department of Government", p. 91.
[13] Lord Mackay, "The Lord Chancellor in the 1990s", p. 243.
[14] Sir Nicholas Lyell, H. C. Debs., 6 November 1997, col. 412.
[15] Lord Mackay, "The Lord Chancellor in the 1990s", p. 243.
[16] Lord Mackay, "The Lord Chancellor's Role within Government", p. 1652.
[17] Ibid.

Government as a whole considers should be sought from the taxpayer. This involves a competition with all the departments of state".[18]

Prior to the implementation of the 1971 Courts Act, the Lord Chancellor's involvement in this competition was slight and non-contentious and he was sometimes cast in the role of conciliator or mediator, being seen as standing to one side of the political rangling. Such a role was attributed to Lydhurst, when Lord Chancellor in the mid-nineteenth century, who "was the great solvent; if there was any difficulty and difference among the Ministers they all deferred to Lydhurst, and he made it up".[19] Indeed, when the Lord Chancellor's Department was "small and rarely in conflict with other substantial departments", he was seen as making "an ideal impartial member of the Cabinet to sit on committees dealing with differences between other departments".[20] Thus Lord Gardiner noted that, upon taking office, his permanent secretary explained to him; "if two Ministers fail to agree on a course of action, and if they don't want a dispute to go to Cabinet, they ask the Lord Chancellor to act as arbitrator and decide for them".[21] He subsequently found himself having to adjudicate between the Foreign Office and the Commonwealth Office over the return of the Burmese royal regalia, deciding in favour of the Commonwealth Office that they should be returned. Lord Elwyn-Jones also reported that he was sometimes asked by the Prime Minister to chair special committees on questions of public policy, "about which there were inter-departmental differences, for instance, whether we should persevere with Concorde, housing finance and other issues".[22] However, the assumption of responsibility by the Lord Chancellor for the administration of the courts and, subsequently, legal aid, which substantially increased the financial needs of his department and his part in the resource bidding process, involved him in the political battle and thus reduced his usefulness as a mediator.

Linked to the Lord Chancellor's "primary role" is his role as adviser to the Cabinet in matters relating to the law. As such, he has a general responsibility relating to new legislation, which means that; "When new rights or duties are established in legislation, it is the role of the Lord Chancellor to advise on adequate measures of enforcement, and to ensure, so far as is possible, that the enforcement measures are proportionate to the problem".[23] Thus the Lord Chancellor has a general responsibility for ensuring that the machinery of justice meets the requirements likely to be placed on it and that it complies as far as possible "with the needs of justice, namely fairness, comprehensibility, predictability, accessibility, affordability, and timeliness".[24] He is therefore always

---

[18] Lord Mackay, "The Lord Chancellor's Role within Government", p. 1652.
[19] Gladstone, cited in J. B. Atlay, *The Victorian Chancellors*, p. 57.
[20] F. Morrison, *Courts and the Political Process in England*, p. 204.
[21] M. Box, *Rebel Advocate; a Biography of Gerald Gardiner* (London, Victor Gollancz, 1983) p. 172.
[22] Lord Elwyn-Jones, *In My Time; an Autobiography* (London, Futura, 1988) p. 270.
[23] Lord Mackay, "The Lord Chancellor's Role within Government", p. 1652.
[24] Ibid.

a member of the Legislation and the Future Legislation and Queen's Speech committees, which scrutinise Bills to be included in the Government programme, and he may chair either or both of these. How effective he is in this role depends on the individual Lord Chancellor. Lord Gardiner, who "never claimed to be a politician",[25] was described by a ministerial colleague, Anthony Crossland, as "amiable" but "completely ineffective", being "a brilliant advocate but . . . no chairman or politician".[26] As a consequence, there was "no hard work done" on Bills put before the committees and ministers presenting them, "got through pretty easy".[27] In contrast, it has been reported that Lord Irvine has given ministers a rough ride.

In his position as "supreme legal adviser to the Cabinet",[28] Lord Chancellors "may be asked to undertake tasks which do not fall clearly within the sphere of the Law Officers, or of some other departmental minister".[29] In this connection Lord Hailsham noted that "a custom . . . had grown up of asking the Lord Chancellor to investigate internal government scandals which were not thought to be important enough for public inquiry"[30] or over which there was uncertainty as to whether a public inquiry was required. Thus in 1949 Lord Jowitt was asked to undertake a preliminary inquiry into the Sidney Stanley affair, which concerned allegations that Belcher, a junior minister at the Board of Trade, had granted licences improperly to a businessman and thus abused his position. He reported to Attlee that "there was unfortunately enough suspicion to justify the establishment of a tribunal of inquiry"[31] and such an inquiry was subsequently convened. Similarly, in 1962 Lord Dilhorne was involved in a preliminary investigation into the security aspects of the Profumo affair. His report to the Prime Minister likewise resulted in a judicial inquiry which was headed by Lord Denning.[32]

Investigations, such as these, which recommended the setting up of a judicial inquiry, were uncontroversial. The same was not always true when a Lord Chancellor advised no action. Indeed, at times, the integrity of the office was compromised, for rather than being seen as acting as an impartial tribunal, the Lord Chancellor was suspected of acting in the interests of government and of being engaged in a cover-up. This was the situation in 1957 when the Prime Minister, Harold Macmillan, refused to initiate an inquiry into an alleged leak of the Government's intention to raise the bank rate. Instead he referred the matter to the Lord Chancellor "for advice as to whether further investigations were called for".[33] The Lord Chancellor, Lord Kilmuir, subsequently reported

---

[25] M. Box, *Rebel Advocate*, p. 229.
[26] R. Crossman, *The Diaries of a Cabinet Minister* Vol 1 (London, Hamish Hamilton, 1975) pp. 394–5.
[27] Ibid.
[28] R. F. V. Heuston, *Lives of the Lord Chancellors 1940–1970*, p. 113.
[29] Ibid, p. 23.
[30] Lord Hailsham, *A Sparrow's Flight*, p. 382.
[31] R. F. V. Heuston, *Lives of the Lord Chancellors 1940–1970*, p. 113.
[32] (1963) Cmnd. 2152, HMSO.
[33] H. Macmillan, *Riding the Storm 1956–59* (London, Macmillan, 1971) p. 418.

that "all concerned were exonerated and advised against a formal inquiry".[34] This draw the reposte from the Opposition that "an enquiry by the Lord Chancellor was no substitute for one conducted by an 'independent judicial person' ",[35] the implication being that the Lord Chancellor's judicial skills and judgment could not be trusted when he was operating in the political context.

Concern for the integrity of the office would seem to have been in Lord Gardiner's mind when he refused the request of the Prime Minister, Harold Wilson, to investigate "leaks" from the Cabinet to the media. He stated "emphatically that it was quite inappropriate for the Lord Chancellor to be employed in such tasks".[36] Unattributable leaks from Cabinet are a fact of political life and often viewed as a safety valve for those ministers who support the government programme as a whole, and thus do not wish to resign, but are opposed to a particular policy or the style of the Prime Minister. Such leaks amount to breaches of convention not law and the setting up of an inquiry headed by the Lord Chancellor would, like the leaks themselves, be seen as politically motivated. For his part, Lord Hailsham, during his first period in office, came to an arrangement with the Prime Minister, Edward Heath, that the use of the Lord Chancellor to investigate internal government scandals "should be given its final quietus, and the Lord Chancellor should not be asked to act in such matters in future".[37] His reasons for wishing the practice to be abandoned were ones of "principle and to allow him to concentrate on his legitimate duties".[38] He considered it "quite improper that the Lord Chancellor should assume the mantle of Grand Inquisitor" and subsequent Lord Chancellors have not done so, although it seems Lord Irvine played a part in Prime Minister Blair's decision to ask Peter Mandelson to tender his resignation.[39]

Although the Lord Chancellor has a role as general legal adviser to the Cabinet and may be consulted on security matters,[40] this does not extend to giving his Cabinet colleagues legal advice on specific issues. To do so would, first, usurp the function of the law officers, who are the government's legal advisers, and, secondly, interfere with the Lord Chancellor's role as head of the judiciary, members of which "may ultimately have to decide whether these ministers have broken the law".[41] Lord Mackay was adamant that it was "no part of the Lord Chancellor's responsibilities, be he ever so eminent, to act as legal adviser to the Government of the day . . . To offer legal advice to the Government would be inconsistent with my function of providing a legal system under the Crown in my judicial capacity, before which the Crown in its executive capacity is only

---

[34] Ibid, p. 421.
[35] Ibid.
[36] Lord Hailsham, *The Door Wherein I Went* (London, Collins, 1975) p. 204.
[37] Lord Hailsham, *A Sparrow's Flight*, p. 383.
[38] Ibid.
[39] January 2001.
[40] Lord Elwyn-Jones, *In My Time*, p. 270.
[41] J. Rozenberg, *The Search for Justice* (London, Sceptre, 1994) p. 8.

one of many potential and actual litigants and indeed it conducts a good proportion of the work before the courts".[42]

Not all Lord Chancellors have been as restrained as Lord Mackay and there is evidence of some holders of the office giving advice, as well as, or instead of, the Attorney-General. Prior to the 1960s, when ministerial decisions were rarely subject to judicial review, the giving of legal advice by the Lord Chancellor was less likely to be seen as conflicting with his role as head of the judiciary and compromising judicial independence than it was at the time Lord Mackay was writing. However, on occasions, it resulted in a less than harmonious relationship with the Attorney-General.[43] In 1873 Gladstone, as Prime Minister, also assumed the office of Chancellor of the Exchequer and sought advice from the Attorney-General as to whether, under the Representation of the People Act 1867, this amounted to "accepting ministerial office". The advice was politically important for if his additional role was seen in this light, he would be held to have vacated his seat and thus required to seek re-election. His concern was that he would not win such a contest. Both the Attorney and Solicitor-General advised him that he was safe. However, to the discomfort of Gladstone and no doubt the irritation of the Attorney-General, the Lord Chancellor, Lord Selbourne, who was supported by the Lord Advocate , intervened and took a contrary view. The matter was eventually settled by the Clerk of the House of Commons, Sir Erskine May, who stated that Gladstone's seat was not vacant.[44]

In 1947 when the Colonial Secretary "defended his refusal to intervene on behalf of six men under sentence of death for sacrificial murder on the Gold Coast by a reference to 'the highest legal advice' that he could not do so; the advice was Jowitt's [the Lord Chancellor] and the Attorney-General, who had advised in the contrary sense, was furious".[45] Similarly, during the Suez crisis, Lord Kilmuir gave the Cabinet advice on international law "in conjunction with, or maybe in competition with, the law officers of the time".[46] On other occasions the Lord Chancellor would seem to have been consulted instead of the Attorney-General, as was evident from the request to the Prime Minister, Clement Attlee, by the Attorney-General, Shawcross, that he ensure that the Lord Chancellor send copies to the law officers of any opinions given to Cabinet.[47] More recently, during his first term as Lord Chancellor, Lord Hailsham was described as "ebullient, assertive, talking at large, offering instant, gratuitous legal advice to the Government, often usurping the role of the Attorney-General".[48]

---

[42] "The Lord Chancellor in the 1990s" p. 247.
[43] P. Polden, *Guide to the Records of the Lord Chancellor's Department*, p. 42.
[44] R. Jenkins, *Gladstone* (London, Macmillan, 1995) p. 374.
[45] P. Polden, *Guide to the Records of the Lord Chancellor's Department*, p. 42.
[46] J. Rozenberg, *The Search for Justice*, p. 8, n. 18.
[47] P. Polden, *Guide to the Records of the Lord Chancellor's Department*, p. 42.
[48] A description drawn by Lewis from conversations with Lords Whitelaw and Rawlinson (G. Lewis, *Lord Hailsham*, p. 318).

The failure of a Lord Chancellor to observe the territorial boundaries of his Cabinet responsibilities may threaten his relationship with the Attorney-General, a relationship which is of necessity a close one, first, because until 1991 the Attorney-General was the Lord Chancellor's only representative in the House of Commons, and still represents him on some matters,[49] and, second, because the Attorney-General's position as head of the Bar brings him into a close working relationship with the Lord Chancellor. In addition, conflict with the Attorney-General may affect the Lord Chancellor's ability to oversee the administration of justice effectively, for while this responsibility resides with his department, there are areas of overlap, particularly in respect of the criminal justice system, where the Attorney-General has responsibility for prosecutions and the Home Secretary for the police and the criminal law. It is therefore essential for the three ministers to have a good working relationship.

This was recognised by Lord Mackay who had "very regular informal meetings with both Law Officers' to enable him "to keep in touch with their concerns and their points of view",[50] and set up a system "of regular meetings at Ministerial and official level to co-ordinate information, policy and practice relating to the criminal justice system".[51] The holding by officials of "trilateral" meetings is recorded in the Strategic Plans of the Lord Chancellor's Department as co-operation with the Home Office and Law Officers and throughout the 1990s this co-operation at departmental level increased. Whether, after new Labour assumed power in 1997, it was successfully sustained at ministerial level is a matter for conjecture, given reports of the relationship between the Lord Chancellor, Lord Irvine, and the Home Secretary, Jack Straw. There were suggestions that they "flew at each other during the first six months"[52] and there were certainly battles over freedom of information legislation and the issue of judicial membership of the Freemasons. Where freedom of information was concerned, Lord Irvine wanted greater safeguards for transparency than Straw was prepared to concede, while over the freemasonry issue, Straw's proposal that all judges should be obliged to disclosure their membership was resisted by Irvine. Straw seemed to win on both counts, although the disclosure of masonic membership, which was made a condition for new appointees, became voluntary for existing judges.[53]

Irvine also seemed at odds with Straw and other colleagues over the issue of whether the right to privacy, contained in the European Convention on Human Rights and incorporated into the Human Rights Bill, would erode the freedom of the press. He expressed the view that "press freedom will be in safe hands with our British judges and with the judges of the European Court".[54] He also

---

[49] See Chapter Seven for the accountability of the Lord Chancellor to the House of Commons.
[50] "The Lord Chancellor in the 1990s", p. 246.
[51] Ibid, p. 245.
[52] I. Hargreaves, "The Godfather" in *Sunday Independent*, 11 October 1998.
[53] See LCD Press Notice, 217/98 (24 July 1998).
[54] *The Guardian*, 4 November 1997.

rebutted suggestions that the Press Complaints Commission would be subject to the new Act, maintaining it was not a public body. This was a position he was forced to reconsider, after David Pannick QC advised the PCC to the contrary. Irvine's "admission of error dented his Cabinet colleagues' confidence in his legal ability"[55] and subsequently Jack Straw announced that the Bill was to be amended to provide some protection for newspapers, a protection that Irvine had insisted was not necessary.

Despite the reported skirmishes, in 1998 the Lord Chancellor, the Home Secretary and the Attorney-General issued a joint statement on proposals to improve planning and performance across all agencies involved in criminal justice. The overall aims of the new strategic approach, which was "welcomed" by the Lord Chancellor, were; "to reduce crime and the fear of crime, and their social and economic costs; and to dispense justice fairly and efficiently, and to promote public confidence in the rule of law".[56] To this end there was to be greater forward planning, performance measurement, and co-ordination between all criminal justice agencies in order to "produce a more coherent and co-operative approach to developing policy". The initiative was something that the Lord Chancellor "look[ed] forward to taking . . . forward as quickly as possible",[57] as, presumably, did Jack Straw. However, it raised the question of whether "a more coherent and co-operative approach" might not be better achieved by some reassignment of responsibilities within the agencies concerned.

The Home Secretary and the Attorney-General are not the only ministerial colleagues with whom the Lord Chancellor needs to co-operate. His responsibilities for matters of policy arising from law reform, such as divorce, family homes and domestic violence, "are discharged in conjunction with his ministerial colleagues".[58] Proposals go to the relevant Cabinet committee for discussion and, if there needs to be legislation, Cabinet itself has to give its approval for its inclusion within the legislative programme. "In all these areas the Government has collective responsibility for what is proposed",[59] although the Lord Chancellor may have to work particularly hard to get law reforms accepted which are not on the main political agenda, or which, like Lord Mackay's "no fault" divorces, are likely to be politically contentious. In other areas of law reform, he may have to work with ministers from a number of departments and the tendency of the Blair Government towards cross-cutting policies increases the need for ministerial co-operation. It is further increased by the stated intention of the permanent secretary at the LCD that the Department should reach out "into departments as a real engine of social change and economic policy".[60]

[55] Sheila Thompson, Head of Information at the LCD in 1997, quoted in D. Egan, *Irvine: Politically Correct?* (Edinburgh, Mainstream Publishing, 1999) p. 134.
[56] LCD Press Notice, 224/98 (21 July 1998).
[57] Ibid.
[58] Lord Mackay, "The Lord Chancellor's Role within Government", p. 1652.
[59] Ibid.
[60] Sir Hayden Phillips, *The Times*, 27 June 1998 (and see Chapter Three).

This strategy was evident when, following the presentation of a paper on the legal services market by Lord Irvine to the Cabinet Sub-Committee on Productivity and Competitiveness, the Department assumed a sponsoring and co-ordinating role across Whitehall for the development of this market.[61]

In addition to his own responsibilities, the Lord Chancellor may also have an interest in the responsibilities of other ministers. The setting up of a judicial inquiry is one such responsibility and it is usual for the relevant minister to consult the Lord Chancellor over who should chair the inquiry, the Lord Chancellor being the formal mechanism through which ministers and judges officially communicate. Removing a judge from his normal duties may have consequences for the courts and other judges, but how much say a Lord Chancellor has in the ultimate decision is uncertain. When the position of President of the Nuremberg trials was being considered, Jowitt wanted it to be Sir Norman Birkett, a King's Bench judge. However, he "felt obliged to accept [the] request" of the Foreign Office for a law lord.[62]

THE INFLUENCE OF THE LORD CHANCELLOR

According to Lord Jenkins, Lord Chancellors have not been as influential in Cabinet as might be supposed, given their status in the Cabinet ranking. The Chancellor of the Exchequer and the Foreign Secretary tend to be more powerful, which is perhaps not surprising, given their high profile responsibilities. A Prime Minister has to be concerned to keep them onside because of the political damage that can result otherwise, as Mrs Thatcher discovered to her cost when Nigel Lawson and Sir Geoffrey Howe resigned from her Cabinet as Chancellor and Foreign Secretary respectively.[63] The influence exerted in Cabinet by a Lord Chancellor, and the nature of that influence, depends, in part, on how he sees the role of Lord Chancellor and on his ability, and/or willingness, to engage in political debate. Indeed, "whether a Lord Chancellor is a powerful person in the Executive depends very much on his personality".[64] Any judgment regarding his influence is, of course, difficult to make, as the assessment relies to a large extent on the diaries and memoirs of Cabinet members, Lord Chancellors themselves having been reticent in recording political, rather than legal, victories.[65] However, some Lord Chancellors have clearly exerted greater influence than others, as a brief look at some of those who held office during the twentieth century demonstrates.

---

[61] Lord Irvine, *Speech to the Lord Mayor's Dinner for Her Majesty's Judges* (Mansion House, July 2000).

[62] R. F. V. Heuston, *Lives of the Lord Chancellors 1940–1970*, p. 100.

[63] Lawson in October 1989 and Howe in November 1990.

[64] Lord Desai, H. L Debs., 17 February 1999, col. 716.

[65] As illustrated by Lord Hailsham's memoirs, which contain little on his role in Cabinet, when Lord Chancellor.

For his part, Lord Birkenhead (1919–22) was a "valuable councillor".[66] He "seldom spoke and then only when he was certain he had something to say", but his "opinions were generally on the side of moderation and conciliation".[67] Lord Haldane (1912–15; 1922) was more politically inclined and, as a Liberal, was only prepared to accept the position of Lord Chancellor in Labour's first administration of 1923 if he could be actively involved in particular areas of political decision-making, namely home affairs and defence. Because of ill health, he felt unable to fulfil both judicial and executive functions and asked to be relieved from the former so that he could concentrate on the executive side of his office, chairing the Home Affairs Committee and sitting on the Committee of Imperial Defence throughout Labour's ten months in office.[68] In contrast, Sankey's position in Cabinet (1929–35) "does not seem to have been very strong"[69] and neither does that of Lord Simon (1940–5). He was Lord Chancellor during the Second World War but was not a member of the War Cabinet and was not known as an active Cabinet minister. Jowitt (1945–51) had a "detached attitude to political matters",[70] although he "served the Labour government well",[71] while Lord Simmonds (1951–4) was described as being as innocent of politics as "a newly baptised baby".[72]

Lord Kilmuir (1954–62), a member of the Conservative Government, headed initially by Anthony Eden and, subsequently, by Harold Macmillan was from a different mould. He was ready to undertake "almost any public service outside Parliament at the request of the Government".[73] One such service was taking soundings from Cabinet ministers, when Eden resigned on grounds of ill health, to determine whether the Queen should be advised to appoint Macmillan or Butler as Prime Minister. At this time the Conservative Party had no system for electing its leader, so the Lord Chancellor and the Lord President, Lord Salsbury, who were the senior members of the Cabinet and "whose position in the Lords left [them] unconcerned in the succession",[74] saw each Cabinet minister to determine who had the majority support. The assumption by Lord Kilmuir of the role of elder statesman is one frequently undertaken by Lord Chancellors and suggests, rightly or wrongly, a degree of detachment from factions within government. Kilmuir was certainly not detached from party politics. After becoming Lord Chancellor, he continued to address political party gatherings and campaigned vigorously in the run up to the general elections of 1955 and 1959, in the second election acting as chair of the Party's election

---

[66] R. F. V. Heuston, *Lives of the Lord Chancellors 1885–1940*, p. 384.
[67] Ibid.
[68] Cave, the previous Lord Chancellor, continued with the judicial side (Ibid, p. 233).
[69] Ibid, p. 527.
[70] R. F. V. Heuston, *Lives of the Lord Chancellors 1940–1970*, p. 14.
[71] Ibid.
[72] By Lord Kilmuir (R. Stevens, *Law and Politics: The House of Lords as a Judicial Body 1800–1976* (London, Chapel Hill,1983)) p. 342.
[73] R. F. V. Heuston, *Lives of the Lord Chancellors 1940–1970*, p. 171.
[74] Earl of Kilmuir, *Memoirs: Political Adventure*, p. 285.

committee.[75] He was also, it seems, more involved in Cabinet than many Lord Chancellors, in 1960 being a member of twenty-three Cabinet committees and chairman of sixteen.[76] Not surprisingly Macmillan described him as part of a "powerful team"[77] and was particularly grateful for Kilmuir's support for the Bill for the appointment of life peers, noting, "I owe a great deal to Butler and Kilmuir for their help over this measure".[78] Kilmuir also had his own agenda for the administration of justice, believing that "the courts must be available for the people and the people able to enter them, in order to establish their rights",[79] and undertook a programme of reform to give effect to this belief.

Dilhorne (1962–4), like Kilmuir, also found himself presiding over the selection of a prime minister, this time when Harold Macmillan, Eden's successor, resigned, again on grounds of ill health. However, Dilhorne was only in office for two years and his role in Cabinet seems to have been unremarkable. Lord Gardiner (1964–70), likewise, seems to have exerted little influence over his colleagues. In Cabinet he was "somewhat silent".[80] This was "partly because of a natural reserve which inhibited him from interfering in matters of which he knew little, and partly because he was preoccupied with his great measures of legal reform".[81] In his diaries Tony Benn spoke of him having an "essential naivety",[82] while Richard Crossman described him as "a real political innocent, uncertain and unsure of himself and . . .out of place in our world".[83] The Lord Chancellor, it seems, was "appalled by the way Cabinet business was done"[84] and his lack of political acumen almost lost him his Bill for the establishment of a law commission, which he was so anxious to introduce. The Bill, although "an excellent proposal", was only saved by a Cabinet decision to set up a sub-committee.[85] He had similar problems with his ombudsman Bill, "not because Cabinet did not like it, but because he is so ineffectual,"[86] hence Crossman's conclusion that he was "an extra-ordinary inept politician".[87] Although Gardiner clearly did not assert himself politically, at times he spoke out against policies, which offended against his "left wing views".[88] He, for instance, denounced Tony Benn's proposal for increasing postal tariffs as a "capitalist document",[89] "bashed" the proposal of the Home Secretary, Frank Soskine, for

[75] Earl of Kilmuir, *Memoirs: Political Adventure,* pp. 310–11.
[76] R. F. V. Heuston, *Lives of the Lord Chancellors 1940–1970*, p. xx.
[77] The other members being Eccles, Maudling, Macleod, Hare, Brookes and Sandys (H. Macmillan, *Riding the Storm*, p. 704).
[78] Ibid, p. 731.
[79] Earl of Kilmuir, *Memoirs: Political Adventure*, p. 99.
[80] R. F. V. Heuston, *Lives of the Lord Chancellors 1940–1970*, p. 223.
[81] Ibid.
[82] Tony Benn, *Out of the Wilderness: Diaries 1963–67* (London, Arrow Books, 1988) p. 328.
[83] R. Crossman, *The Diaries of a Cabinet Minister*, p. 131.
[84] Ibid.
[85] Ibid, p. 55.
[86] Ibid, p. 202.
[87] Ibid, p. 55.
[88] Lord Hailsham, *A Sparrow's Flight*, p. 376.
[89] Tony Benn, *Out of the Wilderness*, p. 204.

a royal commission on immigration,[90] and declared Crossman's suggestion for an interim rate rebate Bill, prior to the planned rating reform, to be "unjust, unhappy, unpopular".[91] However, in terms of setting the political agenda or deciding matters of policy his influence was very limited. His big achievements related to law reform.

Less easy to assess is the influence of more recent Lord Chancellors, the practice of keeping diaries having been mainly confined to Harold Wilson's premiership. Lord Hailsham (1970–4; 1979–87) sat in the Cabinets of both Edward Heath and Margaret Thatcher and was the longest serving Lord Chancellor this century. He "followed a fine tradition of brilliant intellectuals as Lord Chancellors'[92] and, in addition, had held ministerial positions in the wartime government and under Eden and Macmillan. However, he said little in his autobiography about his role in Cabinet, during the time he was Lord Chancellor. He recorded his view that "the Lord Chancellor does play an important part in the work of Cabinet"[93] and noted his membership not just of the main Cabinet but of the Legislation Committee, the Future Legislation Committee, and, like Haldane, the Home Affairs and Defence and Overseas Committees. He also noted that while in Mrs Thatcher's Cabinet, he did "not hesitate from time to time to voice considerable disagreement when [he] differed with her views and opinions", revealing; "Sometimes I have come off best, and sometimes she has prevailed".[94] Hailsham was categorised as an "outer wet", who was "unpersuaded by the new ideology but unable or unwilling to do anything about it".[95] This suggests his influence in Cabinet was limited, although he joined with other "wets" in opposing the proposed budget cuts for 1982–3 and the Central Policy Review Staff's radical proposals for reducing public expenditure, referring to their consideration by Cabinet as "the worst mistake the Government has made since it came to power".[96]

Despite his length of service in Mrs Thatcher's Cabinet, Lord Hailsham received only two small mentions in her autobiography, one concerning his appointment to Cabinet and the other his attendance at Chequers. Similarly, Lord Mackay (1987–97) warranted just two entries. These both related to Mrs Thatcher's loss of the Party leadership. The first explained that, while she sought the opinion of most of her Cabinet ministers as to whether she should fight on after her initial defeat, she had not asked the view of the Lord Chancellor or the Leader of the House of Lords, because they "were not really significant players in the game".[97] The second described how, after her resignation speech to Cabinet, "the Lord Chancellor then read out a statement of

[90] R. Crossman, *The Diaries of a Cabinet Minister*, p. 366.
[91] Ibid, p. 349.
[92] S. Lee, *Judging the Judges* (London, Faber and Faber, 1988) p. 140.
[93] Lord Hailsham, *A Sparrow's Flight*, p. 380.
[94] Ibid, pp. 407–8.
[95] H. Young, *One of Us* (London, Macmillan,1990) p. 200.
[96] Ibid, p. 301.
[97] M. Thatcher, *The Downing Street Years* (London, Harper Collins, 1993) p. 851.

tribute to me, which ministers agreed should be written into the Cabinet minutes".[98] These entries would seem to indicate that Lord Mackay, like some of
his predecessors, had a role in Cabinet, which equated with that of elder statesman rather than a politician. He was certainly not "a politician's politician" and
some questioned his political acumen, blaming him for "the rumpus that blew
up" over the reform of the divorce law.[99] However, he was respected by his colleagues and reports suggest that although, like Birkenhead, he rarely spoke in
Cabinet, when he did make a contribution, colleagues paid attention to what he
had to say.[100]

LORD IRVINE: AT THE CENTRE OF GOVERNMENT

Without doubt the Lord Chancellor who has exerted the greatest political influence in modern times is Lord Irvine (1997–   ). The difference between him and
his predecessor is that while "Mackay was a noiseless politician. Irvine wants to
be in the textbooks . . . going down in history as a great, reforming lord chancellor".[101] Moreover, his reforming zeal has not been confined to those areas for
which he has direct responsibility. Lord Chancellors are always in a position to
have "a voice in the proposals of others"[102] and in the overall government programme, but Lord Irvine has sought a louder voice than is usual for a Lord
Chancellor. This was evident in his assumption of a "pivotal role" in Labour's
"constitutional revolution".[103] Upon taking office, he became the chair of the
sub-committees on devolution, freedom of information, the incorporation of
the ECHR and, subsequently, the reform of the House of Lords, arguing that the
"merit of having the Chairmanship of these Committees in a single pair of
hands" was "to get the interconnections and linkages right".[104] He was, it
seems, a "very successful chairman . . . in the sense that the business has been
shifted quickly, efficiently and rationally".[105] Indeed, reports speak of him as "a
very brusque, very businesslike chair . . . but very, very efficient".[106] He may not
have been liked by some of his colleagues, but then, as Lord Richard, Leader of
the House of Lords in Blair's first Cabinet commented; "You haven't got to like
your colleagues, thank goodness".[107] His abilities were, however respected by

---

[98] M. Thatcher, *The Downing Street Years* (London, Harper Collins, 1993) p. 857.

[99] F. Gibb, *The Times*, 2 May 1997.

[100] Ibid.

[101] Baroness Smith (wife of the late John Smith, leader of the Labour Party) quoted by T.
Rayment, *Sunday Times*, 18 October 1998.

[102] Lord Mackay, "The Lord Chancellor's Role within Government", p. 1652.

[103] Lord Irvine, *The Times*, 12 July 1997.

[104] Public Administration Committee, *Your Right to Know: The Government's Proposals for a
Freedom of Information Act* (1997–98) 398–v, Q. 294.

[105] P. Hennessy in M. Berlins, *A Man for All Roles*.

[106] Ron Davies, who had been SOS for Wales, *Blair's Way*, Channel 4, 2 May 1999.

[107] Ibid.

many and the fact that so much was achieved so quickly was to a large extent due to Irvine's "technical and intellectual gifts".[108]

Irvine's role has not been confined to constitutional reform. In 1998 he held positions on ten committees in total. This included a leading role on the Public Expenditure Committee, where he acted as "prosecuting counsel . . . shredding ministers who sought budgets they could not defend",[109] and, for a time, being chair of the Future Legislation and Queen's Speech Committee, a committee on which the Lord Chancellor always sits.[110] He was therefore seen as having an "octypus-type grip on whole areas of government policy"[111] even though, towards the end of the year, with the work of some of the constitutional committees completed, the proportion of his time spent on Cabinet committee work was reported to have reduced from a half to a quarter.

It is not unusual for Lord Chancellors to spend time in Cabinet committees, as evident from Lord Hailsham's revelations and from those of his father, who noted in 1935 that he was "a member of about a dozen committees, and Chairman of more than one of them".[112] Moreover, for those Lord Chancellors who assumed a mediating role in Cabinet, committees took up "a substantial part" of their time.[113] However, until Lord Irvine held office, membership of Cabinet committees was not accorded such a prominent position within the portfolio of Lord Chancellor functions, perhaps because the role played by Lord Chancellors within them was politically low key, or because Lord Chancellors were circumspect about revealing its extent. This has not been the case with Lord Irvine for whom membership of key Cabinet committees has been an important and well-publicised aspect of his job as Lord Chancellor. He has, it seems, used his position within Cabinet to exert a greater political influence than any Lord Chancellor this century, to the extent that ministerial colleagues came to believe that "a deal done with the Lord Chancellor was effectively a deal done with the prime minister".[114] By so doing, he has given the office of Lord Chancellor a strong political dimension. Under Lord Irvine's stewardship, the position of Lord Chancellor has become overtly at the centre of government.

Lord Irvine's central role in government has arisen not just formally, through his role on Cabinet committees, particularly those concerned with constitutional reform, but also informally, through his closeness to the Prime Minister. He is not the only Lord Chancellor to have been on good terms with the first minister. Many Lord Chancellors have moved in the same social circles as the head of government. Lord Hailsham and his wife were part of the circle whose attendance at the Prime Minister's country residence was said by Mrs Thatcher

---

[108] P. Hennessy in M. Berlins, *A Man for All Roles*.
[109] T. Rayment, *Sunday Times*, 18 October 1998.
[110] He gave up the chair to Margaret Beckett in 1998.
[111] M. Berlins, *A Man for All Roles*.
[112] Viscount Hailsham, "The Duties of a Lord Chancellor", p. 199.
[113] F. Morrison, *Courts and the Political Process in England*, p. 204.
[114] D. Egan, *Irvine*, p. 131.

to be "fairly typical of a Chequers weekend',[115] while Lord Kilmuir was described by Harold Macmillan as "one of my oldest and dearest friends",[116] and one he felt "particular sorry" to lose after his major overhaul of Cabinet meant that Kilmuir had to be asked to go. He noted; "I shall miss him very much".[117]

However, the relationship between Lord Irvine and Tony Blair would seem to have another dimension to it. Irvine is not just a friend of the Prime Minister, he was his mentor when Blair and his wife, Cherie Booth, were working in his chambers. Reports from other Cabinet ministers, shortly after new Labour took office, suggested "that in some respects the prime minister-lord chancellor relationship is still the same as it was when he was his pupil and Derry Irvine was the pupil-master".[118] Lord Irvine's influence within the Labour leadership in fact predates Blair. He advised Neil Kinnock on his dealings with Militant, devising terms which enabled the Labour leadership to drive out its Trotskyite fringe on the grounds of "bringing the party into disrepute", without bringing the Party into conflict with the courts.[119] He also helped the leadership overhaul the Labour Party's constitution, and was "the brains behind Labour's reformulation of its crucial relationship with the unions".[120] He was rewarded with a peerage and when John Smith, a close friend, succeeded Kinnock after the general election defeat in 1992, he was named as Labour's shadow Lord Chancellor. However, it was after Blair became leader in 1994 that "Irvine's personal role [became] seminal"[121] and he moved into the thick of backroom party politics.

To an extent, Lord Irvine's position has continued the trend, apparent since the 1970s, whereby the office of Lord Chancellor has moved more into the political arena. Lord Hailsham, although fairly successful in concealing the changes happening in the LCD, did not escape entirely from the criticism that his actions were dictated by political considerations and, since then, "the Lord Chancellorship has become even more political and more bruising".[122] However, Lord Irvine seems to have raised the political stakes still further with his personal desire to be at the heart of policy making. Yet in his early days in office there appeared to be "a contradiction between Lord Irvine's influence and his political nouce".[123] This was evident in his handling of the controversy surrounding the refurbishment of the Lord Chancellor's residence in the House of Lords. The decision to refurbish it, "to the highest possible standards" at a cost of £650,000, was taken by the House of Lords, with the "strong support and approval" of the Lord Chancellor, who in a letter to the Offices Committee had

---

[115] M. Thatcher, *The Downing Street Years*, p. 370.
[116] H. Macmillan, *At The End of the Day* (London, Macmillan, 1973) p. 93.
[117] Ibid, p. 98.
[118] P. Riddell in M. Berlins, *A Man for All Roles*.
[119] I. Hargreaves, "The Godfather".
[120] Ibid.
[121] Ibid.
[122] M. Berlins, *A Man for All Roles*.
[123] Ibid.

noted that if the work were to be undertaken, it should be "to a very high and historically authentic standard" which would "transform the residence and make it as it should be".[124] Because of the cost, Lord Irvine had suggested that, although not "ideal", the renovation could be completed "in phases, with the first phase confined to the State Rooms".[125] In the event two sub-committees of the Offices Committee (the Administration and Works and the Finance and Staff sub-committees) and the Offices Committee itself approved the full refurbishment and this was confirmed by the full House of Lords on 30 July 1997.[126]

The Lord Chancellor's apartment has been seen as worthy of comment at other times this century and there are obvious contrasts in the attitudes of Lord Chancellors to their surroundings. When Cave was an occupant "it was filled with furniture a second-hand dealer would have treated as scrap",[127] while when Jowitt became Lord Chancellor in 1945 and took up residence with his wife, "the flat was redecorated with their accustomed artistic skill, and parties there were noted for their glitter in the sombre atmosphere of post-war London".[128] It had obviously deteriorated by the time Lord Elwyn-Jones was in occupancy. He described it as "simply a long train of large, draughty rooms over twenty feet high (with two freezing cold bathrooms curiously contrived at the far end of a long corridor)",[129] comparing it unfavourably with "Mr Speaker's perfect Pugin house".[130] During his period as Lord Chancellor, he and his wife oversaw "the long overdue redecoration of the River Room . . . which was in a sorry state of dilapidation", with the aim of restoring it to "its original Pugin concept"[131] and, to that end, "books of Pugin's original wallpaper were examined, lighting and furniture were discussed, . . . perfect sofas and armchairs" were tracked down and "upholstered in mulberry velvet to blend with everything else".[132] Moreover, twenty-two stained glass panels for the windows were produced with the heraldic coat-of-arms of twenty-two former Lord Chancellors. As it happened, Elwyn-Jones was no longer in office when the process was completed, but the windows were in place for the reception which marked Hailsham's opening of Parliament. No adverse comment seems to have been attracted by the renovation, perhaps because it only related to the reception room and not to the private areas of the apartment, but the refurbishment by Lord Irvine was not the first time the issue had created controversy. There had been similar complaints about the spending of public money in 1919 when Lord Birkenhead was Lord Chancellor. Then, as in 1997, the response given was

---

[124] See letter of 1 July 1997, published in *The Times* (25 February 1998).
[125] Ibid.
[126] H.L. Debs., 30 July 1997, col. 181.
[127] G.B. Grundy, "Fifty-Five Years at Oxford" (1944) p. 144 quoted in R. F. V. Heuston, *Lives of the Lord Chancellors 1940–1970*, p. 98.
[128] Ibid.
[129] *In My Time*, p. 298.
[130] Ibid.
[131] Ibid.
[132] Ibid, p. 299.

that it was not a decision taken by the Lord Chancellor, or even by the government of which he was a member, but by a committee of the House of Lords, responsible for the repair and upkeep of the building.

In 1997 this explanation was not seen as adequate. Such a project, undertaken so soon after Labour had taken office, was always likely to attract criticism. Labour ministers, unlike their Conservative counterparts, are, somewhat unreasonably, not expected to enjoy the trappings of office. However, the controversy was fuelled by the Lord Chancellor's personal involvement and obvious pleasure in the refurbishment, which included choosing fittings and furnishings reflecting the original schemes designed by Barry and Pugin, and his lack of sensitivity in addressing criticisms. Particularly controversial was his choice of the wallpaper at nearly £170 a roll and his comment that "we are talking about quality materials which are capable of lasting for 60 or 70 years ... not ... something down at the DIY store which may collapse after a year or two".[133]

Also controversial was the borrowing by the Lord Chancellor of pictures and statues from art museums throughout the country. None of the works of art was actually on show to the public, all being in reserve collections, and Lord Irvine claimed that displaying them in his apartment would make them accessible in a way that they would not have been otherwise. However, the number of items, which amounted to more than one hundred, compared with the thirty-six on loan to 10 Downing Street and the eighteen borrowed by 11 Downing Street, seemed to border on the excessive, and the fact that many of them had been transported to London from Scottish galleries suggested an insensitivity to possible feelings in Scotland that their treasures were being plundered. Moreover, although subsequently the Lord Chancellor announced that the residence would be made available, free of charge, for charitable fund raising occasions, thus ensuring the works of art would be seen by some sections of the public, initially the public access he had in mind was more limited.

The manner in which the refurbishment took place and the way in which Lord Irvine responded to questions about it, added to unease that a senior member of a Labour government, who was also head of the judiciary, should see it as appropriate to exert so much of his energy and interest, not to mention public money, in this direction. The public had just shown its dissatisfaction with a government which seemed to place self-interest above everything. Lord Irvine seemed to be demonstrating the same characteristic and he became "the hate figure" of the new Labour Government.[134] He was "self-confident, abrasive, arrogant" but, most of all, he was "politically naive".[135] In the end, the Prime Minister found it necessary to rescue his beleaguered colleague by confirming that the decision had been made by a committee in the House of Lords, on which Conservative peers had a voice, and advising that the residence would be used

---

[133] Public Administration Committee, *Your Right to Know: The Government's Proposals for a Freedom of Information Act* (1997–98) HC 398-v, Q.354.
[134] F. Gibb, *The Times*, 17 November 1998.
[135] M. Linklater, *The Times*, 4 March 1998.

for official government entertaining, when the rooms in No 10 were too small. His support confirmed the Lord Chancellor's position as a senior government minister who was part of, rather than apart from, the mainstream executive government and this position was further emphasised by Lord Irvine's appointment of Gary Hart, as a special adviser to help him change his image.[136]

POLICIES

Many of the initial concerns surrounding Lord Irvine's position as Lord Chancellor arose from his style and personality. In contrast to the low profile of Lord Mackay, Lord Irvine was "impossible to ignore".[137] However, these concerns should not mask the underlying issue which is whether the executive responsibilities of the Lord Chancellor are now so dominant and of such a nature that they affect the ability of the Lord Chancellor to fulfil his other functions and retain the confidence of the judiciary. The involvement of Lord Chancellors in giving effect to government policies, particularly relating to efficiency and expenditure, which may not be seen by judges and the legal profession as in their interests, has undoubtedly put a strain on the relationship.

When Lord Hailsham was Lord Chancellor, he was generally deferential to the legal profession and the judiciary and, as Nigel Lawson, Chancellor of the Exchequer at that time, subsequently noted, he was not predisposed to undertake reforms which might be seen by these groups as contrary to their interests.[138] Nevertheless, as budgetary restraints began to bite, he found himself under fire from the Bar over several issues relating to expenditure, in particular the level of remuneration for criminal legal aid, about which the Bar had become increasingly dissatisfied. Eventually Lord Hailsham commissioned consultants to investigate how far fees had fallen behind. They reported in 1985 that an increase of between thirty and forty per cent was needed and, concerned at the growing agitation within the profession, Lord Hailsham put a proposal before Cabinet for an interim increase in fee scales of twenty per cent. He had not, however, consulted the Treasury over the proposal and Treasury ministers, "who felt they had been bounced, argued forcefully against the Law Officers and the Lord Chancellor . . . Relations with the Treasury were damaged and Hailsham was left with no more than a routine updating to offer".[139] As far as the Bar was concerned, such an updating, which amounted to a rise of five per cent, was unacceptable and it instigated judicial review proceedings.[140] The Lord Chancellor had therefore managed to upset both the Treasury and the

---

[136] See Chapter Three.
[137] M. Linklater, *The Times*, 4 March 1998.
[138] N. Lawson, *The View from No. 11 – Memoirs of a Tory Radical* (London, Corgi, 1993) p. 620.
[139] G. Lewis, *Lord Hailsham*, p. 299.
[140] See Chapter Seven for an account of those proceedings.

legal profession. In fact the matter was settled out of court when the Lord Chancellor agreed to a timetable for negotiation and the Bar eventually got some of its claim. However, the hand of the Treasury was not far away and in 1988 new legislation on legal aid made it explicit that rates of remuneration would have regard to public funds and that the regulations which gave effect to the rates would be subject to the consent of the Treasury.[141]

The increasing Treasury control over public expenditure resulted in judges and the legal profession portraying the Treasury "as a sort of bogeyman and the Lord Chancellor . . . as either the lackey or dupe of the Chief Secretary of the Treasury", a view that was strongly challenged by Lord Hailsham as "a complete myth".[142] He insisted that "when contention has taken place at ministerial level, in the main it has not been between the Treasury and the Lord Chancellor's Department so much as with the other spending departments, education, health, defence, prisons, pensions, housing, police, and so on for bigger shares in the available cake, and the total limits to be placed on the size of the cake".[143] Hailsham's view would not seem to be borne out by the episode relating to remuneration for criminal legal aid. Moreover, it does not alter the fact that since the 1970s, and most notably since the 1980s, the philosophy of government has been to cut public expenditure, increase efficiency and reduce the role of the State. It has therefore been Treasury dominated. The Lord Chancellor may not, therefore, be, or at any time have been, a "Treasury lackey" but he, like other ministers, has been part of the team that accepted this philosophy and the change in culture it has produced. Moreover, while Hailsham had "clear ideas of which reforms he would support and which he would not",[144] Lords Mackay and Irvine would seem to be willing accomplices of the Treasury. Indeed, their role in giving effect to the control and reduction of public expenditure seems to have subsumed their other responsibilities, particularly those as head of the judiciary and representative of its views and interests.

Lord Mackay, as Lord Chancellor, made clear his support for the aims of the government of which he was a member when he stated that his proposals for the reform of the legal profession and legal system were made, "within the context of government policy which he fully backed".[145] To improve efficiency and cut costs he sought to end the restrictive practices of the legal profession, make the civil courts pay for themselves, improve the efficiency of the magistrates' courts, and reform the legal aid system. Lord Mackay was not a member of the English Bar and, as a consequence, did not have the deferential attitude towards the legal profession and judiciary of his predecessor, Lord Hailsham. He was therefore prepared to take action, which he knew would upset these groups. Indeed,

[141] Legal Aid Act 1988, s. 34.
[142] Lord Hailsham, "The Office of Lord Chancellor and the Separation of Powers", p. 314.
[143] Ibid.
[144] N. Lawson, *The View from No. 11*, p. 620.
[145] F. Gibb, *The Times*, 2 May 1997.

he warned the Economic Policy Committee of Cabinet, to which he submitted his plans initially, that they "would be bitterly opposed by the judges".[146] He had the Prime Minister's "unqualified support"[147] for the three Green Papers,[148] which followed in January 1989, but he was right about judicial opposition. Moreover, judges and members of the legal profession not only opposed the reforms, they also challenged his role as Lord Chancellor, arguing that Lord Mackay was putting his responsibility to the executive before his responsibility to them.

The plan to end the Bar's advocacy monopoly in the higher courts was greeted with accusations that the scheme threatened judicial independence and moved towards executive control of the judiciary.[149] A new system for licensing advocates was to be established, by which a lay-dominated committee would advise the Lord Chancellor on "the education, qualifications and training of advocates appropriate for each of the various courts"[150] and while the Lord Chancellor was required to consult the judiciary over the licensing standards, the final decision was his. The concern was that the Lord Chancellor, as a member of the executive, would therefore have control over who should appear in court and the qualifications and ethics of the legal professions. Lord Mackay "displayed remarkable steadiness under fire"[151] and the main thrust of the reforms were preserved, although the subsequent Courts and Legal Services Act 1990, which gave effect to the changes, made some concessions to the concerns, requiring the approval of the Lord Chief Justice, the Master of the Rolls, the Vice Chancellor of the Supreme Court and the President of the Family Division to be given where rights of advocacy were concerned. Despite this, the suspicion remained that the Lord Chancellor was first a member of the Government, and only second the head of the judiciary and representative of its interests to the executive.

Proposed changes to the management of magistrates' courts, whereby a structure of control was established, which covered not only the administration of the magistrates' courts but the selection and employment of magistrates' clerks, were also decried as executive interference in the administration of justice. The concern was that the Lord Chancellor and his Department would be able to influence them directly in the discharge of their judicial duties. Similarly, the raising of fees in the civil courts, with the intention that these courts should pay for themselves, was heralded as breaching the constitutional right of access to the courts and as conflicting with Lord Woolf's proposals for the reform of the civil system,[152] which, critics suggested, the Government had little intention of

---

[146] N. Lawson, *The View from No. 11*, p. 621.
[147] Ibid.
[148] *The Work and Organisation of the Legal Profession* (1989) Cm. 570; *Contingency Fees* (1989) Cm. 571; *Conveyancing by Authorised Practioners* (1989) Cm. 572 (and see R. Abel, "Between Market and State: The Legal Profession in Turmoil" (1989) 52 *Modern Law Review* 285.
[149] See e.g. Lord Lane, H. L. Debs., 7 April 1989, col. 1331.
[150] *The Work and Organisation of the Legal Profession* (1989) Cm. 570, para. 5.13.
[151] N. Lawson, *The View from No. 11*, p. 623.
[152] *Access to Justice* (1996).

implementing in full,[153] while plans for the reform of legal aid,[154] which included a substantial reduction in availability in civil law cases and a capping of the overall budget, were met with united opposition from judges and the legal profession.

They were also united in their condemnation of an apparent attempt by the Lord Chancellor to interfere in the running of the Employment Appeals Tribunal in order to save money. In an unprecedented debate in the House of Lords in 1994 Lord Mackay was required to explain his communications with the President of the EAT, Mr Justice Wood, which seemed to suggest that, in the interests of efficiency and cutting costs, he had put pressure on Mr Justice Wood to adopt a procedure, which the judge considered to be unfair. Law lords, past and present, joined in accusing the Lord Chancellor of interfering with judicial independence, acting unconstitutionally and allowing his concern for efficiency and cost to override the interests of justice.[155] In addition, Sir Francis Purchas argued that the episode was "Treasury-driven" in that it arose largely out of the failure of the Lord Chancellor to appoint more High Court judges, and that it acted as a warning that judicial independence requires more than judges being independent in the actual trial of the case. It requires also that they are in charge of the process.[156]

Lord Mackay's tenure in office "prompted some of the most bitter hostility – and the worst personal abuse – directed at a Lord Chancellor this century".[157] Moreover, much of it came from senior members of the judiciary. He was portrayed as yielding to Treasury pressure, being more concerned with saving money than with judicial independence and the interests of justice, and of presiding over a system in which increasingly the executive determined the policy objectives of the court in terms of value for money rather than justice. The notion that he was a "Treasury minion" was one that Lord Mackay was reported to have found "really remarkable", [158] a sentiment supported by others who suggested that in "his negotiations with the Treasury over his budget, legal aid and on judges' pay . . . he secured far more than most other spending ministers". Indeed, "he played his cards as well as he conceivably could to ensure the department was best placed to survive the Eighties and Nineties".[159] Accusations that Lord Mackay gave way to the Treasury would therefore seem ill-founded. The truth was that he believed reform of the legal profession and the legal system to be in the interests of justice. He also supported the

[153] Lord Justice Scott, *The Times*, 2 December 1996; 14 January 1997.
[154] *Legal Aid: Targeting Need* (1995) Cm. 2854; *Striking the Balance: The Future of Legal Aid in England and Wales* (1996) Cm. 3305.
[155] See H. L. Debs., 27 April 1994. For an account of the incident, see D. Woodhouse, *In Pursuit of Good Administration; Ministers, Civil Servants and Judges* (Oxford, Clarendon Press, 1997).
[156] Sir Francis Purchas, "Lord Mackay and the Judiciary" (1994) 144 *New Law Journal* 6644, pp. 527–30.
[157] F. Gibb, *The Times*, 2 May 1997.
[158] Ibid.
[159] Ibid.

Government's philosophy of reducing public expenditure and the role of the State. His policies therefore both coincided and contributed to this philosophy.

His policies also provoked one of his most strident critics, Sir Francis Purchas, to ask "whether this repeated scenario in which the Lord Chancellor is found time after time in head-on collision with nearly all the senior members of the judiciary, whose integrity and independence it is part of his constitutional duty to uphold, was acceptable, especially in these times of economic domination of the political scene by the Treasury".[160] Sir Francis made his views clear; "constitutional independence will not be achieved if the funding of the administration of justice remains subject to the influences of the political market place".[161] This was a view supported by Sir Nicolas Browne-Wilkinson, who, as Vice-Chancellor, noted; "At first sight many would not regard the control of finance and administration as providing any threat to judicial independence. But if the matter is given more consideration, it is to my mind apparent that the control of the finance and administration of the legal system is capable of preventing the performance of those very functions which the independence of the judiciary is intended to preserve, that is to say, the right of the individual to a speedy and fair trial of his claim by an independent judge".[162] For Sir Nicolas this performance might be hindered by "a failure to finance the appointment of sufficient judges or the provision of adequate courts and court staff to meet society's current demands for justice"[163] and he believed there was an "inherent . . . risk of interference with the independence of the administration of justice" if "Parliament and the minister between them control the provision and allocation of funds".[164] He argued that "until comparatively recently, this risk was not a real one" because, first, the amount of funding provided had not been an issue and, secondly, the Lord Chancellor's "judicial and ministerial hats rested easily on his head".[165] Now, however, funding was an issue and the Lord Chancellor's position "is becoming more and more difficult, since the price to be paid for obtaining funds for the administration of justice is dependent on satisfying the Treasury that any particular course represents, in their terms, value for money".[166]

In addition to the accusation that he was Treasury-driven, Lord Mackay was also accused of failing adequately to consult on the changes he proposed and thus of failing to represent the views of the judiciary to the executive, one of the functions of the Lord Chancellor. Such criticism suggested that judges lacked confidence in the ability, or desire, of Lord Mackay to protect their independence. It was also evidence of a territorial dispute between the judiciary and the

---

[160] Sir Francis Purchas, "What is Happening to Judicial Independence?" (1994) 144 *New Law Journal* 6665, pp. 1306–10 at 1310.
[161] Ibid.
[162] Sir Nicolas Browne-Wilkinson, "The Independence of the Judiciary in the 1980s", p. 44.
[163] Ibid, p. 45.
[164] Ibid.
[165] Ibid.
[166] Ibid, p. 50.

executive over who ran the courts, a dispute in which the Lord Chancellor seemed to side firmly with the executive. The truth is that "the Lord Chancellor may be too bound into the collective programme of the government of the day to stand up for the eternal independence of the courts, not least in the grim practicality of ensuring that they have the money to dispense justice in a timely and efficient fashion".[167]

The tension that was evident between Lord Mackay and the judges suggested that the increased importance of the Lord Chancellor's executive role had made his position as head of the judiciary untenable. He could not, it seems, fulfil his executive responsibilities effectively and retain the confidence of the judiciary. This was confirmed by his successor, Lord Irvine. Many of the reforms he sought to implement were a continuation of those begun by Lord Mackay and he too met hostility from judges and the legal profession in respect of them. However, in the main, this was not of the same order as that experienced by Lord Mackay. There were a number of reasons for this. First, many of Lord Mackay's reforms were introduced during a period of exceptional tension between judges and the executive, particularly the Home Secretary, Michael Howard. The mistrust this generated diminished with the change of government and Lord Irvine was therefore not faced with the same confrontational situation. Secondly, Lord Irvine benefited from the fact that his predecessor had taken the brunt of the anger and had "softened up" the judges and the legal profession for assaults upon their status. He was therefore bound to be given an easier time. Thirdly, while in many respects the policies were continuations of those started by Lord Mackay, their emphasis was different. Although they were concerned, in many cases, with cutting costs, they were presented in terms of improving access to justice rather than improving efficiency. Moreover they had a softer edge to them, which, after the Conservative years, came as something of a relief. The policies may have produced results of which any Conservative government would have been proud, but they seemed more caring and more concerned to protect the under-privileged than those that preceded them. They were therefore more acceptable to many of the judges who had spoken out against the measures proposed by Lord Mackay, or, at least, it was more difficult for judges to oppose them.

One area where this was evident concerned the requirement that the civil court system should pay for itself. Lord Mackay sought to further this aim by not only raising court fees, but also by removing the power of the courts to waive fees for those who could not afford to pay. He was strongly criticised both in debate in the House of Lords and in the High Court for breaching the constitutional right of access to justice, and, as a result of the High Court ruling,[168] restored the discretion in respect of litigants on income support. Lord Irvine, while vowing support for the aim of a self-financing civil court system and

---

[167] I. Hargreaves, "The Godfather".

[168] *R v. Lord Chancellor, ex parte Witham* [1998] 576, 586 (and see Chapter Seven for an account of the case).

insisting that "what the state provides free, or at a charge, is a matter for government",[169] nevertheless went a step further in softening its consequences by extending the exemption to those in receipt of the income-related jobseeker's allowance, family credit and disability.[170] Although he stated; "I do not accept that there is a constitutional right of access to a free court system, anymore than I would accept that before the National Health Service was set up in 1948 . . . a 'constitutional' right to free medical services was being denied,"[171] he recognised, by implication, that there was a constitutional right of access to justice, which might only be available to some individuals if it were free. This provided some reassurance to the judges. Moreover, he reassured them further by adopting the Woolf reforms [172] and making their implementation a priority, something his predecessor had been slow to do.

Fourthly, Lord Irvine no doubt learnt from the mistakes of his predecessor and, indeed, his own mistakes during his first months in office, and adopted a more consultative approach. This was again evident with regard to controlling the costs of civil actions when his announcement of the introduction of fixed costs for fast-track trials was coupled with a statement that he intended to continue to consult with the legal professions, consumer groups and other interest groups on costs regimes.[173] He stated that he had "listened very carefully" to the views expressed by those who responded to his consultation paper, *Justice at the Right Price*,[174] and, in the light of the reservations about the introduction of a pre-trial costs regime in fast-track cases, he had decided to postpone it "until we can obtain the information we need" through a monitoring system. Moreover, rather than the objective of the exercise being framed in terms of saving the tax payer (interpreted as the Treasury) money, it was presented as aiding access to justice, through cutting costs, allowing consumers "to make informed decisions about their litigation" and providing "transparency to what can be a very confusing system for the man in the street".[175]

Thus while the policies were much the same, their presentation was very different, owing much, perhaps, to Lord Irvine's special adviser, Gary Hart, and his new public relations office. It was difficult for judges and members of the legal profession to contest the Government's commitment to the provision of "a modern, fair and effective legal system which operates on behalf of the people who use the courts, radically increases public access to justice and makes the most effective use of taxpayers' money".[176] In a similar way, opposition was reduced by the presentation of the reform of legal aid in terms of refocusing it "on social welfare issues to be of most help to the most disadvantaged in

---

[169] H.L. Debs., 9 December 1997, col. 47.
[170] Came into effect 1 December 1997.
[171] *Speech to the Lord Mayor's Dinner for Her Majesty's Judges* (Mansion House, July 1997).
[172] After the report by Sir Peter Middleton (October 1997).
[173] LCD Press Notice, 317/98 (15 October 1998).
[174] Published June 1998; see LCD Press Notice, 317/98 (15 October 1998).
[175] Ibid.
[176] LCD website.

society", maintaining "quality of service" and driving down costs through competition, and extending access to justice through new "no win no fee" arrangements. Within a year of Lord Irvine taking office, the public relations machine in the Lord Chancellor's Department was obviously working well.

However, despite a change in style and presentation, Lord Irvine was as concerned as his predecessor to keep control over spending and not to loosen the grip of the executive on the administration of justice.[177] The executive role of the Lord Chancellor therefore continued to dominate, resulting in the implementation of policies which challenge judicial views of their role in the administration of justice. Disagreements about who runs the courts are therefore likely to continue. These seriously weaken the Lord Chancellor's constitutional role, as a bulwark or buffer between the executive and the judiciary, and cast doubt on his position as head of the judiciary.

Particularly contentious, as far as Lord Irvine was concerned, was the continuation of Lord Mackay's reform of the rights of audience. Again this was presented in terms of driving down costs for those who use the courts and thus improving access to justice, rather than making the administration of justice more efficient – a subtle, but important, distinction. Despite this, Lord Ackner noted that Lord Chancellors, "like all spending Ministers, . . . are subject to Treasury constraints. There is . . . inevitably conflict between the desire and the need . . . to contain the costs of justice and the equally important need to maintain standards".[178] Moreover, Lord Irvine's comments on the amount of money earned by "fat cat" lawyers [179] suggested there was another motivation for the removal of the Bar's restrictive practice and, although his remarks had popular appeal and even received some judicial support, they also cast the Lord Chancellor in the role of poacher turned gamekeeper and thus someone not to be trusted. This seemed to be borne out by the fact that while reducing the power of the Bar through the Access to Justice Bill, the Lord Chancellor was, at the same time, increasing his own statutory power.

This was not the first time in the 1990s that judges had had cause to be concerned at an increase in the statutory powers of the Lord Chancellor. The Deregulation and Contracting out Act 1994 had given the Lord Chancellor "practically unlimited powers to contract out his obligations under section 27 of the Courts Act 1971 to contractors who in turn may subcontract to others with no control over experience and qualification of the persons engaged and without any apparently effective parliamentary supervision".[180] However, the Access to Justice Bill, introduced by Lord Irvine, was subject to sustained criticism and defeats during its passage through the House of Lords. Moreover, it was not only judges who voiced concern about the new powers given to the Lord Chancellor under the Bill. It also came from the respected Select Committee on

---

[177] See H.L. Debs.,15 June 1996, col. 1308; 9 December 1997, col. 41.
[178] "More Power to the Executive?" (1998) 148 *New Law Journal* 1512.
[179] H. L. Debs., 14 July 1997.
[180] Sir Francis Purchas, "What is Happening to Judicial Independence?" p. 1310.

Delegated Powers and Deregulation[181] and could not, therefore, be dismissed as vested interest. As well as continuing Lord Mackay's reform of the rights of audience and conditional fees, the Bill set up the Community Legal Service and the Criminal Defence Service. Of particular concern were the powers given by the Bill to the Lord Chancellor to set up the Legal Services Commission (in place of the Legal Aid Board), to run the legal aid scheme and to direct the Commission in running the Community Legal Service and the Criminal Defence Service. This concern related not only to the extent of these powers but to the fact that "policy objectives and national principles are not set out in the Bill, which contains no parameters or criteria for the exercise of [these] powers".[182] This meant that although ". . . the nature and scope of directions given by the Lord Chancellor will be crucial to the operation of the Commission and the way in which it provides access to justice . . . the power of the Lord Chancellor to give directions is almost untrammelled". This, the select committee viewed "with considerable concern".[183]

It therefore recommended that, if such powers were to be granted; "The Bill should be amended so as to contain (a) a clear statement of principle that the objectives of the Community Legal Service is to promote and enhance the opportunities for citizens to have access to legal advice and the opportunity to resolve disputes, and (b) the criteria which the Lord Chancellor is entitled to take into account in giving directions". It considered "that it is more important to circumscribe the Lord Chancellor's powers in this way since, as the Explanatory Notes explain, the Community Legal Services Fund will not be an open-ended fund, as the legal aid fund is now".[184] There was therefore a danger that directions could be given "in the interests of financial stringency" rather than justice. The select committee was also critical of the Lord Chancellor's power to give directions on the running of the Criminal Defence Service, noting that given the State was a party to criminal actions and a defendant's liberty and reputation were at stake, "it would be disturbing if a minister has an undefined power to change the arrangements for giving legal assistance to the impecunious defendant".[185] It therefore requested amendments to ensure the defendant's rights were protected and to ensure that the power of the Lord Chancellor was limited to giving directions on administrative matters.

The select committee further expressed concern about the powers given to the Lord Chancellor with regard to granting rights of audience, particularly as the Bill gave no indication as to how these powers would be exercised, and it suggested, first, that such powers should be limited by the requirement that the Lord Chancellor could only intervene if the profession acted "unreasonably"

---

[181] Delegated Powers and Deregulation Committee, Fifth Report (1998–99) HL 17.
[182] Ibid, para. 2.
[183] Ibid.
[184] Ibid, para. 5. Indeed, the fund amount for 2000–01 is £748m and has provisionally been set at £624m for 2001–02,the decrease being explained by the fact that during 2000–01 some funding started under the Legal Aid Act. (LCD *Departmental Report*, April 2000, para. 99).
[185] Ibid.

over granting rights of audience and, second, that the power should be subject to the affirmative procedure in Parliament rather than to negative resolution. Ironically, given the treatment he had received in debates in the House of Lords, Lord Mackay's statement that, because of its importance, the regulation of the rights of audience should be subject to the approval of Parliament rather than to the negative procedure, was cited approvingly in the House, where the Bill was seen as a continuation of the control the executive claimed over the administration of justice. Lord Rawlinson noted; "Hitherto, no party political politician – that is, no Member of the Cabinet, of the party political administration – has had a say in regulating who represents a subject in Her Majesty's courts. It has been left to the independent judiciary to do that. The 1990 Act brought in by the Conservative Administration went down that road. The Bill is a giant stride further". [186] Lord Lane, for his part, asked; "Is it too much to ask that the noble and learned Lord the Lord Chancellor will not forget that he has a judicial as well as an executive obligation?".[187]

In addition, concern was expressed on the floor of the House of Lords about the power given to the Lord Chancellor in the appointment of the Commission. The Bill provided for a Commission consisting of not less than seven and not more than twelve members but it also allowed that "the Lord Chancellor may by order substitute for either or both of the numbers for the time being specified . . . such other number or numbers as he thinks appropriate".[188] This, Lord Kingsland suggested, meant that a "future Lord Chancellor" might wish to use the power "to increase the number of members because the decisions they were making were unattractive to him".[189] Moreover, the order was subject only to the negative procedure, which "more often than not, is not reached in the other place and is dealt with perfunctorily" in the House of Lords.[190]

Lord Irvine accepted a number of the recommendations, agreeing to include a statement of the purpose of the Community Legal Service and the Criminal Defence Service on the face of the Bill[191] and to set out in the Bill the kinds of direction that could be given to the Legal Services Commission about the exercise of its functions and, where appropriate, to provide that they should be made by order, subject to parliamentary approval.[192] He accepted the importance of "clearly distinguishing" the use of his power to make directions, which "establish new factors to which the Legal Services Commission must have regard in setting the criteria in the funding code"[193] and of subjecting the funding code to affirmative procedure. He also said that he would look to strengthen the word-

[186] H. L. Debs, 19 January 1999, col. 478.
[187] Ibid, col. 1175.
[188] Ibid, col. 491.
[189] Ibid.
[190] Lord Simon, Ibid, col. 491.
[191] Ibid, col. 484.
[192] Ibid, col. 485.
[193] Ibid.

ing of the Bill to enshrine the importance of advocates having the necessary skills.

Policies relating to the administration of justice have therefore continued throughout the 1990s to raise questions about the role of the Lord Chancellor. However, somewhat ironically, it is the constitutional reform programme, steered through by Lord Irvine, which may raise the most difficult questions about the continuing position of Lord Chancellor. The employment of "all his gifts" to push the Government's constitutional reform programme forward may be at the cost of keeping "the integrity of the job intact".[194] This is because, first, the position Lord Irvine assumed at the centre of government has drawn attention to the ease with which the power of a non-elected politician/judge, a creature of the Prime Minister's patronage, can be extended. Joking comparisons with Cardinal Wolsey, made by Lord Irvine, provided ammunition for the cartoonists and the opportunity for wit among members of the House of Lords, including the suggestion by Baroness Young that that he should be called "Your Eminence", Lord Longford's observation that "in the Catholic Church we genuflect in front of a cardinal"[195] and Lord Simon's comment; "we raised no objection when my noble and learned friend appeared to be trying on a cardinal's hat. It is only when he goes on to claim the triple tiara of infallibility that we beg to demur". The Wolsey comparisons also gave Lord Ackner the chance to make a play on words, during the debate on the Access to Justice Bill, when he said; "I propose to take this as the principle point, as the cardinal point, or perhaps I should say as 'the cardinal's point'. It has a significant Wolsey undertone".[196] But, more seriously, the comparisons had the ring of truth about them.

Secondly, there was concern among some senior judges about Irvine's intimate involvement in government policy making, Lord Ackner referring to "the macho image that has recently been spun around the Lord Chancellor and the unparelleled powers he apparently wields in and out of Cabinet, imposing his authority on warring political heads of departments".[197] This was intensified by the incorporation of the ECHR through the Human Rights Act, which reawakened long-existing concerns about judicial appointments and the responsibility of the Lord Chancellor for them.[198] It also raises questions about the constitutional viability of the Lord Chancellor continuing as head of a judiciary, whose responsibility is to uphold rights against a government, of which he is also a member. These questions are particularly pertinent when, as in the case of Lord Irvine, the Lord Chancellor himself is very much involved in policy making and with determining legislation. Inevitably judges will become more than ever engaged in making decisions which have an impact on government policies and which are seen as political. Also inevitably, questions will be raised about

---

[194] M. Berlins, *A Man for All Roles*.
[195] H. L. Debs., 19 January 1998, cols. 1326–7.
[196] H. L. Debs., 14 October 1998, col. 1179.
[197] H. L. Debs., 9 December 1997, col. 56.
[198] As expressed by J. A. G. Griffith, *The Politics of the Judiciary*.

whether, given the Lord Chancellor's executive role, judicial appointments have been made entirely independent of political considerations.[199] There is therefore a danger that judicial independence will be compromised by the very person who is meant to protect it.

Lord Irvine's response to the concerns demonstrate part of the problem. He stated; "Much of the criticisms that have been mounted on the Office recently have been because I chair the committees on constitutional reform . . . I find that criticism quite remarkable because it seems to me that a Lord Chancellor is the most natural choice from among Cabinet ministers to chair committees concerned with constitutional change". He continued, "It doesn't make much sense to attack the office at the moment that the office has come into its own and can be of the greatest use to government".[200] Lord Irvine failed to appreciate that it is the "use" of the office to government that has caused the concern. There is also the fact that he very much wants to be "a great Lord Chancellor, responsible for a major constitutional resettlement and a genuine reform of the justice system".[201] The problem is that, unlike the law reform aspirations of previous Lord Chancellors, such as Gardiner, Irvine's aspirations are seen as political.

CONCLUSION

The key to the effectiveness of the Lord Chancellor, that is his ability to retain the trust and confidence of both Cabinet colleagues and the judiciary, rests on the fact that "participants in the partisan political system . . . view him as a peculiar member of the political system", who while a participant, is not expected to take part in all partisan activities. Similarly, "participants in the judicial system . . . also view him as a peculiar kind of member of their system", who participates but not in all judicial activities.[202] Indeed, "The Office of Lord Chancellor itself can be justified only if the distinction between the Lord Chancellor and other Ministers is meticulously observed".[203]

This suggests that the position for a Lord Chancellor should be that of "decent obscurity".[204] This is not a position to which Lord Irvine has easily adapted, rather he has been very much centre stage in the Labour Government, not to one side of the political fray but at the heart of it . Indeed, "the key question that Lord Irvine provokes is whether or not someone who is so close to the epicentre of political power and to the Prime Minister personally can also constitutionally fulfil the other functions of the Lord Chancellor, those which demand political impartiality and independence".[205]

---

[199] See Chapter Six.
[200] in M. Berlins, *A Man for All Roles.*
[201] Lord Falconer, quoted by I. Hargreaves, "The Godfather".
[202] F. Morrison, *Courts and the Political Process in England*, p. 209.
[203] Lord Woolf, H. L. Debs., 25 November 1997, col. 938.
[204] M. Linklater, *The Times*, 4 March 1998.
[205] M. Berlins, *A Man for All Roles.*

During Lord Mackay's period in office it seemed it was impossible for the Lord Chancellor to fulfil his executive functions effectively and retain the confidence of the judiciary. This was because of his policies. Lord Irvine is faced with the same problem. "Whatever his personal proclivities, [he] has no option but to make hard and controversial decisions that will bring significant public exposure".[206] Moreover, that is not the only problem he faces. During his time in office, there has also been concern that his political profile is damaging to the judiciary, particularly given the incorporation of the ECHR and the inevitable focus there will be on the appointment of judges. He maintains that because of the legal background of Lord Chancellors, "they come to the office imbued with the values that underpin our democracy: the rule of law; freedom under the law; the independence of the judiciary from any Executive interference; the duty of the courts to order the Executive to comply with the law and not overreach itself. . . . The public can [therefore] have confidence that, for any Lord Chancellor, these values would be armour against Executive mindedness or Executive pressure".[207] However, the public may no longer have that confidence as it seems that "the conventions or understandings about proper political conduct" which, in the past, have made it "possible for the individual who holds the office of Chancellor to accommodate the conflicting pressures upon him", are no longer operating.[208] This makes the office in its present form untenable and suggests that the Lord Chancellor should "follow his department into constitutional integration with other spending departments".[209]

---

[206] R. Smith (Director, Legal Aid Group), "The Lord Chancellor under the Spotlight" (1998) 148 *New Law Journal* 6822, p. 24.

[207] H. L. Debs., 17 February 1999, col. 734.

[208] F. Morrison, *Courts and the Political Process in England*, p. 214.

[209] Roger Smith, "The Lord Chancellor under the Spotlight", p. 24.

5

The Lord Chancellor as Judge

THE LORD CHANCELLOR, in his judicial role, is president of the Supreme Court,[1] an ex officio member of the Court of Appeal[2] and president of the Chancery Division.[3] He also represents the Queen as Visitor at ecclesiastical institutions[4] and those universities and Oxbridge colleges where the Crown or founder has not nominated someone else. In this capacity Lord Mackay was called on in 1997 to determine a petition in respect of a complaint by a student at Warwick University about her marks and the disciplinary proceedings brought against her,[5] while in 1998 it fell to Lord Irvine, as Visitor, to hear a dispute involving the Dean of Westminster Abbey.[6] In fact, he pleaded lack of time because of his many duties in government, and, on his advice, the Queen appointed a special commissioner to exercise the jurisdiction on her behalf.[7] Visitorial duties and those related to the Court of Appeal and Chancery are limited and in most instances, when the Lord Chancellor sits in a judicial capacity, it is in the Appellate Committee of the House of Lords or the Judicial Committee of the Privy Council, and here he presides when he so chooses.

The positions held by the Lord Chancellor, as judge, may suggest that the development of this role followed a logical progression. In fact, like most of the functions of the Lord Chancellor, it evolved more by accident than design. There were two strands to its development, both of which stemmed from the Lord Chancellor's closeness to the sovereign. The first developed from the king's practice of passing petitions concerning injustices of the common law to the Lord Chancellor for him to decide on an equitable basis. This lead, ultimately, to the establishment of the Court of Chancery, over which the Lord Chancellor presided and of which, until the mid-nineteenth century, he was, in most instances, the sole judge.[8] The second developed from the Lord Chancellor's position in the House

---

[1] Supreme Court Act 1981, s.1.

[2] Ibid, s.2.

[3] Ibid, s.5(1)(a).

[4] For example, St Stephens Chapel, Windsor; Westminster Abbey.

[5] He ruled that there was no cause for intervention over the marks but that, for a number of reasons, the disciplinary proceedings were a nullity and the decision should be set aside (*Fine* v. *McLardy*, QBD, 19 Nov. 1997). For a discussion of the Visitor's jurisdiction see H. W. R.Wade and C. F. Forsyth, *Administrative Law* (7th edn., Clarendon Press, Oxford, 1994) p. 564.

[6] *Dr Martin and Mrs Nearey* v. *The Dean of Westminster*.

[7] Lord Jauncey of Tullichettle – a retired law lord. (LCD Press Notice, 203/98 (10 July 1998)).

[8] A change in the rules in 1833, which allowed the Master of the Rolls to sit in open court, and the appointment of two vice-chancellors in 1841 altered this position.

of Lords, where his role as Speaker, which had its origins in the Lord Chancellor's position as representative of the sovereign, went hand-in-hand with his role as a judicial officer.

While today the role of Speaker and judge are separate, in previous centuries the roles were inter-changeable with the Chamber of the House alternating between sitting as a legislature and a judicial court of appeal. It is therefore appropriate to consider briefly the Lord Chancellor's position as Speaker, before moving on to consider his judicial role.

THE LORD CHANCELLOR AS SPEAKER

The representative role of the Lord Chancellor as Speaker is apparent in his introduction to the House of Lords. In a ceremony, steeped in tradition, he "advance[s] to the empty throne and [places his] Patent and Writ upon it, in order to show that [he places himself] at the disposal of the Queen".[9] In this representative capacity he remains "the royal instrument to convey the monarch's words", delivering the Queen's speeches "when she is not desirous of being present".[10] He also sits on the Commission to signify the Royal Assent to Bills, wearing his peers robes and his black tricorn hat, and has a major ceremonial role in the opening of Parliament, carrying the Queen's Speech in the purse, which used to carry the Great Seal,[11] handing it to her and taking it back once read.[12]

In his representative role he also presides over the presentation of the Speaker of the House of Commons after a general election, communicating to him or her the Queen's approval, and, in response to the Speaker's claim to the rights and privileges of the Commons, confirming, on behalf of the Queen, "all the Rights and privileges which have ever been granted to or conferred upon the Commons by her Majesty or any of her Royal Predecessors".[13] In addition, he presides over the introduction of new peers to the House, accepting their writs of summons as they kneel on one knee before him and doffing his black tricorn hat three times.

Since the transfer of executive power to the Cabinet, his role as representative of the sovereign is combined with answering for the government. However, despite the increasing importance of this role, his position in the House of Lords is still largely governed by the traditions and customs of the seventeenth century or before. Thus the Lord Chancellor's attendance in the House is required by a standing order which goes back to 1660 and it is the practice of Lord Chancellors to seek the leave of the House if they are to be absent for more than

[9] Earl of Kilmuir, *Political Adventure,* p. 234.
[10] Ibid, p. 235.
[11] It is made of "crimson velvet embroidered in gold thread and pearls with the royal arms and the lion and unicorn with attendant cherubin" and is "heavily tassalled" (Lord Elwyn Jones, *In My Time,* p. 271).
[12] But thanks to Lord Irvine, he no longer has to walk backwards down the steps from the throne.
[13] Lord Elwyn-Jones, *In My Time,* p. 263.

a day.[14] Moreover, until 1998, the normal dress of the Lord Chancellor, when sitting as Speaker, remained a black cloth court suit, breeches, cotton and silk stockings, silver buckled shoes, a black silk gown with train and a full-bottomed late seventeenth-century wig. However, shortly after assuming the Lord Chancellorship, Lord Irvine, not a man for tradition except when refurbishing his apartment or defending the office of Lord Chancellor, secured the permission of the House of Lords to wear plain trousers and shoes on a day to day basis with the breeches, tights and buckled shoes being reserved for ceremonial occasions. He also won the right to spend more time behind the dispatch box, when steering through his own legislation, and thus to take off his wig and gown.[15]

The need for different dress may seem outdated. It does, however, distinguish between the Lord Chancellor as Speaker and the Lord Chancellor as government minister, even if, at times, holders of the office appear to get the roles confused. Unlike his counterpart in the Commons, as Speaker in the Lords, the Lord Chancellor has no regulatory function and no control over the proceedings of the House. Such power resides with the House itself with "any question of order being a matter for the Leader of the House or his deputy or as a last resort a whip".[16] Indeed, the only function of the Lord Chancellor, as Speaker, is to put procedural questions to the House and read out the result of any divisions. Lord Hailsham thought "that in compensation for his impotence the Chancellor had no need to be impartial in debate" and exercised "this self-designed privilege more freely than any Chancellor within living memory".[17]

It is not necessary for the Lord Chancellor to be a peer or to have a seat in the House of Lords, the Woolsack being technically outside the House, but, in practice, Lord Chancellors are always awarded the honour, the last "commoner" Lord Chancellor having been Sir Thomas More (1529–33). There have been Lord Chancellors, for example, Viscount Hailsham,[18] who have presided as Speaker prior to being introduced to the House. A Lord Chancellor in such a position is technically not a Member of the House and is therefore confined to the Woolsack and to acting as Speaker. Once a Member, if he wishes to speak in debates, he moves three or four paces to the left so as to arrive at "his proper place at the head of the highest bench, the duke's bench".[19] This is provided by the House of Lords Precedence Act 1539,[20] which states that "the Lord Chancellor, Lord Treasurer, Lord President of the Council and Lord Privy Seal, being of the Degree of Barons of Parliament, or above, shall sit and be placed, as well in this present Parliament as in all other Parliaments hereafter to be

---

[14] e.g. Lord Irvine sought leave of absence to attend the opening of the new European Court of Human Rights in Strasbourg on 3 November 1998 and to address a meeting of American lawyers in Rome on 4 November (H. L. Debs., 28 October 1998, col. 1907).

[15] The vote was 145 to 115 (see H. L Debs., 16 November 1998).

[16] Lord Elwyn-Jones, *In My Time*, p. 271.

[17] G. Lewis, *Lord Hailsham*, p. 318.

[18] "The Duties of a Lord Chancellor", p. 197.

[19] Ibid.

[20] Section 4.

holden, on the Left Side of the said Parliamentary Chamber, on the highest Part of the Form on the same Side, above all Dukes. . . ."[21] If he fails to move, and speaks from the Woolsack, "his communications [are] treated as advice to the peers, and not formally recorded in the journals".[22]

Nowadays, the balance that Lord Chancellors make between sitting as a judge and acting as Speaker is partly one of personal inclination, although the need to get government legislation through the House weighs heavily in the balance. Both Lords Dilhorne and Gardiner gave the role of Speaker high priority and had admirable attendance records.[23] In a demonstration of remarkable self-discipline, Gardiner used to "sit for hours, silent and motionless, through debates which were often not of the first importance".[24] Arguably, this was not the best use of a Lord Chancellor's time and, in contrast, Lord Irvine, when he attends, is armed with reading material to keep him occupied. The other duties of government have tended to limit the attendance of recent Lord Chancellors, these duties also having an impact on the extent to which they assume a judicial role.

THE HISTORY OF THE JUDICIAL ROLE

The original jurisdiction of the House of Lords "was an offshoot of the power of an absolute monarchy"[25] and included the power to impeach,[26] as well as an appellate jurisdiction from the ordinary courts, which from the fourteenth century was not seriously questioned. The Lord Chancellor played a major part in the exercise of this jurisdiction, not least because, as Speaker, he was "the only peer with a positive duty to attend"[27] and for some time he "virtually performed the Appellate work alone, sitting, but solely to make up a quorum, with a couple of bishops and perhaps a lay peer".[28] This was particularly so after the right of appeal was extended to the Scottish courts by the Act of Union in 1707, as Scottish appeals tended to be mainly based on technical matters of Scottish law in which English judges had no interest. Thus, as well as having a free reign in the development of Chancery law, during the eighteenth century, "Lord Chancellors were left largely to their own devices in shaping Scottish law".[29]

They were also left, as in Chancery, with a considerable workload, which, by the nineteenth century was unmanageable. In the House of Lords the volume of

---

[21] R. F. V. Heuston, *Lives of the Lord Chancellors 1940–1970*, p. 2.

[22] Ibid, p. 14.

[23] Dilhorne had an attendance record of eighty-five per cent during the two years he was Lord Chancellor and Gardiner had a ninety-eight per cent attendance record over six years.

[24] R. F. V. Heuston, *Lives of the Lord Chancellors 1940–1970*, p. 219.

[25] L. Blom-Cooper and G. Drewry, *Final Appeal: A Study of the House of Lords* (Oxford, Clarendon Press, 1972) p. 16.

[26] Lord Melville in 1805 was the last to be subject to such proceedings.

[27] L. Blom-Cooper and G. Drewry, *Final Appeal*, p. 31.

[28] Lord Hailsham, *A Sparrow's Flight*, p. 380.

[29] R. Stevens, *Law and Politics*, p. 9.

the Scottish appeals caused such a backlog[30] that in 1824 Standing Orders of the House increased the number and length of judicial sittings, so that appeals were heard five days a week from ten o'clock until four. In addition, the Orders introduced a rota of peers to attend with fines for non-attendance. The result of this innovation was that; "Two peers [were] summoned in rotation from a list made out at the beginning of every session. . . . [However] as the Chancellor consider[ed] it his peculiar duty to attend to the case before the House, the other Lords, very justly, look[ed] upon themselves as only present for the purpose of producing the necessary quorum of appellete authority".[31] Thus the role of the Lord Chancellor as supreme judge was confirmed.

The judicial workload of the House of Lords subsequently eased, when the right to appeal from the Scottish courts was curtailed in 1825, and, by the late 1830s, the need for lay peers to sit to make up a quorum disappeared, there being sufficient ex-Lord Chancellors and enobled judges in the House to staff a court of professional judges.[32] This not only ended the practice of lay peers voting in appeals, the last instance being in 1834,[33] but also reduced the workload of the Lord Chancellor. However, it was not until the Appellate Jurisdiction Act 1876, which provided for the appointment of Lords of Appeal in Ordinary, that there were sufficient properly qualified judges within the House to ensure a continuation of this reduction.

The Appellate Jurisdiction Act also confirmed the office of Lord Chancellor at "the apex of the judicial pyramid".[34] Section 5 provided that the House in its judicial capacity must include at least three members drawn from the Lord Chancellor, the Lords of Appeal in Ordinary, and former holders of high judicial office, including ex-Lord Chancellors. It also provided[35] for the rules of the court to be made and amended by three or more senior judges, of whom the Lord Chancellor was one, and for the Lord Chancellor to be one of those consulted by the Queen on rules concerning the hearing of ecclesiastical cases.

However, the judicial role of the Lord Chancellor had to co-exist with a political role which was becoming increasingly tied to party politics and while the effect of the Appellate Jurisdiction Act was to separate the court from the legislature, this separation was not formal. The overlap between the two was evident

---

[30] In 1811 the House of Lords decided twenty-three cases but there were over 338 still waiting. These were mainly Scottish appeals, of which there were so many because appeal to the House of Lords gave an automatic stay of execution. (See R. Stevens, *Law and Politics*, for the history of this period.)

[31] Leahy, cited in R. Stevens, *Law and Politics*, p. 21.

[32] Ibid, p. 29.

[33] In 1844 the convention that lay peers should refrain from voting for fear of lessening the authority of the House was established (*O'Connell* v. *R* (1844) 11 Cl. & F. 155 421–6) although Lord Denman attempted to do so in *Bradlaugh* v. *Clarke* (1883) 8 App. Cases 354. It had also been the practice for all petitions to the sovereign from overseas to be heard in an open committee of the Privy Council. However, in 1833 this also ended when the Lord Chancellor, Lord Brougham, "called into being" the Judicial Committee of the Privy Council (J. B. Atlay, *The Victorian Chancellors*, p. 315).

[34] A. Bradney, "The Judicial Activity of the Lord Chancellor 1946–87: A Pellet" (1989) 16 *Journal of Law and Society* 360.

[35] Section 17.

in the way in which Lord Chancellors from the 1880s through to 1913[36] continued to combine political commitment with active judging, thereby ensuring that the House of Lords in its judicial function was still part of the political fray. Indeed, "the most obvious obstacle to a scientific formalism was the office of Lord Chancellor itself",[37] which continued to confound any notion of the separation of powers. Moreover, while some of the other throwbacks to the mix of judicial and political functions, such as the right of peers to be tried for felony or treason by their fellow peers, were subsequently removed,[38] the Lord Chancellor continued, and continues, to exercise this mix in the House of Lords, albeit, in theory and practice, wearing different hats. Of course, "in exercising his judicial functions, the Lord Chancellor does not act as a member of the Government but on his personal responsibility and under judicial oath".[39] Like all judges, the Lord Chancellor is bound not only to "well and truly serve" the Queen, but also to "do right to all manner of people after the laws and usages of this Realm without fear or favour, affection or ill will". He is therefore required to be independent and impartial.

Given that the Lord Chancellor acts, when he chooses, as president of the highest court, it is perhaps surprising that little or no attention is paid to the judicial record of an incoming Lord Chancellor. This may be because, even more surprisingly, some Lord Chancellors, for instance in recent times, Lords Hailsham, Havers and Irvine, have had little or no previous experience as senior judges and, as a consequence, there is "not much evidence to analyse when they [are] appointed".[40] It may also be that any examination of a Lord Chancellor's judicial record seems pointless when there is no opportunity to influence the appointment, and "since recent Lord Chancellors have not spent much time sitting in their judicial capacity . . ., it does not matter much whether or not they are good judges".[41] However, even if Lord Chancellors do not sit frequently, they can still exert considerable influence. As a matter of principle, it would therefore seem appropriate that some attention should be paid to the professional record of a Lord Chancellor but then principle does not rule the British constitution. If it did, a Cabinet minister would not be appointed to preside over the highest court in the land.

---

[36] i.e. Selbourne, Cairns, Halsbury and Loreburn.

[37] R. Stevens, *Law and Politics*, p. 84.

[38] By the Criminal Justice Act 1948 (s. 30). The right had meant that, if Parliament was sitting, the case was heard by the whole House. If it was not, it was heard by a jury of peers. Originally such trials were presided over by the Lord High Steward but in modern times this function fell to the Lord Chancellor, as in 1935, the last time the right was invoked, when Lord de Clifford was tried and acquitted for manslaughter.

[39] Home Affairs Committee, *Third Report, Judicial Appointments Procedures* (1995–96) HC 52-II, Appendix 1, Memorandum from the LCD.

[40] S. Lee, *Judging the Judges*, p. 148.

[41] Ibid.

THE INFLUENCE OF TWENTIETH CENTURY LORD CHANCELLORS

In his judicial role, the Lord Chancellor can exert leadership over the general development of the law, as well as over particular decisions. These are not, of course, discreet, as particular decisions inform the development of the law. It follows, therefore, that Lord Chancellors, who have been very active as judges, are likely to have had a stronger influence over judicial thinking than those who have been less so. However, Lord Chancellors can lead and influence in other ways, most obviously through law reform but also through their expectation of the role the law lords should play.

At the turn of the twentieth century Lord Chancellors were active judges. As such, they were very powerful within the House of Lords and exerted considerable influence. Lord Halsbury (1886–92; 1895–1905) dominated judicial thinking and has been attributed with making the role of the law lords "increasingly mechanistic".[42] It was he who stipulated that the House of Lords should be bound by its own earlier decisions,[43] a rule that was strictly applied until the Practice Direction of 1966 gave some flexibility. He also insisted on the literal interpretation of statutes[44] and stressed the importance of excluding policy issues from review by the courts.[45] The leadership and attitudes of two other Lord Chancellors at the turn of the century, Herschall (1892–5) and Loreburn (1905–12), were also influential in setting the tone for the development, or, perhaps more accurately, the non-development, of administrative law, while Lord Haldane (1912–15) "sought to lead the House, and hence the legal system, away from any semblance of competition with the political system"[46] and Lord Birkenhead (1919–22) "consolidated the Conservative position" by stressing the subservience of the appeal court to the will of Parliament.[47]

Leadership is not a quality possessed by all Lord Chancellors; neither Finlay (1916–19) nor Cave (1922–4; 1924–8) is noted for providing it. Indeed, as far as Cave was concerned "his vision of the appellate process provid[ed] little rationale or justification for a second appeal"[48] and thus for the House of Lords exercising a judicial function. His attitude, according to Stevens, helped to "set the tone for later decades".[49] Moreover, it was compounded by the first Lord Hailsham (1928–9; 1935–8) who, "although a strong man, . . . in some respects

---

[42] B. Abel-Smith and R. Stevens, *In Search of Justice* (London, Allen Lane, the Penguin Press, 1968) p. 123.

[43] *London Street Tramways Co.* v. *L.C.C.* [1898] C 375 t 379–80.

[44] e.g. *Earl Grey* v. *Attorney General* [1900] AC 124.

[45] e.g. *Janson* v. *Driefontein Consolidated. Gold Mines* [1902] AC 484 at 491.

[46] R. Stevens, *Law and Politics*, p. 220.

[47] R. Stevens, "Judges, Politicians and the Confusing Role of the Judiciary" in K. Hawkins (ed.), *The Human Face of Law* (Oxford, Clarendon Press, 1997), p. 271. Stevens notes that this conservative position, as originally proposed by Dicey, might be thought the role model for Birkenhead's successors from Dilhorne to Mackay.

[48] R. Stevens, *Law and Politics*, pp. 238–9.

[49] Ibid.

let the power and prestige of the office of Lord Chancellor drift. He did not maintain the pressure of law reform work developed by Sankey (1929–35), and he did not give the leadership to the judges that the office made possible".[50] Maugham (1938–9) and Caldecote (1939–40), who followed him to the position of Lord Chancellor, are similarly criticised. Their Chancellorships "were the culmination of a long period, when instead of providing a role model for the judges, successive Chancellors either had not articulated a clear role for the appellate work of the House or had somewhat mindlessly regurgitated what sounded acceptable to the typical High Court judge".[51] The failure of these Lord Chancellors of the interwar years to clarify the role of the House of Lords and provide it with purpose suggests lack of leadership. However, leaving the law lords without direction itself influenced their role and the development of the law. It was a negative influence, but influence all the same.

In contrast to his predecessors, Lord Simon (1940–5) provided strong leadership and his influence on the direction taken by the House of Lords was considerable. Not only did he sit with "remarkable frequency during his tenure as Chancellor", but "the combination of his intellectual and political power was forbidding".[52] Moreover, "the political animal in Simon was strong, and there is no doubt that he sometimes steered the House wisely".[53] However, while "he advocated civil liberties and the importance of the independence of the judiciary . . . he subordinated their significance to that of the legislature and the executive in a way that, in terms of power, made the courts increasingly appear to be but an arm of the executive".[54] It was, of course, wartime, so perhaps he felt restrained, as a judge, from acting otherwise.

His successor Jowitt (1945–51) also felt restrained in his role as judge but for different reasons. He felt a tension between his judicial position and his membership of the Labour Party. This was no doubt exacerbated because of the part he had played in government, both as a law officer and, prior to that, as a departmental minister.[55] He sat in few leading cases, perhaps because his energies were directed towards the extensive legislative programme of the Attlee Government. He was the first Lord Chancellor to be faced with the choice of sitting judicially or as Speaker, the Appellate Committee of the House of Lords being established in 1948, and he chose most often the legislative role.

The concepts of law expounded by Simon, Jowitt and his successor, Simonds (1951–4), were reflected in the minimal judicial role assumed by the House of

---

[50] R. Stevens, *Law and Politics*, p. 242.

[51] Ibid, p. 245.

[52] Ibid, p. 329.

[53] Ibid, p. 331.

[54] Ibid, p. 332. This was evident in his leading judgment in *Duncan* v. *Cammell, Laird and Co. Ltd.* [1942] AC 624 in which he laid down the rule that the courts could not question a claim of Crown privilege, regardless of the nature of the document, thereby giving government departments legal power to override the rights of litigants whenever they chose.

[55] He had been Solicitor-General, Attorney-General, Paymaster General, Minister without Portfolio and Minister of National Insurance.

Lords, which confined itself to declaring the law. Those they appointed "were not a group of Lords of Appeal who might be expected to swim against the tide of their de facto appointers. . . . For the most part they acquiesced in the articulated jurisprudential views of (and normally the actual policies pursued by) the Lord Chancellors".[56] They were "either consciously or unconsciously aware of the political dangers of any move that might be seen in the political world as judicial legislation",[57] choosing therefore a "deliberate withdrawal from an activist judicial role and the cultivation of an apparently 'neutral' political position".[58] In so doing, they were adopting a position which had been "consciously fostered" and "encouraged by successive Lord Chancellors and politicians, particularly of Liberal and Labour parties", since the latter part of the nineteenth century.[59]

It was not until Lord Kilmuir (1954–62) became Lord Chancellor in 1954 that "the first major effort to halt the decline of the courts" importance was made".[60] For this, as Lord Chancellor, Stevens suggests, "he deserves to rank as one of the most important figures in twentieth century English law".[61] Kilmuir, who had previously held the position of Home Secretary as well as Attorney-General and was therefore a politician and a lawyer, wanted the courts to have "greater usefulness in the modern world".[62] He was "apparently prepared to risk exposing the judges to the winds of politics by encouraging them to be less formalistic and to undertake many more practical functions".[63] Despite opposition for his permanent secretary, Sir George Coldstream, Chancery judges and the Labour benches, he established the Restrictive Practices Court in 1956. Moreover, while taking little part in the judicial work of the House of Lords, he was "conscious of [his] responsibility for the high standards" of the judicial system.[64]

Kilmuir was followed by Lord Dilhorne (1962–4), who had no judicial experience and was in office for too short a time to gain much while Lord Chancellor, and then by Lord Gardiner (1964–70). He provided little leadership as president of the Appellate or Judicial Committees. Indeed, he sought to abolish the House of Lords, believing it had no role to play. He did, however, give direction through his forward looking programme of law reform and the establishment of law commissions for England and Scotland, which, Lord Hailsham suggests, "gave him the right to claim an important place amongst twentieth century Chancellors".[65] He also led the House of Lords to a reconsideration of the rules relating to judicial precedent, the Practice Statement of 1966,[66] formally freeing

[56] R. Stevens, *Law and Politics*, p. 357.
[57] Ibid, p. 354.
[58] J. Bell, *Policy Arguments in Judicial Decisions* (Oxford, Clarendon Press, 1983) p. 5.
[59] Ibid.
[60] R. Stevens, *Law and Politics*, p. 420.
[61] Ibid.
[62] B. Abel-Smith and R. Stevens, *In Search of Justice*, p. 297.
[63] Ibid, p. 295.
[64] Earl of Kilmuir, *In My Life* (London, Allen Lane, the Penguin Press, 1968) p. 298.
[65] *A Sparrow's Flight*, p. 382.
[66] Practice Statement (Judicial Amendment) [1966] 1 WLR 1234.

the House of Lords from the rule imposed by Halsbury some seventy years previously that it was bound by its own decisions, and aided the development of judicial creativity in the Privy Council by allowing dissenting opinions.

Lord Gardiner was, in many respects, a political innocent. By contrast, his successor, Lord Hailsham, was a "party workhorse" who "brought to the judicial work many of the positions he had articulated politically, for he had complete confidence in the English system of justice and the traditional concepts of judicial objectivity and law".[67] Moreover, unlike many of his predecessors, he was unconcerned about being seen as making law or his decisions being seen as political. Indeed he argued that judging was "a political activity, involving definite stands on political issues, where all that can be expected is an openness to argument".[68] Thus, he believed, that the decision whether or not to assume jurisdiction was itself a political one. Whatever judges decided, they were "in politics".[69]

Hailsham, and for different reasons Kilmuir and Gardiner, "breathed a new life into the appellate process",[70] a process which gained new momentum during the late 1980s and 1990s as the consequences of membership of the European Community became apparent and judicial review increased dramatically. It was, however, frustrated by Lord Mackay's refusal to countenance a Bill of Rights. This had to wait for Lord Irvine, although his view that "the courts may not decide either on the validity or desirability of legislation"[71] meant that the Human Rights Act, passed in 1998, gives the courts less power than some judges would have liked.

Hailsham and Mackay, through their decisions to sit as judge, whenever possible, were also able to exert their influence as president of both appeal courts. The presiding judge can do this in a number of ways. As "the individual with potentially the greatest influence on the oral exchange",[72] he can "exercise considerable influence over the course of the argument to be presented in court".[73] Indeed, according to Lord Denning, "in a way he conducts the argument".[74] Moreover, the manner and speed with which an appeal is undertaken largely depends upon him. He can intervene to curtail counsel or allow interventions by the judges or, in Lord Hailsham's case, "interject [himself] during the course of the argument".[75]

In addition, the presiding judge "may . . . play a disproportionate part in drafting the final decision".[76] In the case of Lord Simon, "his judicial duty did

---

[67] R. Stevens, *Law and Politics*, p. 440.

[68] J. Bell, *Policy Arguments in Judicial Decisions*, p. 5.

[69] Lord Hailsham, H.L. Debs., 29 November 1978, col. 1384.

[70] R. Stevens, *Law and Politics*, p. 444.

[71] Lord Irvine, "Judges and Decision Makers: the Theory and Practice of *Wednesbury* Review" [1996] *Public Law* 59 at 61.

[72] A. Paterson, *The Law Lords* (Macmillan, London, 1982) p. 66.

[73] L. Blom-Cooper and G. Drewry, *Final Appeal*, p. 66.

[74] Quoted in A. Paterson, *The Law Lords*, p. 66.

[75] G. Drewry, "The Lord Chancellor as Judge" (London, Macmillan, 1982) p. 856.

[76] L. Blom-Cooper and G. Drewry, *Final Appeal*, p. 179.

not end with the day's argument. He was active in the weeks, which followed, pursuing his own researches and ready to engage in correspondence about different points. He kept a close eye on the preparation of opinions, and was always ready with a courteously phrased amendment or correction to a colleague's draft".[77] One effect of his close supervision was that "other law lords dissented from his speeches only with some trepidation".[78] In *Liversage* v. *Anderson* (1942)[79] Lord Simon's assumption of a supervisory role controversially extended to an appeal over which he had not presided. The case concerned whether the courts could review the exercise of the Home Secretary's power to intern individuals without trial,[80] and in a ruling, which was subsequently much criticised, the House of Lords held they could not. Lord Atkin dissented and in his judgment he described the majority as being "more executive-minded than the executive".[81] Moreover, he ridiculed his colleagues by citing extracts from "Alice through the Looking Glass". Lord Simon, who rightly had not heard the appeal himself, wrote to Atkin asking him to omit the paragraph concerned. This action can be seen either as an acceptable request from a Lord Chancellor, concerned that the passage and the comments might give offence and undermine the authority of the House of Lords, or as an unacceptable interference in judicial discretion, "as it was these phrases which give the judgment its peculiar force and lift it into the category of greatness".[82] More seriously, Lord Simon's intervention, described by Robert Stevens as "most sinister",[83] could be viewed as having "passed over the line which marks the boundary between a permissible intervention by a Lord Chancellor in his capacity as a presiding judge and an impermissible interference by a Lord Chancellor in his capacity as Cabinet Minister".[84] The danger that a Lord Chancellor might seek to influence his judicial colleagues for political reasons is endemic in the mix of roles that Lord Chancellors are expected to fulfil. The safeguard against it happening is the integrity of the Lord Chancellor and the robustness of the law lords in defending their independence.

There is, of course, no safeguard against a Lord Chancellor with little or no judicial experience assuming the role of president in the House of Lords or Privy Council. Indeed, this position is his by right, a situation which would seem unlikely to add to the reputation of these bodies. The idiosyncratic nature of this situation was recognised, in part, in 1969 when Lord Gardiner, the Lord Chancellor, announced that, as "in modern times, Lord Chancellors have little opportunity by virtue of their executive and legislative duties to acquire that

---

[77] R. F. V. Heuston, *Lives of the Lord Chancellors 1940–1970*, p. 58.

[78] R. Stevens, *Law and Politics*, p. 329.

[79] [1942] AC 206.

[80] Under Regulation 18B, made under the Emergency Powers Act 1939.

[81] For a full account see R. V. F. Heuston (1970) "The Office of Lord Chancellor" 86 *Law Quarterly Review* 33.

[82] R. F. V. Heuston, *Lives of the Lord Chancellors 1940–1970*, p. 59.

[83] R. Stevens, *Law and Politics*, p. 333.

[84] R. F. V. Heuston, *Lives of the Lord Chancellors 1940–1970*, pp. 58–9.

high degree of judicial expertise and experience required in the presiding judge of the ultimate tribunal", the rule that, an ex-Lord Chancellor, if sitting, automatically presided in the absence of the Lord Chancellor would be amended and the senior Lord of Appeal would preside instead.[85] However, the change in the rule did nothing to prevent a Lord Chancellor, when in post, from exerting his influence as presiding judge, even if he has no judicial experience. Thus the position is retained whereby an individual who has argued a case before the law lords one day, may preside over them the next. While his colleagues, at least in recent times, have been appointed because of their judicial record, he has not, and the evidence of the judicial capabilities of Lord Chancellors is mixed.

THE JUDICIAL RECORD OF LORD CHANCELLORS

A quick review of some of the Lord Chancellors, during the last hundred years or so, reveals considerable variation in the judicial reputations of holders of the position, as well as, at times, differences of opinion among those making the assessment. The judicial capabilities of Herschell (1886; 1892–5) are praised by Heuston, who notes that, "as Lord Chancellor, [he] is remembered by lawyers today for his judgments. They are of the highest order of achievement and entitle him to a place in the front rank of English judges".[86] He is less fulsome in his praise of Halsbury (1895–1905), nevertheless suggesting; "His learning, with the help skilfully supplied by counsel, was sufficient for the disposal of the appeals which came before him".[87] Others describe Lord Halsbury as "capable of producing . . . creative [decisions]" and as an expert at "construing precedents narrowly in order to avoid the rules he had cast" both for himself and for the rest of the House of Lords (see above).[88] Indeed, he "had the nineteenth century ability to avoid 'precedents' when they conflicted with 'principles' ". [89] Halsbury is noted for being influenced by his political views when making judicial appointments.[90] However, except for the field of labour law, where his refusal to recognise the legitimacy of strike action demonstrated his bias against trade unions, there would seem to be "no ground for the suspicion that his political views had any influence upon him in the discharge of his judicial functions".[91]

Haldane (1912–15; 1924) is seen as somewhat inconsistent in his approach to law. Despite the fact that he "did not hesitate to use the political power of his office to reshape English administrative law or the Canadian constitution",[92] in

---

[85]   H. L. Debs., 22 May 1969, cols. 469–70, cited in L. Blom-Cooper and G.Drewry, *Final Appeal*, p. 179.

[86]   R. F. V. Heuston, *Lives of the Lord Chancellors 1885–1940*, p. 110.

[87]   Ibid, p. 74.

[88]   B. Abel-Smith and R. Stevens, *In Search of Justice*, p. 123.

[89]   Ibid.

[90]   See Chapter Six.

[91]   R. F. V. Heuston, *Lives of the Lord Chancellors 1885–1940*, p. 74.

[92]   R. Stevens, *Law and Politics*, p. 222.

the case of the latter carefully choosing the panel and presiding over the Privy Council in all constitutional appeals,[93] he "claimed little or no control over the interpretation of statutes or development of the common law",[94] using "the declaratory theory" as a "convenient political device" to limit the role of the courts.[95] Sankey's contribution as a judge (1929–35) was also limited, particularly where private law was concerned, although he undertook "crucial work" in the field of law reform.[96] His main interest was in politics and, as a result, he was attracted to areas of law "where the public interest was at stake" and in these "he was capable of taking an active and important part".[97] In the Privy Council "he understood better than his contemporaries those nuances of political life necessary to the handling of constitutional cases" with the result that his work in Commonwealth affairs was "important and sophisticated".[98] Nevertheless, according to Heuston, while, in general, his "judgments are clear, careful and correct . . . they do not entitle him to a place among the great English judges".[99]

Of Finlay (1916–19), little complimentary is said by academic commentators, while Lord Birkenhead (1919–22) is described by Stevens, as "one of the most complex and controversial Chancellors of all times".[100] Birkenhead had been "a brilliant lawyer"[101] but he "never fulfilled his potential as a lawyer and a judge, not through any lack of ability but through lack of application".[102] Cave (1922–8) is noted as having left "little imprint",[103] while the first Lord Hailsham (1928–9; 1935–8), whose "contribution to the common law was not outstanding", is criticised for failing to put his mark on the appellate work of the Lords",[104] giving the impression of "being more interested in the political than the legal side of his work".[105]

Lord Maugham (1938–9), unlike most Lord Chancellors who held office before the Second World War, found little time to sit as a judge. On the positive side, Heuston praises his "versatility" and states that "the sweep of his learning and the clarity of his style show to peculiar advantage in his judgments on common law topics, even though he had training on the chancery side".[106] In contrast, Stevens suggests that as both law lord and Lord Chancellor, Maugham

---

[93] Between 1912–29 there were forty-one cases from Canada involving judicial review and Haldane sat in thirty-two, delivering judgment in nine. He also dominated those from Australia and played an active part in Indian appeals (Ibid, pp. 219–20).

[94] Ibid, p. 222.

[95] Ibid, p. 223.

[96] Ibid, p. 227.

[97] Ibid.

[98] Ibid.

[99] R. F. V. Heuston, *Lives of the Lord Chancellors 1885–1940*, p. 525.

[100] R. Stevens, *Law and Politics*, p. 232.

[101] Ibid.

[102] Ibid, p. 235.

[103] Ibid, p. 238.

[104] Ibid, p. 240.

[105] Ibid, p. 241.

[106] R. F. V. Heuston, *The Lives of the Lord Chancellors 1885–1940*, p. 573.

was unimpressive and notes; "it is arguable that he carried to the Woolsack all the worst failings and prejudices of the least distinguished type of English judge".[107] Stevens is also dismissive of Lord Caldecote's brief term as Lord Chancellor (1939–40), noting that he was "generally agreed to have been one of its least distinguished incumbents".[108]

The same cannot be said of Lord Simon (1940–5), who is praised by Heuston as being "superb" in his role in the House of Lords.[109] He notes; "it is impossible to open any volume of the Appeal Cases from 1941–1946 without being struck by the scale and distinction of his achievement – an achievement accomplished in spite of the fact that he had not been a practising member of the Bar for more than a dozen years before his elevation to the Woolsack".[110] Simon's successor, Jowitt (1945–51), receives no such plaudits, although Heuston defends him from the criticism that he was a "reactionary", arguing that rather than putting his energies into delivering judgments, his "creative energies found release in legislative reform".[111] That said, in the total of twenty-eight appeals on which he sat as Lord Chancellor or ex-Lord Chancellor, he produced seven single judgments, which is more than any other post-war Lord Chancellor until Lord Hailsham.[112] It is the nature of these judgments which has provoked the criticism.

Lord Kilmuir (1954–62) seems to have had little interest in his role as judge, the only reference in his memoirs to an actual case is in his description of one of his working days which "involved delivering a judgment on a rating appeal in the House of Lords, attending [a] lunch . . ., some twelve speeches in the Committee stage of the Restrictive Practices Bill, and a speech at the Lord Mayor's dinner to the judges".[113] This apparent lack of interest in his judicial role is reflected in his judgments, which Heuston states "are not remarkable either in quantity or quality . . . The abiding impression is that of a judge who was simply uninterested in the development of legal concepts by analytical reasoning".[114] Moreover, in an indictment of Kilmuir as Lord Chancellor, Heuston notes; "This is not unusual amongst trial judges, but it is not only unusual but also inappropriate in a Lord Chancellor".[115] Heuston's verdict on his judgments contrasts with Stevens' praise for the way in which he "halt[ed] the decline of the courts" (see above), demonstrating that judicial leadership does not necessarily depend upon judicial ability.

Lord Dilhorne's two years in office (1962–4) was too brief to determine how, as Lord Chancellor, he performed as judge, other than that "he saw his task to

---

[107] R. Stevens, *Law and Politics*, p. 243.
[108] Ibid, p. 245.
[109] R. F. V. Heuston, *The Lives of the Lord Chancellors 1940–1970*, p. 57.
[110] Ibid.
[111] Ibid, p. 123.
[112] A. Bradney, "The Judicial Activity of the Lord Chancellor 1946–87: A Pellet", p. 367.
[113] Earl of Kilmuir, *Political Adventure*, p. 265.
[114] R. F. V. Heuston, *Lives of the Lord Chancellors 1940–1970*, p. 175.
[115] Ibid.

ascertain and apply the law".[116] Gardiner (1964–70), although in office for longer, also provided little evidence of his capabilities. The limited view taken by Gardiner of his judicial function is regretted by Heuston, both because of the high quality of his judgments and because "the interests both of litigants and of the legal system as a whole require that the Lord Chancellor should be as assiduous as possible in the discharge of his judicial functions".[117] This may be the case when the Lord Chancellor concerned is a good judge but in many respects it would seem better for those Lord Chancellors who lack the necessary talent or expertise to leave judging to their colleagues.

Lord Elwyn-Jones' (1974–9) view of his function as judge was even more limited than Gardiner's. He gave only one leading judgment,[118] otherwise simply agreeing with the conclusion of one or more of his colleagues.[119] This was in marked contrast to Lord Hailsham (1970–4; 1979–87), who, despite the fact that he had never sat in any judicial capacity before, enjoyed this part of his job more than any other,[120] giving judgment himself in all but twelve of the seventy-two appeals he heard as Lord Chancellor and ex-Lord Chancellor.[121] However, his enthusiasm did not make him "an outstanding Judge".[122] Although he sat whenever possible, he was "not able to sit frequently enough to build up a body of jurisprudence bearing his own personal mark"[123] and, more importantly, "he lacked the detachment necessary to the judicial temperament".[124] According to Lewis, "he talked a good deal during the hearing and few, if any, of his speeches in the law reports are capable of serving as a guiding light".[125] This view is supported by some of Hailsham's contemporaries. Lord Wilberforce thought Hailsham "was not, perhaps, cut out to be a judge; there was always much of the debating instinct about him", while Lord Templeton described some of Hailsham's decisions as "lucid fog". For his part, Lord Lane considered his opinions "a pleasure to read" but because they "lacked crispness, they would not be of much help to a recorder sitting in a provincial town trying to make sense of a House of Lords decision and to direct a jury properly".[126] This sentiment was echoed by Lord Bridge, who commented of Hailsham's judgment in *Hyam*[127] that he could not "regard it as providing practical guidance to judges who have to direct juries . . .".[128] Part of the problem may have been Lord

---

[116] Ibid, p. 197.
[117] Ibid, p. 222.
[118] *R* v. *Majewski* [1977] AC 443.
[119] A. Bradney, "The Judicial Activity of the Lord Chancellor 1946–87: A Pellet", p. 367.
[120] G. Lewis, *Lord Hailsham*, p. 314.
[121] A. Bradney, "The Judicial Activity of the Lord Chancellor 1946–87: A Pellet", p. 367.
[122] G. Lewis, *Lord Hailsham*, p. 315.
[123] Ibid.
[124] Ibid.
[125] Ibid.
[126] Ibid.
[127] *R* v. *Hyam* [1975] AC 55; [1974] 2 WLR 607; [1974] 2 All ER 41.
[128] S. Lee, *Judging the Judges*, p. 145.

Hailsham's lack of previous judicial experience. He had never directed a jury himself and thus was unaware of what was required.

Despite the dedication he showed to his judicial role when Lord Chancellor, Hailsham was by temperament a politician first and a judge second. Lord Mackay (1987–97), in contrast, was "more judge first and politician second".[129] He had been a Lord of Appeal in Ordinary for two years, prior to his appointment as Lord Chancellor, only the fourth Lord Chancellor since the Appellate Jurisdiction Act 1876 to have come via this route.[130] He quickly gained a reputation for an openness of approach to the law, which took account of academic views and legal developments in other jurisdictions. Within the first few months of being in office, he led the law lords "to impeccably progressive decisions in two important cases".[131] In *Polkey*[132] "he made it much more difficult for employers to justify a procedurally unfair dismissal by claiming that the employee deserved to be dismissed anyway" and in *Haywards* v. *Cammell Laird*,[133] "he opened up the floodgates for claims of unequal pay through sex discrimination".[134] His judgments, according to Simon Lee, "are exhaustive analyses of previous case law to determine the 'principle' which underlies the precedent",[135] this search for the principle also characterising his formulation of government policy.[136] Moreover, even on those occasions when he did not give a full opinion, he frequently added a "pertinent paragraph instead of relying on the formula that there is nothing one can usefully add".[137]

Lord Mackay was an experienced and distinguished judge prior to his appointment as Lord Chancellor. Lord Irvine (1997–), by contrast, not only lacked experience as a judge but also of criminal cases. He took silk at thirty-seven thus becoming the country's youngest QC, but his legal world "is one where you make money rather than a reputation for landmark cases".[138] That said, "his personal record does include some such highlights, such as the case he won in the House of Lords as a young silk where the right of a Sikh student to wear his turban to school was at stake".[139] It was reported that some law lords had reservations about his ability as a judge.[140] However, it was not his lack of

---

[129] Ibid, p. 147.
[130] The others were Cave (1922), Maugham (1938) and Simonds (1951). Sankey had been a Lord Justice of Appeal when appointed in 1929.
[131] S. Lee, *Judging the Judges*, p. 149.
[132] *Polkey* v. *AE Dayton Services Ltd* [1988] 1 AC 344.
[133] *Haywards* v. *Cammell Laird Shipbuilders Ltd.* [1988] IRLR 257.
[134] S. Lee, *Judging the Judges*, p. 149.
[135] Ibid, p. 150.
[136] N. Lawson, *The View from No. 11*.
[137] S. Lee, *Judging the Judges*, p. 149.
[138] I. Hargreaves, "The Godfather".
[139] Ibid.
[140] D. Egan, *Irvine*, p. 232. The first case that Irvine heard was *Boddington* v. *British Transport Police* [1998] 2 WLR 639; [1998] 2 All ER 203 and he gave the leading judgment in what was a unanimous decision. However, in dicta he contended that an invalid by-law was a nullity and thus had no legal effect. This view was not supported by his colleagues. Lord Browne-Wilkinson, who preferred to express "no view at this stage", nevertheless suggested that people would have regulated

judicial experience, which resulted in the position of Lord Chancellor, as judge, being questioned so strongly during his Chancellorship. Indeed, Geoffrey Robinson proclaimed that he would be happy for Lord Irvine to hear his case,[141] although whether this is because he considered him to be a good judge or because they shared the same commitment to human rights is not certain. Rather the issue of the Lord Chancellor sitting as judge came to the fore at this time because of Lord Irvine's personality, his high profile position in the Labour Government and the policies he was instrumental in pushing through.

THE FREQUENCY WITH WHICH LORD CHANCELLORS SIT AS JUDGES

Many Lord Chancellors have proclaimed their belief that holders of the office should sit as frequently as possible.[142] Most recently, Lord Irvine noted; "Both my predecessors, the noble and learned Lord Mackay and Lord Hailsham, attached real importance to the Lord Chancellor sitting in the Chair and so do I".[143] The traditional argument as to why a Lord Chancellor should sit as judge relates to his responsibility for judicial appointments. As a consequence, when the Appellate Committee of the House of Lords was established, making it more difficult for Lord Chancellors to sit as frequently as before, Lord Simon, "bewailed the fact that by reason of this change, Lord Chancellors would lose their personal contact with Bench and Bar so essential to their role in appointing judges".[144] He was not only concerned that this might handicap the Lord Chancellor in making judicial appointments but also that it might end the practice by which Lord Chancellors were themselves appointed from the ranks of barristers.[145] This was a sentiment shared by Lord Hailsham, who was adamant that the office of Lord Chancellor should be restricted to "members of the profession adequately equipped with academic legal scholarship and practical experience".[146] He believed that the only way of ensuring this was to subject "each successive Lord Chancellor to the ordeal, if it be such, or as I would prefer to put it the pleasure and privilege, of presiding over the highest of tribunals".[147] This would ensure that "a politically motivated prime minister does not give the office to a no-good lawyer".[148] He also thought that sitting frequently was necessary to keep in touch with the profession.

their lives on the basis that the act was valid, while Lord Steyn stated, "in a practical world . . . a court will usually assume that subordinate legislation, and administrative acts, are valid unless it is persuaded otherwise".

[141] *The Times*, 6 July 1999.
[142] e.g. Lord Gardiner (G. Drewry, "The Lord Chancellor as Judge", p. 855); Lord Mackay (C. Anderson, *Unreliable Evidence* (BBC Radio 4, 6 April 1999)).
[143] H. L. Debs., 17 February 1999, col. 736.
[144] G. Drewry, "The Lord Chancellor as Judge", p. 855.
[145] L. Blom-Cooper and G. Drewry, *Final Appeal*, p. 112.
[146] Lord Hailsham, "The Office of Lord Chancellor and the Separation of Powers", p. 318.
[147] Ibid.
[148] Lord Hailsham, *A Sparrow's Flight*, p. 379.

Today, these justifications seem somewhat thin, given the large number of appointments that need to be made, the changes in appointment practices and the concerns that exist about the Lord Chancellor's appointing role.[149] Yet Lord Irvine has noted; "sitting gives the Lord Chancellor a practical awareness of the development of the common law at the highest level [and] it enables him to assess the quality of the most senior advocates".[150] Moreover, he added; "It is just possible that the Lord Chancellor may himself have a contribution to make". This may be so, although whether it is appropriate for a person who has never sat as a full-time judge before to be in a position suddenly to make "a contribution" is a different matter. A further justification put forward for the Lord Chancellor sitting as judge is that, at the turn of the twenty-first century, far fewer law lords have held political office or had experience of politics than has previously been the case. The presence of the Lord Chancellor, which throughout the century had been "of added value, particularly in the fields of public law, public administration and judicial review" is, therefore, "of even greater value".[151] This view, put forward by Lord Borrie, was one with which Lord Irvine agreed. Yet the types of cases listed are the very situations in which the Lord Chancellor has to be careful about sitting, for, as discussed below, they are ones in which the government may have an interest.

Until the Second World War, the evidence suggests that Lord Chancellors sat regularly, the judicial function dominating the other functions of the Lord Chancellor. This is apparent from the description, given by Viscount Hailsham, of "his ordinary day's work". This entailed arriving at his office at 9.45am to allow about half an hour to attend to administrative duties, sitting judicially on four days of the week (Wednesday being Cabinet day) in the House of Lords or Privy Council until 4.00pm with a break of half an hour for lunch, returning to his rooms to "array himself in his full panoply of robes as Speaker of the House of Lords" and sitting in that capacity until the House rose, usually between 7.00pm and 8.00pm, having dinner, frequently at some public function, and, finally, attending to his red boxes.[152]

This pattern changed during the War, when the bombing of London ended evening debates, and immediately after, when building works resulted in the law lords having to retreat from the chamber to a committee room to hear appeals. Thus "the constitutional split between the judicial and legislative functions, which had occurred during the nineteenth century, was translated into a physical division"[153] and while the Lord Chancellor at the time, Lord Jowitt, emphasised the temporary nature of the change, his predecessor, Lord Simon, was not reassured, fearing that it "would mark a departure from the time-honoured role

---

[149] See Chapter Six.
[150] H. L. Debs., 17 February 1999, col. 736.
[151] Lord Borrie, H. L. Debs, 24 June 1999, col. 1062.
[152] Viscount Hailsham, "The Duties of a Lord Chancellor", p. 196.
[153] L. Blom-Cooper and G. Drewry, *Final Appeal*, p. 112.

of the final appellate court as the alter ego of Parliament".[154] Judgments continued to be given in the House but here too there was change as they were "in the form of a report from what was henceforth known as the Appellate Committee".[155]

The change in the arrangements for judicial sittings was, as Lord Simon feared, permanent and, as the House of Lords has continued to sit in its legislative capacity from 2.30pm rather than just in the evening, Lord Chancellors have been unable to combine the roles of Speaker and judge in the same way as their predecessors. The result has been that no Lord Chancellor since the Second World War has "sat [as judge] very frequently".[156] This by itself may not be a very good measure of the part played by Lord Chancellors, not only because what constitutes "sitting frequently" is not defined, but also because of the differences in the political and judicial climates in which Lord Chancellors have operated. As Bradney suggests, the contribution of Viscount Simon immediately after the Second World War was, for instance, "of a different order to that of Lord Gardiner's in the mid-60s".[157] Similarly, "the weight to be attached to the work of Lord Elwyn-Jones and Lord Hailsham in the 1980s might be different to that to be attached to the work of Viscount Jowitt and Lord Kilmuir in the mid–1950s".[158] One relevant factor is obviously the difference in the caseload. This has varied from a total of thirty-nine cases heard by the House of Lords and Privy Council in 1949 to seventy in 1964 and one hundred and eight in 1984.[159] While in 1998 and 1999, the House of Lords alone heard fifty-six and fifty-five cases, respectively.[160] Related to the number of cases is the proportion heard by different Lord Chancellors. All Lord Chancellors have exercised their right to sit, although the percentage of cases heard has ranged from a high of around ten to a low of one per cent in 1969.[161]

The actual number of times individual Lord Chancellors sit during their time in office therefore has to be considered in context and comparisons between different Lord Chancellors are not necessarily meaningful. Nevertheless, it still provides a useful indicator of the importance Lord Chancellors place upon the judicial role.[162] Figures show that Lords Jowitt (1945–51), Simonds (1951–4) and Kilmuir (1954–62) sat, on average, somewhere between two and three times

---

[154] Ibid.

[155] Lord Hailsham, *A Sparrow's Flight*, p. 378.

[156] G. Drewry, "The Lord Chancellor as Judge", p. 855.

[157] A. Bradney, "The Judicial Activity of the Lord Chancellor 1946–87: A Pellet", p. 362.

[158] Page 366.

[159] Ibid, p. 362.

[160] Figures from House of Lords website.

[161] From figures from A. Bradney, "The Judicial Activity of the Lord Chancellor 1946–87: A Pellet".

[162] N.B. There is some discrepancy between the figures cited by different authorities and it is not always clear whether they include Privy Council cases as well as those heard by the House of Lords. Where more recent Lord Chancellors are concerned, there are also differences between the number of cases revealed by a Lexis search and those listed on the House of Lords website.

a year,[163] although, Lord Kilmuir, for one, indicated that this was less often than he would have liked.[164] Even so, he sat with greater frequency than Lord Gardiner (1964–70), who managed only four days during his six years in office,[165] hearing just seven appeals, only two of which were House of Lords cases.[166] He chose instead to devote himself to the role of Speaker, a trend followed by the next Labour Lord Chancellor, Lord Elwyn-Jones (1974–9) who sat in only two House of Lords and two Privy Council appeals in five years.[167]

Lord Hailsham (1970–4; 1979–87), who first succeeded Lord Gardiner and, subsequently, Lord Elwyn-Jones, commented that under Lord Gardiner the judicial function "had almost begun to atrophy".[168] He set about reviving it and, within his first two years as Lord Chancellor, had already sat in eight appeals in the House of Lords and heard two appeals and eight petitions in the Privy Council.[169] Moreover, he prepared a full judgment in each instance. In total he sat in forty-five appeals during his two terms as Lord Chancellor,[170] producing an average of three and a half cases a year, which, with the exception of Lord Dilhorne (1962–4), whose average over his two years in office had been five, was more than any other judge since Lord Simon. Lord Mackay (1987–97) continued the revival of the judicial role. He tried to hear six to eight cases a year[171] and, although he did not always achieve this, he managed an annual average of nearly five over his ten years in office, clocking up a total of sixty days.[172] The increase in the number of occasions on which Lords Hailsham and Mackay sat, when compared with their immediate predecessors, reestablished the role of Lord Chancellor as judge and with it the debate about the appropriateness of such a role, a debate which continued and gained momentum when Lord Irvine became Lord Chancellor.

It is not always clear why different Lord Chancellors have chosen to give different weightings to the judicial role, although their background, prior to becoming Lord Chancellor, may be influential. Lord Kilmuir had been primar-

---

[163] According to Bradney, Jowitt sat twelve times in six years, Simonds eight times in three years and Kilmuir twenty times in eight years; figures include the House of Lords and the Privy Council (A. Bradney, "The Judicial Activity of the Lord Chancellor", p. 267). Heuston states that Simonds sat six times and Kilmuir twenty-four (R. F. V. Heuston, *The Lives of the Lord Chancellors 1940–1970*).

[164] Earl of Kilmuir, *Political Adventure*, p. 298.

[165] Lord Irvine, H. L. Debs, 17 February 1999, col. 736; Heuston says he sat for only two days.

[166] *Button* v. *DPP; Swain* v. *DPP* HL [1966] AC 591 and *N. Ireland Commissioner of Valuation* v. *Protestant Board of Education* [1969] 3 All ER 352. He also heard a Chancery case, concerning an application for bail (*Re Kray* [1965] Ch 736).

[167] Figures from Lexis.

[168] *A Sparrow's Flight*, p. 279.

[169] A. Bradney, "The Judicial Activity of the Lord Chancellor" p. 367.

[170] Ibid. Heuston, however, says he heard thirty-eight cases in his first term alone. It may be that this number included petitions to the Privy Council as well as appeals. Lord Irvine, translating Hailsham's judicial effort into days, states that he sat for twenty-eight days and fifty-three days, respectively (H. L. Debs., 17 February 1999, col. 736).

[171] Lord Mackay in C. Anderson, *Unreliable Evidence*.

[172] Lord Irvine, H. L. Debs., 17 February 1999.

ily a politician and it is therefore not surprising that he preferred a role in the legislature rather than in the court. Lords Dilhorne and Mackay, on the other hand, had been law lords and were likely to choose to continue to hear appeals, whenever possible. However, the positions of Gardiner and Hailsham present "something of a paradox" in that Gardiner "always conveyed the image of the apolitical "lawyer's lawyer" but chose to devote his time to being Speaker", while Hailsham's "roots are deeply embedded in his long and active career in Conservative Party politics" yet he "took every opportunity to don the non-partisan mantle of judge".[173] Indeed, he increased the number of deputy speakers from twenty-one to twenty-six to enable him to do so. Explanations may lie, at least in part, in Lord Hailsham's personal ambition to follow in his father's footsteps and in Lord Gardiner's sensitivity to Labour Party suspicions of any hint of judicial activism.

Differences in the frequency with which Lord Chancellors sit are not only evident when they are serving government ministers. They are also apparent afterwards. Those who have held the office of Lord Chancellor receive a pension, derived from the Lord Chancellor's Pension Act 1832, together with a lump sum and a widow's pension. This was initially awarded by way of compensation for the abolition of "certain valuable patronage hitherto vested in the Lord Chancellor", as is apparent from the long title of the Act which states its objective as being "to abolish certain Sinecure Offices connected with the Court of Chancery and to make provision for the Lord High Chancellor on his retirement from Office".[174] The pension was not originally tied to continued judicial service but in a debate in 1965 over increasing the pension to which Lord Chancellors are entitled, an amendment was proposed to make the pension dependent upon his "not receiving earned income from any other source" and "upon the pensioner making himself available to participate in the legal work of the House of Lords".[175] The amendment was rejected on the understanding that by convention an ex-Lord Chancellor was under an obligation to sit judicially, if drawing the pension.

Most Lord Chancellors since the War have continued to sit when retired, although just as there are differences in the number of times they sit while in office, there is considerable variation in the frequency with which ex-Lord Chancellors hear appeals. Lord Simon, consistent with his record as Lord Chancellor, sat in fifty-eight appeals in the House of Lords and the Privy Council, and Lord Dilhorne in two hundred and forty-one, thirty-six as retired Lord Chancellor and the remainder after he became a law lord in 1969.[176] Somewhat surprisingly, Lord Elwyn-Jones, who sat rarely as Lord Chancellor, had a higher than average sitting rate when retired, hearing eighty-seven appeals

[173] G. Drewry, "The Lord Chancellor as Judge", p. 855.
[174] R. F. V. Heuston, *Lives of the Lord Chancellors 1885–1940*, p. 21.
[175] See H. C. Debs., 22 July 1965, cols. 2069–74.
[176] A. Bradney, "The Judicial Activity of the Lord Chancellor", p. 367.

in ten years, although he only gave full judgment in five cases.[177] Less surprisingly, Lord Gardiner sat in only three appeals as ex-Lord Chancellor, on each occasion simply concurring with the majority, while Lord Mackay heard thirteen cases during the first thirty months he was out of office.[178]

The number of appeals that an ex-Lord Chancellor is able to hear is, of course, limited by the age at which he relinquishes office. He is subject to the same disqualification rules as the law lords[179] and this accounts for Lord Hailsham's relatively low total of twenty-seven appeals.[180] He was already approaching eighty when replaced, briefly, by Lord Havers and then by Lord Mackay. Sitting in appeals is also limited to those who refrain from other employment. Kilmuir, who surrendered his pension and went to the City, was thus not eligible to sit as ex-Lord Chancellor. It may seem somewhat strange that Lord Chancellors, who had no judicial experience prior to being appointed and acquired little while in office, should still be expected to undertake judicial duties when no longer in government. The need for them to earn their pension would seem to outweigh considerations of judicial competence.

THE SELECTION OF JUDICIAL PANELS; THE DIMINISHING ROLE FOR THE LORD CHANCELLOR

The way in which Lord Chancellors combined political commitment with active judging in the nineteenth and early twentieth century was evident in their attempts to influence the outcome of cases by packing the appeal bodies of the House of Lords and Privy Council.

Halsbury (1895–1905) who wanted to see the power of the trade unions reduced, sought to manipulate the composition of judicial panels to secure these ends, a strategy which proved to be effective when the House of Lords held that unions could be sued for losses arising from a strike,[181] while the "careful selection" of panels by Loreburn (1905–12) "helped to return some powers to the dominion government in Canadian appeals and in English appeals ensured that the courts would abandon attempts to interfere directly with policy decisions by the Executive".[182] He also manipulated split decisions of the House of Lords to secure the outcome he wanted, allowing the decision to stand and the ruling of the Court of Appeal therefore to remain, when he approved of it, and ordering the case to be reheard, when he disapproved.

Haldane (1912–15; 1924) can also be seen to have exercised "political" judgment in the selection of panels, choosing them carefully "when vital domestic

---

[177] Lexis.
[178] Ibid and House of Lords website.
[179] See now Judicial Pensions and Retirement Act 1993, which came into effect in 1995.
[180] A. Bradney, "The Judicial Activity of the Lord Chancellor", p. 367.
[181] *Taff Valley Railway Co.* v. *Amalgamated Soc. of Railway Servants* [1901] AC 426 (R. Stevens, *Law and Politics*, pp. 93–7).
[182] *Board of Education* v. *Rice* [1911] C 179 (Ibid, p. 85).

issues were being litigated before the House of Lords".[183] He chose four Liberal law lords to hear *Local Government* v. *Arlidge* (1915),[184] thereby securing a decision which removed the danger of the courts imposing procedural requirements on government departments and had long term effects for the growth of administrative law. Similarly Viscount Hailsham (1928–9; 1935–8) "was not above packing the House in order to curb [Lord] Atkin's activities", namely, his determination to develop the common law in line with changing social conditions.[185] Moreover, evidence suggests that Haldane, Sankey and Hailsham "all chose their Privy Council panels in order to further their own particular concerns about the dominion".[186]

The ability of Lord Chancellors to manipulate panels for political purposes, which would seem to have been relatively easy at the beginning of the twentieth century, became increasingly difficult as the century progressed and the appellate workload expanded. It also became politically unacceptable for Lord Chancellors to be seen to engage in such manipulation and, by the time the second Lord Hailsham held office, although the selection of Appellate Committees was still "theoretically in the hands of the Lord Chancellor", it was "actually delegated" to his permanent secretary who consulted the Lord Chancellor in cases of difficulty.[187] Moreover, the guidelines for selecting a panel, noted by Lord Hailsham, suggested very different considerations from those made by Lord Chancellors at the beginning of the century. Relevant to the selection was the subject matter, in that, wherever possible, judges who were specialist in the area under consideration should hear the case, and, if it was an appeal from the Scottish courts, a Scottish law lord should be on the panel. A further consideration was the nature of the case. Where a case had party political implications, as for instance, when it related to a trade dispute, it was important that adjudication should normally be by judges who have had no political experience. Indeed, in 1972 when the House of Lords was due to hear the appeal of *Heaton's Transport Co.* v. *TGWU*,[188] Lord Hailsham not only ensured that those on the panel had no political experience, he also announced, a week before the hearing was due to begin, that this was the case. This contrasts with the behaviour of his father, when Lord Chancellor, and the behaviour of other Lord Chancellors at the beginning of the century.[189]

[183] Ibid, p. 200.
[184] [1915] C 120 (See Ibid, p. 192).
[185] B. Abel-Smith and R. Stevens, *In Search of Justice*, p. 125.
[186] R. Stevens, *Law and Politics*, p. 192.
[187] A. Paterson, *The Law Lords*, p. 87. There are in fact two types of judicial committees of the House of Lords, the Appeal Committees, which give leave to appeal where there is no right to do so and no leave has been given by a lower court, and the Appellate Committees which hear the appeal. Appeal Committees are selected by the Principal Clerk to the Judicial Office, who tends not to ask the senior law lords to sit. The Judicial Office, which is a branch of the Office of the Clerks of Parliament, is also responsible for organising the lists.
[188] [1972] IRLR 25.
[189] Lord Irvine might likewise have taken responsibility over the rehearing of the Pinochet case (*R* v. *Bow Street Metropolitan Stipendary Magistrate and Others, ex parte Pinochet Ugarte* (No. 3)

However, these considerations aside, Hailsham reported that "the normal practice is to select the most convenient panel available".[190] There is, in any case, often little choice to make. Given the need to synchronise hearings in the Appellate Committee with those in the Judicial Committee of the Privy Council, together with the need to exclude any law lord who has heard the case in the Court of Appeal, and to discount law lords who may be unavailable because they are acting as chair of a royal commission or public inquiry or are overseas, "in practice the permanent secretary often has remarkably little room for manoeuvre".[191] This is also true where the Lord Chancellor is concerned and "a present day Lord Chancellor would find it exceedingly difficult to 'pack the court' in cases of a particular type, even if he were minded to do so".[192]

In fact, as Lord Irvine confirmed, the choice of the panel is now delegated to the senior law lord. He noted; "Responsibility for determining the composition of the House of Lords in its judicial capacity and of Appellate and Appeal Committees, lies with the Lord Chancellor. However, for many years it has been the policy of successive Lord Chancellors in practice to delegate this responsibility to the senior Lord of Appeal in Ordinary".[193] Yet, as delegation is only by convention, this may not prevent suspicions arising about whether a Lord Chancellor has had a hand in the composition of a particular panel. There is, as Lord Wilberforce pointed out, "no legal provision"[194] and while the practice "works quite well, as do many other informal elements in our constitution", it relies once again on the integrity of the Lord Chancellor and on the senior law lord resisting any attempt by the Lord Chancellor to interfere in the selection of panels. Moreover, it seems that it is still the Lord Chancellor who determines whether he sits on a particular case. This becomes increasingly controversial with the increase in judicial review and the role given to the House of Lords in the Human Rights Act 1998 and to the Privy Council by devolution legislation. As Lord Lester noted, in relation to these developments; "It is no answer to the problem for the Lord Chancellor to delegate the function of appointing the members of the court to the senior Law Lord. That leaves a potentially embarrassing tension within the rather opaque system of choosing the court, especially were the Lord Chancellor to be unwise enough to seek to persuade the senior Law Lord to agree to his sitting as a member of the Judicial Committee or the Appellate Committee".[195]

[1999] 2 WLR 827), instead of which he publicly chastised the law lords and told them that they must "put procedures in place to ensure that this does not happened again". (Interview with J. Rozenberg, *Radio 4*, 25 March 1999).

[190] Quoted in A. Paterson, *The Law Lords*, p. 88.
[191] Ibid.
[192] Ibid, p. 89.
[193] H. L. Debs., 30 July 1998, col.WA220.
[194] H. L. Debs., 28 October 1998, col. 1965.
[195] Ibid, cols. 1970–1.

While the Lord Chancellor has discretion as to whether to sit in a particular case in the House of Lords or Privy Council, there are certain factors which may guide him. During the period 1885–1945, "there seems to have been a convention that the Lord Chancellor should preside on the hearing of appeals raising important issues of Dominion Constitutional Law".[196] More recently, Lord Hailsham maintained that his choice was governed by the needs of staffing. He stated; "I have always put myself to sit in a case which would not and could not have been heard then if I hadn't been willing to sit myself".[197] It can also be assumed, at least in modern times, that the Lord Chancellor listens to any concerns that the senior law lords may have about him sitting in a particular case.

Limitations upon the Lord Chancellor's choice to sit as judge are linked to the need to protect judicial independence and integrity and to maintain confidence in the legal system. To this effect, it is important that justice is not only done but is seen to be done. Cases must therefore be heard by an unbiased tribunal. This does not mean that judges have to be apolitical. This would be an impossible requirement, particularly of a Lord Chancellor, who is appointed because of his support for the governing party. Nor does it mean that Lord Chancellors cannot have a view of what the role of the courts should be and attempt to steer the House of Lords in that direction. It does mean that Lord Chancellors should not sit in cases, in which there is a party political element or in which the government, of which he is a part, has a direct or indirect interest. As Lord Lester has said; "The time has surely come to recognise that inevitably it would be constitutionally inappropriate and improper for the Lord Chancellor to sit in any case where the Government or a Minister has an interest as a party litigant or in which constitutional or political issues are involved".[198]

Lord Chancellors, at least in the twentieth century, have seldom heard cases in which government interest is direct, although Lord Loreburn's involvement in *A.G.* v. *West Riding of Yorkshire CC*[199] provides an exception. The case concerned whether, under the Education Act 1902, education authorities could be ordered to pay teachers for the time they spent teaching religious education. The Court of Appeal had held that they could not, an uncomfortable decision for the government and one which was likely to result in it being "bombarded with questions" in Parliament. Loreburn advised an appeal, "as a matter of policy and fair play" and four months later presided over a "generally liberal House", chosen by him, which reversed the decision, Loreburn delivering the leading judgment.[200]

---

[196] R. F. V. Heuston, *Lives of the Lord Chancellors 1885–1940*, p. xvii.
[197] Quoted in G. Drewry, "The Lord Chancellor as Judge", p. 855; and see H. L Debs. 26 January 1971, col. 821.
[198] H. L. Debs., 28 October 1998, col. 1971.
[199] [1907] AC 29.
[200] R. Stevens, *Law and Politics*, p. 87.

Cases where there is an indirect interest are, however, more problematic. Lord Irvine has been reluctant to accept such a category stating that the furthest he was prepared to go in offering a definition of cases in which a Lord Chancellor should not sit is "any appeal where the Government might reasonably appear to have a stake in a particular outcome; apart from that the issue should be addressed on a case by case basis".[201] This was not a view held by Heuston, when writing in the early 1960s, who stated; "It has been settled for some years that it would be unconstitutional for a Lord Chancellor to take part in a criminal trial, as he is a Minister of the Crown holding office at the pleasure of the Sovereign".[202] However, subsequently, Lord Hailsham sat on a number of criminal appeals, often giving the leading judgment, as did Lord Mackay. Thus Lord Irvine's observation that; "Lord Chancellors have . . . frequently sat in criminal . . . appeals"[203] was correct and the rule proclaimed by Heuston would seem no longer to apply. This may be justified on the basis that the looser link between the Crown and the executive arm of government distances the Lord Chancellor from the charge of being judge in his own cause. Yet, arguably, such a rule is still relevant, not least because of the importance to the governing party of its "law and order" policies being seen as effective and the indirect interest it therefore has in the criminal jurisdiction.

A problem may also arise when a law lord is appointed Lord Chancellor but has yet to give judgment in an appeal, which it would have been inappropriate for him to hear in his new position. Two such instances arose when Lord Mackay was appointed Lord Chancellor in 1987. The first, a Privy Council case from New Zealand, concerned the statutory power invested in a government minister to grant consent for the issue of shares to a foreign investor and the duty of care owed by the minister to the company involved.[204] Although not a domestic case, the ruling was likely to have implications for the British Government and so was not a case in which, as Lord Chancellor, Lord Mackay should have given judgment. It would therefore have seemed appropriate for him to withdraw from the case, prior to judgment being given. In practice, this would have made no difference, as the Privy Council was unanimous in finding for the New Zealand Minister of Finance. However, Lord Mackay chose not to withdraw. Neither did he withdraw from the second case, which concerned a prisoner's right to legal representation when on a disciplinary charge. Yet the case had implications for the legal aid budget, for which, as Lord Chancellor, he was now responsible.[205] He therefore had a ministerial interest in the case.

More controversial, was Lord Mackay's decision to preside over the House of Lords in *Pepper* v. *Hart*,[206] an Inland Revenue case. While accepting that the

[201] H. L. Debs., 17 February 1999, col. 735.
[202] R. F. V. Heuston, *Lives of the Lord Chancellors 1885–1940*, p. 199.
[203] H. L. Debs., 28 October 1998, WA137.
[204] *Rowlings* v. *Takaro Properties Ltd*. [1988] 1 All ER 163.
[205] *Hone* v. *Maze Prison Board of Visitors* [1988] 1 All ER 3210.
[206] [1993] AC 593.

Lord Chancellor "would not sit in a case involving decisions of his own nor of members of the government in their executive capacity",[207] Lord Mackay argued that the application of taxing statutes to individuals is not a matter for government but for the independent board of the Inland Revenue. He was not therefore sitting in judgment on his political colleagues and there was no government interest in the case. Further he noted that it "has always been customary for the Lord Chancellor to sit in cases involving important questions of law, even if government agencies are involved, where the decisions are not those of ministers but of independent persons appointed for the purpose".[208] *Pepper* v. *Hart*, he said, fell within this category of cases. Whether or not it had been customary, his view that the Government had no direct interest in revenue cases was disputed by some, including Lord Lester and Lord Goodhart, who believed Lord Mackay was wrong to sit in the case.[209]

His decision to sit was criticised not only on grounds of the substantive issue involved but also because an important aspect of the case was whether judges should be allowed to refer to *Hansard* where the intention of a statute is unclear. Several of the law lords hearing the case, including Lord Mackay, had expressed strong feelings for or against the principle in a debate in Parliament two years previously and there was therefore a danger of confusion between legislative and judicial roles. More importantly, the issue was one in which the Government had an interest as it related to the responsibility of ministers, when presenting Bills to Parliament. Indeed, the Attorney-General contended before the Appellate Committee that "recourse to *Hansard* would breach parliamentary privilege and weaken the good governance of the country",[210] a view which was accepted by Lord Mackay, who dissented from the decision of the majority that reference to *Hansard* was admissible.

The participation of the Lord Chancellor, who is also a Cabinet minister, in the decision raised "issues of conflict of interest, and it [did] not engender confidence in the independence of the judiciary and the immunity of the system from pressures emanating from government".[211] Lord Irvine's decision to hear *Director of Public Prosecutions* v. *Jones*[212] also gave rise to criticism. The case concerned the Public Order Act 1986 and the limitations it placed upon the right to peaceful assembly on the public highway. It therefore involved the rights of the individual against an organ of the State of which the Lord Chancellor is a

---

[207] Lord Mackay, *The Administration of Justice* (Hamlyn Lecture, 1994) p. 24.
[208] Ibid, p. 25.
[209] H. L. Debs., 17 February 1999, col. 729.
[210] Lord Lester, H. L. Debs., 28 October 1998, col. 1971.
[211] D.Oliver, "Pepper v. Hart; a suitable case for reference to Hansard?" [1993] *Public Law* 5 at 5. Interestingly, Lord Mackay's successor, Lord Irvine, suffered the consequences of the ruling in *Pepper* v. *Hart* when the Human Rights Bill was before the House of Lords. Lord Lester and others made repeated attempts to "Pepper and Hart" him by getting him to expand upon how the act should be interpreted, with a view to subsequently using his statements before the courts as indications of parliamentary intent.
[212] [1999] 2 AC 143.

member. Moreover, it involved an Act around which there remained consider-able controversy and against which Lord Irvine had spoken as an opposition politician in the House of Lords. Lord Irvine gave the leading judgment for the majority,[213] in which he used the European Convention on Human Rights to affirm the development of the common law to hold that, subject to certain qual-ifications, there was a public right of peaceful assembly on the public highway. He therefore found for the individual against the State. But, he might not have done so. In any case, regardless of the outcome, the question was raised, first, about the validity of someone, who had expressed strong views about a partic-ular piece of legislation, subsequently hearing a case which concerned it, and, secondly, of someone, who was a minister, giving judgment in a case which con-cerned individual rights against the State.

Lord Irvine's decision to sit on this case, and his earlier decision to hear a case concerned with judicial review of public authorities,[214] gave rise to "real con-cern" about "the recent practice, in the light of the modernisation of the system, to sit in cases of that character"[215] and was one of the reasons why the Lord Chancellor's role as judge became a significant issue during his Lord Chancellorship. There were others. His overt role in policy making, together with his close relationship with the Prime Minister, indicated he was at the heart of government. This resulted in reservations from some of the law lords about him sitting as judge[216] and rumours that at least one of them was refusing to sit with him. However, more important for the long term future of the office of Lord Chancellor, were the implications of the Human Rights Act and devolu-tion legislation, which, ironically, had been overseen by Lord Irvine as part of the Government's reform programme, and the case of *McGonnell* v. *United Kingdom*, which came before the European Court of Human Rights in 1999.

THE EFFECT OF THE HUMAN RIGHTS ACT 1998

The passing of the Human Rights Act, which gives effect to the European Convention on Human Rights, inevitably involves the Appellate Committee of the House of Lords in making judgments, which will be seen as political. This is likely to result in greater scrutiny of its members. A foretaste of this scrutiny was evident in 1998/99 in the *Pinochet* cases,[217] where the disclosure of Lord

---

[213] Lords Clyde and Hutton concurred and Lords Slynn and Hope dissented.

[214] *Boddington v. British Rail Police* [1999] 2 AC 143.

[215] Lord Lester, H. L. Debs., 28 October 1998, col. 197. He stated that this concern was shared by a number of leading lawyers and judges, including Heather Hallett QC, Chair of the Bar Council of England and Wales, Philip Dry and Antoinette Curran, Presidents of the Law Societies of Scotland and Northern Ireland, respectively, Roy Amlot, QC, recent chair of the Criminal Bar Association, and Michael Lavery, QC, chair of the Standing Advisory Commission on Human Rights in Northern Ireland.

[216] Lord Steyn, "The Weakest and Least Dangerous Department of Government" p. 92.

[217] *R v. Bow Street Metropolitan Stipendiary Magistrate and Others, ex parte Pinochet Ugarte* [1998] 3 WLR 1456; (No. 2) [1999] 2 WLR 272; (No. 3) [1999] 2 WLR 827.

Hoffmann's interest in Amnesty International resulted in the House of Lords setting aside its own decision on the basis that the panel which had heard the case "was not properly constituted".[218] Similar attention will, no doubt, also be paid to the Judicial Committee of the Privy Council when, under legislation, which devolved powers to Scotland, Wales and Northern Ireland, it hears disputes concerning *vires*. After the Hoffmann episode, Lord Irvine wrote to Lord Browne-Wilkinson, the senior law lord, stating that, in the light of that episode, judges should always consider, prior to a trial, whether any of their number might appear subject to a conflict of interest.[219] However, he appeared to see himself exempt from the test, when in early 1999 he sought to sit on a panel which was due to hear an appeal concerning police liability for the suicide of a man in police cells. He was obliged to stand down after the barrister acting for the dead man's family argued that his presence on the bench would breach their right under section 6 of the European Convention on Human Rights to a fair hearing by an independent and impartial tribunal. Lord Irvine had again failed to appreciate that a judge, who is also a Cabinet minister, should not hear cases in which an organ of the State is a party.[220]

For the Lord Chancellor to hear human rights or devolution cases would clearly suggest a conflict of interest and it is presumed that no Lord Chancellor would participate in such a decision. However, as far as Lord Irvine is concerned, "there is no category of cases that could be labelled 'constitutional' which should be 'no-go areas for the Lord Chancellor'".[221] He refused to provide assurances regarding his role in the House of Lords or Privy Council, stating that it was "not desirable to lay down any rigid rules".[222] This provokes the obvious question – why not? If the position of Lord Chancellor as judge is to be maintained, then rigid rules relating to when he is debarred from sitting would seem to be required. Statements from Lord Irvine that he would "exercise [his] discretion not to sit", when he considered "it would be inappropriate to do so", are insufficient, as was his comment that he had "no doubt that future Lord Chancellors will do likewise".[223] They may or may not, but where cases such as these are concerned, it would seem inappropriate for them to have any discretion to exercise.

The effect of the Human Rights Act on the position of Lord Chancellor is likely to extend beyond the confines of human rights cases. It seems inevitable that it will spill over into all cases where there is a public interest, making it

---

[218] Lord Hoffmann was Chairman of Amnesty International Charity Ltd, a registered charity which undertook the charitable aspects of Amnesty International's work in the UK. He was not paid for this work, nor was he a member of Amnesty. He failed to disclose his connection with Amnesty, which, unusually, was given leave to intervene in Pinochet 1, thereby making it a party to the case, and in Pinochet 2 the House of Lords held that Hoffmann had been automatically disqualified from sitting in the case. It therefore vacated its previous decision.

[219] Reported in *The Times*, 18 December 1998.

[220] For a fuller account see D. Egan, *Irvine*, pp. 230–2.

[221] H. L. Debs., 17 Feb. 1999, col. 736.

[222] H. L. Debs., 20 October 1998, col. WA138.

[223] Ibid.

difficult for a Lord Chancellor to sit in any case, other than one that is entirely within the bounds of private law. More important, the Lord Chancellor's position as judge at all is challenged by the European Convention. Article 6 provides for the right to a fair and public hearing before an independent and impartial tribunal. The European Court of Human Rights has stated that independence is to be determined with regard to the manner of the appointment of a tribunal's members and their terms of office, the existence of guarantees against outside pressures and whether the body appears to be independent.[224] The Lord Chancellor's position would seem to be suspect on all three grounds. First, his appointment by the Prime Minister[225] and the fact that, unlike other judges, he can be dismissed by him at will, suggests that he lacks the security of tenure associated with judicial independence and required by the Convention. Secondly, the only guarantee against outside pressures is the judicial oath, which case law suggests is an inadequate guarantee,[226] and the integrity of the Lord Chancellor himself, which is unlikely to be seen as sufficient. Thirdly, the position of the Lord Chancellor as a government minister undermines the appearance of independence, required by the European Court.

These points were reiterated by the European Commission's decision in *McGonnell*, which was concerned with whether the Royal Court of Guernsey is an independent and impartial tribunal within the meaning of Article 6 of the Convention.[227] The Royal Court is presided over by the Bailiff of Guernsey, or in his absence the Deputy Bailiff or a Lieutenant-Bailiff, whose role is "to determine questions of law and to direct the Jurats on the relevant law and as to the matters which they should consider in determining issues of fact".[228] The Bailiff, who is appointed by the Queen and holds office during Her Majesty's pleasure, is also President of the Court of Appeal and in fact spends most of his time discharging judicial functions. However, like the Lord Chancellor, he also has legislative and executive roles. In the former, he is President of the Island's legislature, the States of Deliberation, and the electoral college, the States of Election, which is responsible for appointing the jurats. In the latter, he is head of the administration of the island, chairing four States Committees.

The European Commission, by twenty-five votes to five, held that the Royal Court did not accord with the requirements of Article 6. Significantly, the British member of the Commission, Sir Nicholas Bratza, who subsequently became a judge in the Court, agreed with the majority. While accepting that

---

[224] *Bryan* v. *United Kingdom* (1995) EHRR 342, para 37.

[225] Technically he, like all ministers, is appointed by the Queen on advice from the Prime Minister.

[226] See *Starrs* v. *Procurator Fiscal, Linlithgow* (1999) *The Times*, 17 November and *R* v. *Lippe* (1990) 60 CCC(3rd) 34, 76–7 and [1991] 2 SCR 114; see also the Canadian case, *Ref. Re Territorial Court Act* (NWT) section 6 (2) (1997) 152 DLR (4th) 132, 141.

[227] Mr McGonnell was refused planning permission to build a dwelling house on his land, on the basis that the land was reserved for agricultural use and/or visual amenity, and exercised his right under the relevant legislation to appeal to the Royal Court.

[228] *McGonnell* v. *United Kingdom*, No. 28488/95 (20/10/98) European Commission of Human Rights, para. 39.

"the Bailiff's other functions did not directly impinge on his judicial duties in the case and that the Bailiff spends most of his time in judicial functions", the Commission considered "that it is incompatible with the requisite appearances of independence and impartiality for a judge to have legislative and executive functions as substantial as those in the present case". The Commission therefore found that the Bailiff's "independence and impartiality are capable of appearing open to doubt"[229] and the case proceeded to the European Court of Human Rights.

McGonnell has obvious relevance to the position of the Lord Chancellor, who appears considerably more vulnerable. The Bailiff of Guernsey seems to have satisfied the Commission in relation to "the objective guarantees of independence and impartiality", as he is appointed by the Queen, and unlike the Lord Chancellor holds office during Her Majesty's pleasure subject to a retirement age of seventy years. Thus he is not subject to the vagaries of Cabinet reshuffles and prime ministerial whim. He failed the test on the grounds of "appearance of independence", despite the fact that he could claim that most of his time was spent on judicial functions. This is not a claim that could be made by the Lord Chancellor, whose legislative and executive functions are considerably more "substantial" than those of the Bailiff. Moreover, a defence by the Government that this combination of functions was compatible with Article 6, due to the special historical and geographical conditions pertaining in the United Kingdom, is likely to be rejected, as it was in *McGonnell*. It therefore seems likely that an action for breach of Article 6 against any court in which the Lord Chancellor sits would be upheld, a prospect which is unlikely to be relished by his judicial colleagues.[230]

In February 2000 the European Court of Human Rights followed the Commission in finding, unanimously, that the requirements of Article 6 had not been met. Its decision centred on the fact that the Bailiff had, when Deputy Bailiff, presided over the States of Deliberation, when it passed the planning regulations against which McGonnell subsequently appealed. The Court refused to accept that "when the Bailiff acts in a non-judicial capacity he merely occupies positions rather than exercising functions". It noted; "even a purely ceremonial constitutional role can be classified as a 'function'".[231] The Court found that "any direct involvement in the passage of legislation, or executive rules, is likely to be sufficient to cast doubt on the judicial impartiality of a person subsequently called on to determine a dispute over whether reasons exist to permit a variation from the wording of the legislation or rules at issue".[232]

Lord Irvine insisted that the position of the Lord Chancellor was unaffected by this case. He stated; "The decision in *McGonnell* is confined to the special

---

[229] Ibid, para. 61.
[230] It is possible that the law lords themselves might be suspect because of their legislative role.
[231] *McGonnell* v. *United Kingdom*, No. 28488/95 (8/02/00) ECHR.
[232] Ibid.

position of the Bailiff of Guernsey and his role in the particular case".[233] Moreover, he argued that the Court "had accepted the Government's submission that neither Article 6 nor any other provision of the Convention requires States to comply with any theoretical constitutional concepts as such" and that the reason the requirements of Article 6 had not been met was because of "the judge's direct involvement in the passage of legislation".[234] This may be an overly restrictive view of *McGonnell*, particularly when viewed alongside the opinion of the Commission, and Lord Irvine's affirmation that "the Lord Chancellor would never sit in any case concerning legislation in the passage of which he had been directly involved nor in any case where the interests of the executive are directly engaged"[235] may not be insufficient to prevent a future challenge of his own position.

Reference to the European Convention on Human Rights, through the Human Rights Act 1998, or, if this fails, through the European Court of Human Rights, provides the only formal mechanism for checking the role of Lord Chancellor as judge. The only other restraints are informal and largely depend upon the legal profession, denouncing any attempt by the Lord Chancellor "to use the office for purely political ends".[236] The office of Lord Chancellor, like many of our constitutional arrangements, therefore relies on imprecise rules to restrain it rather than constitutional enactments. Moreover, these rules are operated by a powerful interest group to which the Lord Chancellor belongs and which may expect him to protect the professional and financial interests of its members as well as the interests of justice. Modern Lord Chancellors are unlikely to use the office overtly for "political ends". They may, however, fail to recognise that they compromise themselves and their fellow judges if they sit in cases where there is an indirect government interest, because of possible policy and financial repercussions, or where they have previously spoken politically on the issue in question. Such situations, while rare, do nothing for the principle of judicial independence and the requirements of impartiality and further detract from any credibility of the Lord Chancellor as judge.

CONCLUSION

On several occasions in the past the Appellate Committee of the House of Lords has been under threat with inevitable consequences for the Lord Chancellor. In the 1870s it would have become a separate court, but for the concerted opposition of a group of Conservative backbenchers, and in the 1960s the then Lord Chancellor, Lord Gardiner, proposed its abolition on the basis that it did not do anything. This is no longer the case. As well as the House of Lords hearing the

[233] H. L. Debs., 23 February 2000, col. WA33.
[234] Ibid.
[235] Ibid.
[236] M. J. C. Vile, *Constitutionalism and Separation of Powers*, p. 342.

range of criminal and civil appeals, a further dimension has been added to its work by membership of the European Union. It is also increasingly concerned with judicial review appeals, many of which are high profile and politically sensitive, and, since the Human Rights Act 1998 came into effect in October 2000, with upholding human rights against public bodies, including government departments. These developments create the need for a formal and stricter separation of powers between the courts and the executive and thus make the position of the Lord Chancellor in the House of Lords untenable. It may be that, as the textbooks say, he "rarely sits for judicial business" and that he chooses the cases over which he presides with great care. However, the retention by a government minister of the right to sit in the final court of appeal which, in effect, has also assumed the role of a constitutional court, undermines judicial independence. Appearances matter and for the Lord Chancellor to take part in any House of Lords decision creates a danger of his judicial colleagues being perceived as biased towards the executive.[237]

Moreover, Lord Irvine's argument that the constitutional reforms make it necessary for there to be a strong Lord Chancellor to act as a buffer between the Government and the judiciary is unsustainable, particularly if, as he argues, his role "as effective guarantor of judicial independence" requires him to preside over important appeals.[238] Rather, they require the law lords to be distanced from the Lord Chancellor, who is part of the government from which they need protection. The reforms would also seem to require them to be distanced from the legislature, so that the situation cannot arise whereby judges, who have engaged in debate in the House, hear a case, in which the issue or legislation debated arises, as it did in *Pepper* v. *Hart* (above). Such a situation does nothing for the well-being of the system of justice. It embarrasses counsel, who know what the law lords have said as legislators,[239] and raises doubts in the minds of the parties that their case will be heard impartially.[240]

The statement by Lord Browne-Wilkinson, following *McGonnell*, in which he emphasised the need for law lords to refrain from expressing opinions, which might make them ineligible to sit judicially, sought to reinforce and strengthen the conventional position, which has long existed, that judges do not speak on matters which are politically contentious. However, it would seem an inadequate response to their changed constitutional position, as was Lord Irvine's confirmation that he would abide by the same rules and "bear in mind that he might render himself ineligible to sit judicially on a matter which might later be relevant to an appeal to the House".[241] The only effective response would seem to be for the Appellate Committee of the House of Lords to separate itself from

---

[237] See, for instance, A. W. Bradley and K. D. Ewing, *Constitutional and Administrative Law* (11th edn., London, Longman, 1993).

[238] Speech to the *Worldwide Common Law Judiciary Conference* (Edinburgh, July 1999).

[239] Lord Lester in C. Anderson, *Unreliable Evidence*.

[240] Lord Steyn has in fact accepted "a self-imposed vow of perpetual silence in the legislative chamber while he sits as a Law Lord". (Lord Lester, H. L. Debs., 17 February 1999).

[241] *The Times*, 18 July 2000.

the legislature and become a supreme court. The creation of such a court, which in all probability would assume a role analogous to that of supreme courts elsewhere, would make it inappropriate for the Lord Chancellor to sit and thereby end his role as judge. Moreover, the historical link, which gave him the dual role within the House of Lords, would be gone.

This dual role might also end with the reform of the House of Lords. Despite the recommendation of the Wakeham report that the law lords should remain in a reformed upper chamber,[242] a move to an elected, or even part elected, House might, in the long run, challenge the position of the law lords in it and could result in the creation of a supreme court. This would be unlikely to have the Lord Chancellor presiding over it. It might also challenge the Lord Chancellor's position as Speaker,[243] as a chamber with an elected element might be less prepared to accept the conventions and traditions, whereby the House, at present, regulates itself and require a different role of its Speaker. It might then prefer to decide for itself who should take this role. The Lord Chancellor could therefore find himself with neither a judicial nor a legislative role, being the victim of a constitutional reform programme in which, ironically, the current Lord Chancellor, Lord Irvine, played a major part.

---

[242] Royal Commission on the Reform of the House of Lords (Chairman, Lord Wakeham), *A House for the Future* (2000), Cm. 4534.
[243] Although Wakeham did not see why it should.

6

Judicial Appointments

INTRODUCTION

THE RESPONSIBILITY OF the Lord Chancellor for most judicial appointments has its origins in his position as the sovereign's first minister. In modern times it is more easily reconciled with his role as head of the judiciary. However, recognition of this role actually arose, at least in part, from his responsibility for appointments.[1] Today the patronage he exercises, both directly and indirectly, through such appointments is vast. His responsibility for the appointment of the fifty or so of the most senior members of the judiciary, that is the Lords of Appeal in Ordinary, Heads of Division and Lords Justices of Appeal, is indirect.[2] They are appointed by the Crown on the recommendation of the Prime Minister and, in practice, are therefore in his or her gift. However, the Prime Minister "normally expects the Lord Chancellor to advise him in the first instance".[3] Moreover, Lord Hailsham's contention that he "would have considered resigning if the Prime Minister had rejected all his suggested names and made an appointment from outside his list",[4] suggests there is expectation on the Lord Chancellor's part that the advice will be accepted.

The procedure by which the Lord Chancellor advises the Prime Minister is confidential, and Lord Chancellors have refused to give details. It is, however, evident that some prime ministers expect to be more involved in appointments than others. Mrs Thatcher, it seems, "liked to discuss appointments",[5] Lord Hailsham recalling that she seemed to think "that 'somewhere above the ceiling' there was always The Best Man". She did not, according to Lord Hailsham, "appreciate the need to balance the Bench"[6] and, as a result, Hailsham noted after one meeting with her; " 'We must be careful in future minutes *not* to pan our candidates, and *not* to put too many names' ".[7] It seems thereafter that he submitted a shortlist with two or three names in order of preference, with

---

[1] See Chapter one.

[2] Who total a maximum of fifty-one i.e. twelve law lords, the Lord Chief Justice, Master of the Rolls, President of the Family Division, Vice Chancellor and thirty-five Appeal Court judges (*Judicial Appointments: Annual Report* (LCD,1998–99), Cm. 4449).

[3] Home Affairs Committee, *The Work of the Lord Chancellor's Department* (1991–92) HC 214-I, HMSO.

[4] G. Lewis, *Lord Hailsham*, p. 267.

[5] Ibid.

[6] Ibid, pp. 267–8.

[7] Ibid.

reasons for his preference.[8] Lord Mackay, when Lord Chancellor, noted of the process; "I give confidential advice to the Prime Minister. He receives it confidentially and makes his recommendation".[9] He expanded a little on the advice he gave, saying that he regarded it "as appropriate to advise the Prime Minister fully on the field from which this choice should be made".[10] This included giving the Prime Minister "such views as I might have with respect to the possible candidates". He also noted; "I am neither surprised nor disappointed by any appointment advised during my term of office, and I have supported wholeheartedly every one of them".[11] However, this is not to say that his preferred candidate was always accepted. Indeed he "was careful not to say that".[12]

It is to be assumed, however, that someone from his shortlist was always appointed and that the Prime Minister did not introduce a different candidate, for "[a]lthough Prime Ministers may from time to time suggest that they are not unwilling to exercise their power of appointment, in recent times there is no direct evidence that they have done so. The likelihood is that a modern Prime Minister would depart from the recommendations of the Lord Chancellor only in the most exceptional case".[13] There was a suggestion that Mrs Thatcher refused to accept Lord Hailsham's advice over the appointment of Sir John Donaldson as Master of the Rolls.[14] Indeed, when Hailsham informed her that a number of judges had "expressed the strong opinion that John Donaldson was the wrong man for the job", Mrs Thatcher is reported to have replied; "Fortunately, Lord Chancellor, your judges do not appoint the Master of the Rolls, I do".[15] However, given Lord Hailsham's comments about resignation, it seems likely that Donaldson was one of the names he put forward, even if not his preferred candidate. This would seem confirmed by the contention of his biographer that neither of the prime ministers under whom he served, namely Heath and Thatcher, made an appointment from outside his list.[16]

While the influence of the Lord Chancellor over the most senior appointments is indirect, he has a direct influence over the appointment of the ninety-eight High Court judges,[17] the five hundred plus circuit judges,[18] and over thirteen hundred recorders and assistant recorders.[19] For all these positions he advises the Crown directly, and the Crown, of course, follows his advice. Thus in prac-

---

[8] Lord Hailsham, *A Sparrow's Flight*, p. 427.
[9] Home Affairs Committee, *Judicial Appointments Procedures* (1995–96) HC 52-II, Q. 447.
[10] Ibid, Q. 452.
[11] Ibid, Q. 453.
[12] Ibid, Q. 459.
[13] J. A. G. Griffith, *The Politics of the Judiciary*, p. 22.
[14] Both Wilson and Callaghan had refused to appoint him to the Court of Appeal.
[15] A. Samuels, "Appointing the Judges" (1984) 134 *New Law Journal*, 6139, p. 27.
[16] G. Lewis, *Lord Hailsham*, p. 267.
[17] This is the statutory ceiling; in 1998 there were actually ninety-seven in post (*Judicial Appointments: Annual Report*) and in January 2000, 101.
[18] Statutory Ceiling 565; in 1998 there were 560 in post (Ibid).
[19] In 1998 there were 842 recorders and 385 assistant recorders, with 96 assistant recorders in training (Ibid).

tice, if not theory, the appointments are his. He also appoints directly over one thousand district judges,[20] nearly two hundred stipendary magistrates[21] and most of the thirty thousand lay magistrates.[22] In addition, there are numerous tribunal positions to fill – the industrial tribunals alone requiring over two hundred and seventy chairs, as well as panels members – and the appointment of around seventy Queen's Counsels.

The Lord Chancellor also recommends candidates for the position of Judge Advocate General and Judge Advocate General of Her Majesty's Fleet to the Queen, appointing the Assistant Judge Advocates himself. In addition, he is involved in "joint recommendations", such as those made with the Secretary of State for Employment on the appointment of lay members of the Employment Appeals Tribunal, advises ministerial colleagues on some appointments, for example, the Secretary of State for Transport on possible Trunk Road Inspectors, and has statutory power to authorise serving judges or legal practitioners to sit in capacities other than those covered by any specific appointments they hold.[23]

There has been a fourfold increase in the number of full time judges since the Court Act 1971, the number of circuit judges alone having risen from two hundred and five in 1971 to five hundred and sixty in 1998/99. This inevitably increases the number of appointments that any Lord Chancellor has to make. In 1996 Lord Mackay noted that he made nearly four hundred judicial appointments a year, excluding magistrates, which meant that, in practical terms, on average he considered the details of about twenty-four candidates a week, of whom eight would be appointed. When pressed on whether, given his other responsibilities, he had time to consider each person's file personally, he responded; "I do endeavour to look pretty closely at what is said about everyone I appoint to judicial office".[24] If nothing else, modern Lord Chancellors are conscientious and hard working.

However, given the number of appointments,[25] it is inevitable that officials play a significant part in the process and have done so, to varying degrees, throughout the twentieth century. Stevens notes of earlier times that while some Lord Chancellors were active in the appointment process, "it fell heavily to the permanent secretary to take soundings with Bench and Bar, to make recommendations to the Lord Chancellor . . . and to humour judges who were uncomfortable with the decisions".[26] It is therefore not surprising that judicial

[20] In 1998 there were 349 district judges and 743 deputy district judges (Ibid).

[21] In 1998 there were forty-eight metropolitan stipendary magistrates, forty provincial and 106 acting stipendaries (Ibid).

[22] Except those in the Duchy of Lancaster.

[23] Home Affairs Committee, *Judicial Appointments Procedures*, HC 52-II, Appendix 1, Memorandum from the LCD. So, for example, his authority is required to enable circuit judges to sit in the Criminal Division of the Court of Appeal, under s. 52 of the Criminal Justice and Public Order Act 1994 and in the High Court, under s. 9 of the Supreme Court Act 1981.

[24] Ibid, Q. 522.

[25] In 1997 there were 600 full and part-time appointments; in 1998/99 over 700 (*Judicial Appointments: Annual Report*).

[26] R. Stevens, *The Independence of the Judiciary*, p. 40.

appointments have frequently been seen as putting considerable power in the hands of the Civil Service. While Lord Gardiner may have had the time and inclination in the 1960s to "personally interview . . . applicants for County Court judgeships which no previous Lord Chancellor had done",[27] no Lord Chancellor would now be able to undertake such a feat, even if he were minded so to do. Much is left to officials.

It was evident, during Lord Hailsham's Chancellorship, that "a small group of officials in his Department headed by his Permanent Secretary exercise great influence over appointments",[28] and John Taylor, an ex-junior minister in the LCD, noted of his time there, "it was made perfectly clear that I was excluded from any part of the functions relating to judicial appointments. The permanent secretary had that important role, and it is far from being administrative".[29] The change in emphasis in the role of the permanent secretary, considered in Chapter Three, means that responsibility for judicial appointments is now largely delegated to the head of the unit with that function.[30] The current occupant of that position is, like the permanent secretary, a non-lawyer. She reports directly to the Lord Chancellor but this does nothing to detract from the point that officials control the process.

The Department's role in judicial appointments features in the LCD's Strategic Plan, under the challenge; "to sustain improvements in the quality, efficiency and effectiveness of court services".[31] However, while some responsibilities of the Lord Chancellor's Department, such as the Court Service, are recognised as having been delegated to officials and thus operate at arm's length from the Lord Chancellor, appointments remain his personal responsibility. Judges would, no doubt, be concerned if it were otherwise. Moreover, constitutionally, it accords with the requirements of ministerial responsibility and the Lord Chancellor's accountability to Parliament. Less persuasive is Lord Mackay's assertion that the "personal responsibility of a single individual . . . assuming he is reasonably competent . . . is the best guarantee that the appointments will be good ones".[32] It seems a strange system that has to rely on the competence of one person for the quality of its judiciary. This would not seem a valid constitutional safeguard, even when linked to the Lord Chancellor's responsibility to Parliament.

The Lord Chancellor's responsibility for appointments is not confined to those of a judicial nature. It extends to all those bodies for which he has responsibility, including, for instance, the Legal Services Commission, the Law Commission and the Advisory Committees on Justices of the Peace. Moreover, reforms instigated

---

[27] S. Shetreet, *Judges on Trial*, p. 53.

[28] G. Lewis, *Lord Hailsham*, p. 268.

[29] H. C. Debs., 6 November 1997, cols. 443–4.

[30] Michael Huebner, who had previously been chief executive of the Court Service Agency was succeeded by Jenny Williams, a non-lawyer from the Inland Revenue, at the end of 2000.

[31] LCD, *Strategic Plan* (1996/97–1998/99).

[32] Home Affairs Committee, *The Work of the Lord Chancellor's Department* (1991–92), HC 214-II, Q. 116.

by Lords Mackay and Irvine, although welcome in many respects, have increased the patronage at the Lord Chancellor's disposal. This is evident in the creation of the Civil Justice Council,[33] the role of which is to promote the needs of civil justice and advise the Lord Chancellor on its improvement.

Membership is determined, in part, by legislation. The Council is chaired by the Master of the Rolls, with the Vice-Chancellor acting as his deputy, and, as required by the Civil Procedure Act, includes members of the judiciary and the legal professions, civil servants concerned with the administration of the courts, and representatives of consumer affairs, advisory bodies and litigants. The first lay members were appointed, following advertisements in the national press which requested statements of interest from organisations of national standing involved in the civil justice system. The organisations selected were then asked to nominate internal or external candidates for service on the Council and the Lord Chancellor chose members from these nominees.[34] The process therefore gives him considerable discretion to determine the final membership of the Council.

The patronage of the Lord Chancellor has also increased through the introduction of interview panels for judicial appointments, which have been progressively extended to include circuit judges, district judges, stipendary magistrates, masters and registrars of the Supreme Court, many tribunal appointments and assistant recorders.[35] In exercising these new appointment powers the Lord Chancellor is, once more, dependent upon a small group of officials. Applications for lay interviewers, who are selected from the Lord Chancellor's Advisory Committees on Justices of the Peace, on the basis that they "will bring to their role both expertise in interviewing and a knowledge of the judicial system",[36] are sifted by officials from the Judicial Appointments Group against four criteria, namely, whether they have "well developed skills of assessing people", "sufficient knowledge of the judicial system to carry credibility", "understanding of the impact of the judicial system on all types of court user", and "credibility with the profession and with individual candidates".[37] Short-listed candidates are then interviewed by two officials from the Judicial Appointments Group who make recommendations to the Lord Chancellor. Thus officials not only draw up shortlists of candidates to be interviewed for judicial office, they also make decisions about those who will do the interviewing, suggesting, perhaps, an over-concentration of power in the hands of a small elite.

---

[33] Civil Procedure Act 1997.

[34] The membership was announced on 24 February 1998 and the twenty-one members included representatives from the National Consumer Council, Iron Trades Insurance Group, Trade Union Congress, Citizens' Advice Bureaux, Consumer Association, Legal Aid Board and Legal Action Group. (NB members serve in their own capacity not as representatives).

[35] Not recorders because they are chosen from assistant recorders, who have already gone through the interview process.

[36] Home Affairs Committee, *Judicial Appointments Procedures*, HC 52-II, Appendix 1, Memorandum from the LCD, para. 2.5 18.

[37] Lord Irvine in evidence to the Public Administration Committee, *Your Right to Know: The Government's Proposals for a Freedom of Information Act* (1997–98), HC 398-v, Appendix 2.

The final decision is, of course, for the Lord Chancellor and Lord Irvine has stated that, in making it, he takes into account "the desirability of maintaining a broad balance within the panel in the light of . . . gender, ethnic origin, public/private school background, Justices of the Peace/non- Justices of the Peace, political affiliation and geographical location".[38] While maintaining such a balance is a laudable objective, it is one which may be difficult to satisfy, given the pool from which the applicants are drawn. Indeed, the selection, composition and unrepresentative nature of the Advisory Committees on Justices of the Peace, which have, at times, been criticised, suggest that these committees may not be the best starting point for choosing lay interviewers.

The use of interviews with lay representation has extended even to appointments to international courts, a panel, consisting of two judicial members, two legally qualified government officials – one from the LCD and one from the Foreign Office – and a lay member, being convened in 1998 to interview five candidates for appointment to the European Court of Human Rights.[39] The panel recommendation took the form of a list of three, in order of preference, which was agreed by the Lord Chancellor and the Foreign Secretary, with the candidate at the top of the list, Nicholas Bratza QC, subsequently being accepted by the Parliamentary Assembly at Strasbourg.[40] Such a procedure is much to be preferred to the mystical emergence of possible appointees. Yet, the determination of the composition of the interview panel, excellent though it was, would seem to lack the requisite openness. It is somewhat ironic that the introduction of lay interviewers and the establishment of the Civil Justice Council, which were portrayed as part of a modernising process, not only increased the patronage of the Lord Chancellor, at a time when he is under attack for his role in appointments, but also resulted in the use of procedures which had been criticised in relation to other appointments.

LORD CHANCELLORS AND JUDICIAL PATRONAGE

Until the early eighteenth century, it was the practice of all the counsel who appeared in the Chancery Court to bring to a breakfast with the Lord Chancellor on New Year's Day "a pecuniry present, according to their generosity or their means, or their opinion of his venality or of his stability . . . in the hope of being raised to the Bench or of obtaining silk gowns, or of winning 'the Judge's ear' ". [41] This custom was abolished by Lord Chancellor Cowper in 1706 and with it the notion that the chance of advancement might be improved by

---

[38] Lord Irvine in evidence to the Public Administration Committee, *Your Right to Know: The Government's Proposals for a Freedom of Information Act* (1997–98), HC 398-v, Appendix 2.

[39] The panel was Simon Brown LJ, Lord Rodger of Earlsferry, Sir Thomas Legg, then permanent secretary at the LCD, Sir Franklin Bernam, legal adviser at the Foreign and Commonwealth Office, and Joanna Foster, former chair of the EOC.

[40] Although initially the Assembly preferred the third candidate on the list, Robert Reed QC.

[41] J. Campbell, *Lives of the Lord Chancellors* (5th edn., London, ——, 1868) pp. 251–2.

financial inducement. By the mid-nineteenth century a different factor had come into play. With the increase in the importance of the House of Commons and the growth of political parties, it was evident that a barrister's best chance of advancement lay in becoming a Member of Parliament. One hundred and thirty-nine judges were appointed to the High Court and the Appeal Courts between 1832 and 1906, of whom eighty were MPs at the time of their nomination and eleven others had stood for Parliament. Moreover, of those who were MPs, sixty-three were appointed by their own party while in office.[42] Thus two thirds of the appointments can be classified as rewarding political service, and nearly half as rewarding party political service.

Lord Halsbury, Lord Chancellor for two extensive periods (1886–92 and 1895–1905), is noted for using his patronage to such effect. He not only appointed Tory MPs for "their political service to the Conservative Party".[43] He also "almost invariably put service to the Conservative Party above judicial qualities",[44] appointing judges, "both in the appeal courts and at first instance, as much for their political reliability and for political services performed as for any other reason".[45] As a result he appointed "to the High Court, and to a lesser extent to the county court, men of little or no legal learning whose previous career in public life had been largely in the service of the Conservative Party".[46] His appointees were therefore not always of the quality required. Lord Salisbury, who was Prime Minister for most of Halsbury's time in office, "would never apologise for the practice of making [judicial promotions] a reward for political 'right thinking' ".[47] However, after Halsbury was publicly criticised for some of his early appointments, he did urge the need for caution.

Not all Victorian Lord Chancellors were criticised for their appointments. Lord Lyndhurst (1827–30; 1833–6) was praised by Atlay for displaying a "rare disinterestedness" and for making "excellent" appointments.[48] Similarly, Lord Truro (1850–2) was said by him to have exercised his patronage with "the complete approval of the profession".[49] The situation, in any case, began to change when Loreburn succeeded Halsbury in 1905, and while he "appointed appeal judges because of their politics, the High Court bench became less political".[50] It was, however, Haldane, appointed as Lord Chancellor in 1912, who was credited with ending the use of patronage for political purposes. With the "cordial assent" of Prime Minister Asquith, Haldane introduced a policy of appointing

[42] H. J. Laski, "The Techniques of Judicial Appointments" in *Studies in Law and Politics* (London,1932) p. 168.

[43] D. Pannick, *The Judges* (Oxford, Oxford University Press, 1988) p. 66.

[44] B. Abel-Smith and R. Stevens, *In Search of Justice*, p. 129.

[45] R. Stevens, *Law and Politics*, pp. 84–5.

[46] R. F. V. Heuston, *Lives of the Lord Chancellors 1885–1940*, p. 36.

[47] G. Cecil cited in S. H. Bailey and M. J. Gunn, *Smith and Bailey on the Modern English Legal System*, pp. 215–16.

[48] J. B. Atlay, *The Victorian Chancellors*, p. 146.

[49] Ibid, p. 453.

[50] R. Stevens, "Judges, Politicians, Politicians and the Confusing Role of the Judiciary" in K. Hawkins (ed.), *The Human Face of Law* (Oxford, Clarendon Press, 1997) p. 269.

"only on the footing of high legal and professional qualifications",[51] and although Lord Birkenhead subsequently had difficulty in preventing Lloyd George from making political appointments to the Bench, "this position, as regards puisne judgeships, has more or less been maintained since".[52]

Haldane's policy did not apply to the law lords or to the members of the Privy Council, who, he believed, benefited from training in the House of Commons which brought them into touch with the real world, but while these appointments took account of political service, they were not made on a "party political" basis. Lord Chancellors, since Haldane, have had varying views about the merit of political service. Both Lords Jowitt and Simonds, who covered the period 1945–55, "paid scant attention to political activities; service in the House of Commons was apparently neither an advantage nor a disadvantage".[53] Jowitt's appointments, according to Heuston, were generally regarded as "admirable", with "never the slightest suggestion" they were "in any way influenced by political considerations".[54] Indeed, Jowitt himself drew attention to the fact that he had " 'never let political considerations weigh with [him] to the slightest degree in trying to get the fittest man' and had 'never appointed, incidentally, a member of [his] own party' ".[55] Lord Kilmuir, on the other hand, made known his intention of taking political service into account and so broadening the experience of the Bench. Whether because of this policy, or otherwise, between 1956 and 1976 there was "some resurgence of the political law lord",[56] with five of the ten law lords in 1974 having had political experience.

This did not, however, lead to a revival of the claim of Attorney-Generals and Solicitor-Generals to high judicial position, which, prior to the Second World War, they seemed to have. Fifteen of the twenty-three Attorney-Generals, who held office between 1873 and 1945, were promoted to the Supreme Court or the House of Lords, and nine out of the seventeen Solicitor-Generals, who did not progress to the position of Attorney-General, were promoted to higher judicial office.[57] In contrast, between 1945 and the year 2000 only two out of the eighteen holders of one or both offices have subsequently held judicial positions, namely, Lynn Ungoed-Thomas and Sir (now Lord) Jocelyn Simon.[58] Thus any

[51] R. B. Haldane, *An Autobiography* (1929) cited in S. H. Bailey and M. J. Gunn, *Smith and Bailey on the Modern English Legal System*, p. 216.

[52] S. H. Bailey and M. J. Gunn, *Smith and Bailey on the Modern English Legal System*, p. 216.

[53] B. Abel-Smith and R. Stevens, *In Search of Justice*, p. 176. They noted that in 1956 twenty-three per cent of Supreme Court judges had been MPs or candidates for a parliamentary seat.

[54] R. F. V. Heuston, *Lives of the Lord Chancellors 1940–1970*, p. 118.

[55] Cited in R. Stevens, *Law and Politics*, p. 337.

[56] Ibid, p. 625.

[57] Five went on to become Lord Chief Justice, two Master of the Rolls, four Lords of Appeal, and four Lord Justices. Eight became LC. Figures from S. H. Bailey and M. J. Gunn, *Smith and Bailey on the Modern English Legal System*, p. 216.

[58] Labour Solicitor-General 1951, High Court judge 1962–72 and Conservative Solicitor-General 1952–62, President of Probate, Divorce and Admiralty Division 1962–71 and Lord of Appeal 1971–2.

notion that service as a law officer will be rewarded by promotion to a senior judicial position seems now to be unfounded.

While Lord Chancellors have differed over whether or not it is beneficial for some senior judges to have political experience, in recent times they have been united in their insistence that their decisions on appointments are not influenced by party political considerations. This is, of course, difficult to determine, given that the political leanings of the majority of judges are not a matter of public record. In any case, even if a Lord Chancellor can be shown to have appointed mainly those who lean in one direction, this does not prove that he put party political considerations first; they may have simply been the most suitable candidates. The system, nevertheless, allows a Lord Chancellor to appoint, or recommend for appointment, those who are sympathetic to the government's ideology, and in the unusual circumstances of the 1990s, when tension between the government and senior judges was running high,[59] there was heightened concern about the appointment system and the patronage of the Lord Chancellor.

Such concern was held to be unfounded by the Home Affairs Select Committee's inquiry into judicial appointments. It reported that, despite suggestions that ministerial appointments to the judiciary run the risk of being influenced by political considerations, there was "absolutely no evidence to suggest that the present Lord Chancellor [Lord Mackay] has used his powers of patronage regarding judicial appointments to favour those who share the same ideology as the Government. On the contrary, there was consistent acclaim for the quality of judges appointed by the Lord Chancellor and a recognition that political considerations had not been a factor".[60] Indeed, the Lord Chief Justice, the late Lord Taylor, was adamant that, in making judicial appointments, the then Lord Chancellor "has absolutely no political motivation at all",[61] noting of the appointments made by him; they "could not be described as being of the same political colour as the Executive in power at the moment".[62] Lord Taylor's assertion, together with other evidence, resulted in the select committee concluding that, while it had "some qualms about the role of the Prime Minister in appointments", it had none about the Lord Chancellor.[63]

Thus at the end of the twentieth century, "even the sternest critics of the present arrangements would surely have to concede than any vestige of the old party-political 'spoils' system that prevailed until the early part of this century has been eradicated".[64] Yet, the nature of the process means that its non-revival is dependent on future Lord Chancellors, whose non-political spirit cannot be guaranteed. This is clearly "a weakness in the appointments process".[65]

[59] See Chapter Four.
[60] Home Affairs Committee, *Judicial Appointments Procedures*, HC 52-I, para. 122.
[61] Ibid, HC-II, Q. 285.
[62] Ibid,.
[63] Ibid, HC-I, para. 128.
[64] G. Drewry, "Judicial Appointments", p. 1.
[65] Home Affairs Committee, *Judicial Appointments Procedures*, HC 52-II, para. 123.

Moreover, Lord Mackay's contention that an errant Lord Chancellor would be unlikely to remain in office, if he made dubious appointments, would itself seem dubious. A Lord Chancellor with the Prime Minister's support would be difficult to dislodge. In any case, given the secrecy of the process, particularly as it relates to senior appointments, it would not be easy to secure the necessary evidence. In many instances, the appointments may, in fact, be good ones, but they may, nevertheless, have been influenced by political considerations. Some would argue that with the judges being forced into a more political role, through the Human Rights Act, political considerations, even those of a party political nature, have their place in the appointments process, as they do in the United States. But, as will be discussed later, this requires the process to be open and for there to be adequate safeguards.

THE JUDICIAL APPOINTMENTS SYSTEM

The judicial appointments system has consistently been criticised for the patronage it gives to a Cabinet minister, the secrecy that surrounds it, its dependence upon a network of personal friendships and recommendations, the production of "monochrome" judges,[66] and the perpetuation of a judiciary in its own image. The system centres upon secret soundings, or, using Lord Irvine's preferred phraseology, "a confidential information gathering process",[67] and, until recently, there was little indication as to why certain individuals were appointed or promoted and others were not. Appointments to the judiciary were at best, "governed by well established conventions"[68] and, at worst, "done on the old boy network with a nudge-nudge and wink-wink".[69]

Prior to the Courts Act 1971, the system for appointing the lower judiciary "was somewhat haphazard".[70] When a vacancy arose in the county court a senior official in the LCD would sound out "a few" county court judges in the area and report these to the Lord Chancellor, a procedure that seemed to confirm there was an old boys' network in operation. Although these arrangements "were elaborated and rationalised to great advantage",[71] during Lord Hailsham's period in office, and the consultation process for the appointment of circuit judges, recorders and assistant recorders was delegated to senior officials in the Department, the criticisms remained. Moreover, the corresponding rationalisation of the appointment of Queen's Counsel did little to engender confi-

---

[66] G. Lewis, *Lord Hailsham*, p. 267.
[67] LCD Press Notice, 279/97.
[68] Lord Elwyn-Jones, *In My Time*, p. 265.
[69] G. Robinson (JUSTICE) in evidence to the Home Affairs Committee, *Judicial Appointments Procedures*, HC 52-II, Q. 527.
[70] G. Lewis, *Lord Hailsham*, p. 269.
[71] Ibid.

dence in a system still shrouded in secrecy. Indeed, in 1992 it was described as being based on "the Franz Kafta school of business management".[72]

High Court appointments were likewise surrounded in secrecy, although it was evident that between 1945 and 1960 it became the established practice for the Lord Chancellor to consult the heads of Division. Such consultation was, according to Lords Elwyn-Jones and Hailsham, more than notional, Lord Elwyn-Jones revealing that if two names had equal support, the choice was left to him,[73] and Lord Hailsham noting that he never remembered a case "in which the decision, when made, was not a collective one".[74] The Lord Chancellor, as would be expected, also takes soundings from senior judges about appointments within their ranks. The recommendation that he subsequently makes is likely, in most instances, to accord with the majority opinion, if there is one. However, in October 1996 there were reports that "a furious behind-the-scenes row had broken out between some of Britain's senior judges and the Government over the appointment of the new Lord Chief Justice, Lord Bingham".[75] The appointment came at a time when tension between the Government – particularly the Home Secretary, Michael Howard – and the judiciary was unusually high and, according to newspaper reports, it went against the advice given to the Lord Chancellor, Lord Mackay, by the Lord Justices. They were reported to have opted for Sir Christopher Rose[76] and it was suggested that some judges saw the appointment of Lord Bingham as "political", in the sense that he was seen as less confrontational than Sir Christopher, and as a threat to judicial independence. His appointment can better be explained on the basis that he was seen by Lord Mackay as a reformist, who was "prepared to challenge traditional orthodoxes and practices",[77] and who would therefore be likely to support the Lord Chancellor's agenda for change. Judicial concern may therefore have had more to do with a desire to maintain the status quo than with notions of judicial independence.

Such glimpses of what happens behind the scenes have been rare and the accuracy of such reports difficult to ascertain, for the appointment of judges remains wrapped in secrecy. Yet there have been developments. In 1986 the LCD published a guide to the policies and procedures on judicial appointments. The booklet, according to the preface, written by Lord Hailsham, was intended "to dispel any lingering sense of mystery or obscurity that there may be about how this work is done".[78] It was, however, a slight document and did little to dispel

---

[72] Gareth Williams QC, Chairman of the Bar (who became Lord Williams of Mostyn, a minister in the Home Office) cited in D. Pannick, *The Times*, 6 April 1999.

[73] Lord Elwyn-Jones, *In My Time*, p. 265.

[74] Lord Hailsham, *The Door Wherein I Went*, p. 254.

[75] *The Independent*, 9 October 1996.

[76] It was reported that of seventeen Lord Justices canvassed, fourteen chose Sir Christopher Rose, two opted for Lord Woolf and one was undecided (Ibid).

[77] Ibid.

[78] LCD, *Judicial Appointments: the Lord Chancellor's Policies and Procedures* (May 1986; revised edn. November 1995).

anything. The best that can be said of it was that it indicated that, where appointments were concerned, the LCD recognised the need to engage a little more with the outside world.

Considerations/criteria

There are three guiding principles used by the Lord Chancellor in appointments. The first requires that appointment should be on merit, regardless of ethnic origin, gender, marital status, sexual orientation, political affiliation, religion or disability.[79] The second places significant weight upon the views of serving members of the judiciary, who have knowledge of the candidate's performance,[80] and the third requires that a candidate should have served in a part time judicial post "for long enough to establish his or her competence and suitability".[81] However, until recently, the secrecy surrounding the process has made it difficult to determine the attributes necessary to secure a judicial position, or, indeed, the factors which may disqualify someone from holding office.

The evidence suggested that any conviction for an offence involving "moral turpitude" would automatically disqualify an applicant. However, convictions for traffic offences and others which are relatively minor would not adversely affect a candidate's chances, although drink driving may. More serious was a breach of professional etiquette or ethics, and "unprofessional conduct involving a moral element would no doubt end any chance of promotion to the bench".[82] Similarly, bankruptcy would be likely to exclude, as would conduct in an applicant's private life which "gives rise to a suspicion that [he or she] might not maintain the strict standards expected of judges".[83] However, "short of moral turpitude, the considerations for appointment [were] on the whole a weighing and balancing process . . . some defects in personal character or failures in private life would tend to be outweighed by the remarkable professional record of a barrister considered for appointment".[84]

A "point which held very strongly"[85] against candidates at one time was their marital status. Divorced candidates stood little chance of judicial office when Jowitt was Lord Chancellor. However, by the 1970s, divorce was no longer a bar, although Shetreet noted that an applicant would not be appointed while divorce proceedings were pending or if there had been "disgraceful aspects to [the] divorce proceedings", they "had attracted adverse publicity" or the man

---

[79] Home Affairs Committee, *Judicial Appointments Procedures*, HC 52-II, Appendix 1, Memorandum from LCD, para. 2.3.2.

[80] Ibid, para. 2.3.9.

[81] Ibid, para. 2.3.5.

[82] S. Shetreet, *Judges on Trial*, p. 64.

[83] Ibid, p. 65.

[84] Ibid, p. 61.

[85] R. Stevens, *The Independence of the Judiciary*, p. 88.

was "guilty of notoriously bad conduct, such as physical cruelty".[86] While Jowitt was Lord Chancellor there was also, for a time, a bar on the appointment of Roman Catholics. This arose because of instructions issued by the Pope in November 1949 in which he seemed to instruct Catholic judges not to grant divorces. For a judge to follow the Pope's instructions would have been contrary to the judicial oath, and Jowitt therefore suggested that Catholics should not be appointed to the Probate, Divorce and Admiralty Division and that judges from other divisions should be required to make "a clear statement they did not regard themselves as bound by the Pope's pronouncement".[87] He wrote; "I must soft-pedal on my appointment of Catholics, and for the time being I shall not appoint them without laying down a hard and fast rule which would cover myself for the future".[88] Subsequent clarification of the papal instructions resulted in the restriction being removed and the guiding principles, under which the Lord Chancellor now operates, prevent religion or marital status being a consideration.

As far as the criteria for appointment are concerned, minimum professional requirements were, and continue to be, prescribed by statute. Those relating to rights of audience were changed in 1990 to open the way for solicitors as well as barristers to become judges in the higher courts and are governed by the Courts and Legal Services Act 1990. Thus the Acts which previously laid down the qualifications necessary are all amended by it.[89] Other criteria, which were gleaned as being particularly relevant, include vague qualities, such as having "a fine mind", being "hardworking and eminently competent", being in receipt of "good opinions from Bench and bar", giving "distinguished public service", having the "necessary balance" and being of an "appropriate age and experience".[90] Where initial appointment was concerned, "the size of practice", "temperament", "legal skill and personal integrity"[91] seemed to be what mattered.

Towards a more open system

Under Lord Mackay there was a more tangible reduction of the "sense of mystery", as he sought to make the system more open, both in terms of transparency and opportunity. In July 1993 he announced a "progressive programme" of reform to the judicial appointments system.[92] This included "measures to

[86] S. Shetreet, *Judges on Trial*, p. 61.
[87] R. Stevens, *The Independence of the Judiciary*, p. 86.
[88] Ibid, p. 87.
[89] e.g. High Court judges; s.10 Supreme Court Act 1981: Deputy Judges of High Court; SCA s 9(4): Lords Justice of Appeal and Heads of Division; SCA s. 10: law lords; Appellate Jurisdiction Act 1876: circuit judges; Courts Act 1971 s.16: recorders; CA 1971 s. 21: assistant recorders; CA 1971, s.24; district judges; County Courts Act 1984 s.9.
[90] R. Stevens, *The Independence of the Judiciary*, p. 83.
[91] Ibid, p. 86.
[92] Home Affairs Committee, *Judicial Appointments Procedures*, HC 52-II, Appendix 1, Memorandum from LCD, para. 2.5.2.

improve arrangements for forecasting and planning the numbers and expertise of judges" needed at the various levels, the "progressive introduction of specific competitions for judicial vacancies", the provision of proper job descriptions, which detailed the tasks and the qualities required to fulfil them, and the progressive introduction of open advertisements for positions in the lower courts. He also announced further measures to encourage applications from women and black and Asian practitioners, the review of application forms, a more structured basis for consultation, and the exploration of involving lay people in the selection process.

As a result of the Mackay initiative, in September 1994 the first advertisements for circuit and district judges appeared, followed, subsequently, by advertisements for assistant recorders and Deputy Masters. These positions are now subject to annual competition. Respondents to the advertisements receive an application pack, which includes a leaflet explaining the application process, a job description, a statement of eligibility and details of the selection criteria to be used. It also contains an outline of the terms and conditions of service, together with information on the number of appointments expected to be made and their location. The application form requires candidates to provide biographical and career information and an assessment of their suitability for appointment with reference to the job description and selection criteria, which are fully defined. Applicants therefore have a more informed view of what is required and a better opportunity to present themselves in a way which meets those requirements.

For instance, those aspiring to be circuit judges are told that they must meet the statutory requirements, normally have had at least two years service as a recorder, be aged between forty-five and sixty, although allowance may be made for a career break or for someone who has started their career late, be in good health, have satisfactory sight and hearing, be able to sit and concentrate for long periods of time, and be "persons who conduct themselves at all times, both in their professional and personal lives, in a manner which will maintain public confidence in the standards of the judiciary". Applicants should also live "within reasonable travelling distance" of the courts in which they will sit.

They are also informed of the three sets of criteria against which they will be measured. The first relates to their legal knowledge and experience, including their effectiveness and performance as recorder, their knowledge and understanding of the appropriate area of the law, and their "comprehensive knowledge of the rules of evidence and of court practice and procedure". The second concerns their skills and attributes. Their intellectual and analytical ability must be such as to enable them to concentrate, to understand and assimilate facts and arguments, to recall evidence and information speedily and accurately; "to apply legal principles to particular facts and to determine from a large body of information those issues and facts which are relevant and important and those which are not"; and to "weigh relevant issues and matters of law in order to formulate them for reasoned and coherent presentation to a jury". They must also have sound judgment, be decisive, have good communication skills and author- ity, by which is meant "the ability to command the respect of court users and to maintain fair-minded discipline in the court and chambers without appearing pompous, arrogant or overbearing", and "the ability to promote expeditious despatch of business". The third set of criteria relates to personal qualities and includes integrity, fairness, an understanding of people and society, maturity and sound temperament, courtesy and humanity, and commitment.[93]

The criteria for district judges equate with those outlined above. They require that applicants should have; "an appropriate level of legal knowledge and expe- rience and professional achievement; intellectual and analytical ability; sound judgment; decisiveness; the ability to communicate effectively with all types of court user; and the ability to command respect of court users and maintain the authority of the court". The personal qualities required are the same as for cir- cuit judges. Subsequently the LCD has stated its intention of separating "cour- tesy" and "humanity" in recognition that they "are different traits which require individual identification and discussion",[94] while the Equal Opportunities Group[95] has argued that "fairness" should be replaced by "impartiality", "open- mindedness" should be listed as a personal quality, and "commitment", seen as "favouring male work patterns", should be replaced by "conscientiousness and diligence".[96] In addition, changes brought about by the implementation of the Woolf reforms, with their emphasis on case management, suggest that addi- tional skills may be required. Lord Mackay noted; "in the future, I will have more of a requirement for a degree of management skill in certain types of judge than is required at the moment".[97] As it happened, this was not a consideration that Mackay had to make. However, it may be one that Lord Irvine should see as relevant.[98] The criteria therefore need to be kept under constant review and amended to comply with changing situations. But their publication in such a detailed form has been a considerable step forward and enables those not appointed to at least question the decision, if they believe they meet the require- ments.

Those candidates considered suitable are interviewed by a panel comprising a senior member of the LCD's Judicial Appointments Group, a serving judge and a lay member. Since 1998 the same panel has, wherever possible, also under- taken the shortlisting of candidates and the process therefore now benefits from a continuity, which was missing when shortlisting was done solely by officials.

---

[93] See Public Administration Committee, *Your Right to Know: The Government's Proposals for a Freedom of Information Act*, HC398-v, Annex.

[94] As considered by Sir Leonard Peach, *Report on the Scrutiny of Judicial Appointments and Queen's Counsel Selection Procedures* (1999).

[95] A joint working party comprised of representatives from the Bar, the Law Society, the African, Caribbean and Asian Lawyers Group, the Society of Black Lawyers, the Society of Asian Lawyers, the Association of Women Barristers, the Association of Women Solicitors and the LCD.

[96] As reported by Sir Leonard Peach, *Report on the Scrutiny of Judicial Appointments*.

[97] Home Affairs Committee, *Judicial Appointments Procedures*, HC 52-II, Q. 482.

[98] This was endorsed by Sir Leonard Peach.

The function of the interview panel is not to appoint but "to submit assessments of the candidates to the Lord Chancellor, who then uses the information on the application form submitted by the candidate, the assessment made by the interview panel, and the views on particular candidates collected from members of the judiciary and of the professions, to come to a final decision".[99] It is the reliance on views from members of the judiciary and the profession, who know (or may not know) the candidates, which remains controversial, despite their more structured collection during the 1990s.

"Soundings" are taken either through interviews, conducted by members of the Judicial Appointments Group, or by post and, according to the LCD, are as wide as possible. This is a claim of which some are sceptical, Geoffrey Robertson, QC, noting that although he is head of chambers of fifty barristers, he had "never been sounded for anything".[100] All those who are consulted, which include judges and leading members of the Bar Council and Law Society, are provided with a list of names and invited to comment and to rate the applicants from one to five against the criteria for the position. Their comments are typed up and submitted to them for approval before being added to the files containing comments from earlier years. Thus a profile of prospective candidates is built up, providing, for each candidate, "the views of at least twelve or fifteen usually, actually it is very often many more, professional peers over many years".[101] Thus, according to Sir Thomas Legg, when permanent secretary, the "casual kind of old boy network way of doing it" has been replaced by "a structured, organised, rolling programme of quite extensive consultations which are carried out according to the rules and principles which the Lord Chancellor has laid down".[102] Moreover, in a move towards greater openness, in March 1996 a list of those consulted on the appointment of assistant recorders, was published as a Annex to the Guide for Applicants. It is also now the policy of the LCD to allow candidates to see all statements of fact held on their file and to have an opportunity to correct any errors. They are not, however, allowed to see opinions, although, if requested, officials will give a "general summary of the tenor" of these.[103]

Lord Mackay strongly defended the system which operated under his chancellorship as producing "a quality of judges which commends itself",[104] while the Home Affairs Select Committee welcomed the move to advertisements and interviews which had resulted in a shift so that "the system of appointment is becoming less reliant upon opinion which cannot be guarenteed to be objective".[105] However, opinion still plays a major part, raising concern that there are

---

[99] Home Affairs Committee, *Judicial Appointments Procedures*, HC 52-I, para. 25.
[100] HC 52-II, Q. 573.
[101] Sir Thomas Legg, permanent secretary, Ibid, Q. 49.
[102] Ibid, Q. 8.
[103] Ibid, Appendix 1, Memorandum from LCD, para. 2.3.17.
[104] Ibid, Q. 441.
[105] HC 52-I, para. 62.

"inherent elements of bias" within the system,[106] which are increased by the "random" nature of the consultation and the fact that comments may be "second-hand" opinions, anecdotal or "hearsay".[107] Moreover, high dependence upon the opinions of serving judges suggests that those with advocacy skills and the opportunity to show them will be favoured. There is also the risk of "promotion by opinion poll, as it were, amongst your peers, or . . . that the club becomes a self-reinforcing body and that only people who fit the same criteria as existing members of the club ever make it through to the next stage of the promotion ladder".[108]

Indeed, "recruitment systems which rely principally on the views of existing post holders are inherently vulnerable to inadvertent bias in favour of those from similar backgrounds as current post-holders – in this case, barristers against solicitors, men against women and white candidates against ethnic minority ones".[109] Such bias is not overt, those consulted having "the capacity to dress up comments on a candidate's ability so as to cover up prejudice".[110] Nevertheless, the effect is that women, ethnic minorities, solicitors, employed barristers and those with "paperwork" practices are discriminated against.[111] Moreover, the secrecy still engendered within the appointments system is "the antithesis of openness in government"[112] and thus runs counter to the stated aims of both John Major and Tony Blair to make government more transparent.

Lord Irvine has continued the reform of the appointments procedure started by his predecessor, seeking to broaden the base of judicial recruitment by providing greater flexibility in the sitting arrangements for part-time judges, so that they could accumulate their required twenty days' sitting in a year more conveniently, and increasing the upper age limit for appointment to assistant recorder from fifty to fifty-three, a recognition of the problems for women who take time out to raise a family.[113] Moreover, "to improve the current system and encourage wider applications", he announced the development of a scheme which would enable prospective applicants to "shadow" a judge, so that they can get an understanding of what it is like to sit judicially, the introduction of a "mentoring" scheme, in which district and circuit judges and recorders "would be asked to advise and guide their more junior colleagues in the part-time judiciary", and a system whereby newly appointed assistant recorders would be allocated "pupil-master" judges, who would undertake "a small amount of in-court observation" with their views being disclosed only to the individual concerned.[114]

[106] Aleksander (JUSTICE), Ibid, HC 52-II, Q. 567.
[107] HC 52-I, paras. 46–51.
[108] Public Administration Committee, *Your Right to Know: The Government's Proposals for a Freedom of Information Act,* HC 398–v, Q. 321.
[109] Home Affairs Committee, *Judicial Appointments Procedures,* HC 52-II, Appendix 19, Memorandum by Law Society.
[110] Ibid, Appendix 18, Memorandum by the Law Centres Federation.
[111] HC 52-I, paras. 52–7.
[112] R. Stevens, HC 52-II, Q. 525.
[113] LCD Press Notice, 220/97 (9 October 1997).
[114] LCD Press Notice, 279/97.

In a further move towards open competition, he extended the advertising of judicial vacancies to High Court judges, the first advertisement appearing on 24 February 1998. The system, whereby application was by invitation only, therefore no longer operates, although given that the views of other judges will largely determine the suitability of a candidate, a cynic might suggest that, in practice, nothing has changed; only those judges who would previously have been invited to apply will, in fact, be appointed. Moreover, Lord Irvine has retained "the power to offer appointments to those who have not applied" so that he can reach those "who are able, but unwilling, to press their own claim"[115] and he has used this power, eleven out of the nineteen High Court judges appointed in the two years from February 1998 having been invited to take up the position. If those concerned were from groups under-represented on the bench, such invitations could be seen as helping address problems of inequality of opportunity. However, making appointments from those who have not gone through the full application process would seem to go against the notion of equal opportunities, which requires that all are subject to the same processes, and, arguably, to infringe the spirit of the Code of Practice on the Promotion of Equal Opportunities,[116] which states; "recruitment solely or primarily by word of mouth may unnecessarily restrict the choice of applicants available. The method should be avoided in a workforce predominately of one sex, if in practice it prevents members of the opposite sex from applying".[117]

From the beginning of his Chancellorship in 1997 Lord Irvine emphasised that he would not tolerate discrimination in judicial appointments, and to this end he would seek to make the judicial appointments process "open and more transparent".[118] He also moved to provide mechanisms by which the process could be held to account. He told the Minority Lawyers Conference; "If any of you feel aggrieved about a specific application or incident, and believe you were subject to negative discrimination, I undertake to look at the case personally and provide you with a personal reply".[119] In addition, he flagged the possibility of establishing an ombudsman to examine complaints by applicants that they had been subject to unfair treatment in the appointments process and he indicated that a review would be undertaken of the system, by which the performance of part-time judges was appraised to determine their suitability as full time judges.[120] He further announced that he would report annually to Parliament on the operation of the judicial appointments system, the first report being for 1998–9[121] and that a feedback system was being introduced to

---

[115] LCD Press Notice, 43/98 (23 February 1998).
[116] Equal Opportunities Commission, *Code of Practice for the Elimination of Discrimination on the Grounds of Sex and Marriage and the Promotion of Equal Opportunities in Employment* (1985).
[117] Ibid, para. 19c.
[118] Address by Lord Irvine, *Minority Lawyers Conference* (LCD Press Notice, 279/97; 29 November 1997).
[119] Ibid.
[120] LCD Press Notice, 220/97 (9 October 1997) and H.L. Debs. 15 October 1997, cols. WA 193–4.
[121] The first report was presented to Parliament in October 1999.

make the appointments process fairer, or at least to counter perceptions that it was unfair.

As a consequence, unsuccessful candidates are now able to receive feedback on their applications and although actual comments made by consultees are not divulged to candidates, officials in the LCD "give them as frank an assessment as they properly can of their strengths and weaknesses and whether they think it profitable to apply in another year, and so on".[122] This is also the case for those seeking appointment to Queen's Counsel and, after the 1999 appointments, the Lord Chancellor's Department received one hundred and forty requests for feedback, which amounted to nearly one in four of the unsuccessful applicants. Providing such feedback is expensive, as is the whole selection process, and in an attempt to make the selection of QCs self-funding, the Access to Justice Act 1999 provides the Lord Chancellor with the discretion to levy a fee on applicants, which for the year 2000 he set at £353.00.[123]

Yet, despite the reforms and in apparent contradiction of his aim to ensure better accountability and non-discrimination, Lord Irvine was adamant that the consultation process should remain. He did, however, seek to change its image, objecting to the consultations being referred to as "secret soundings", which, he said, was inaccurate and made them "sound sinister". They were, he insisted, neither "secret" nor "soundings" but a "confidential information gathering exercise", which enables "the ability and performance of individuals [to be assessed] over a very, very long period of time". It is, in his words, "actually very good. You simply would not get that frank assessment unless on a confidential basis".[124] Nevertheless, in order to reassure those who might think that "bile and prejudice" enter the process and that such considerations are taken into account, he instructed his officials that "any allegation of misconduct made during the course of consultation about a judicial candidate must be specific" and "be disclosed to the candidate, to give him an opportunity to present his side of the story".[125] The extensive nature of the consultations is evident from the 1997 competition for assistant recorders, during which "over 1,600 people were consulted, and more than 8,000 comments were received on 1,000 applicants".[126]

Such figures seem impressive. They do not, however, remove the concern about the nature of the information that is collected and the extent to which it favours particular candidates. Moreover, the concern was heightened by the appointment by Lord Irvine of his friend, Gary Hart, as his special adviser.[127] Of course, the appointment of a special adviser is different from that of a judge.

[122] Public Administration Committee, *Your Right to Know: The Governments Proposals for a Freedom of Information Act*, HC 398-v, Q. 319.

[123] *The Times*, 13 July 1999. In total over 500 candidates for judicial or QC positions in 1999 took the opportunity of receiving feedback on their applications.

[124] Public Administration Committee, *Your Right to Know: The Governments Proposals for a Freedom of Information Act*, HC 398-v, Q. 312.

[125] LCD Press Notice, 279/97 (29 November 1997).

[126] Ibid.

[127] See Chapter Three.

Nevertheless, his failure to advertise the job suggested an acceptance of a culture, which, by its nature, is discriminatory. The processes for information gathering may have been formalised, but those giving the information may still be influenced by loyalties to the "club", whether this is school, inn, chambers or a social institution. The background of applicants and their social interaction with others in the profession may therefore still be important. Such concern also arose over the appointment of a barrister from Lord Irvine's old chambers to the position of First Treasury Junior. Treasury Juniors or Devils are not appointed by the Lord Chancellor but by the Attorney-General. However, their appointment, like that to Queen's Council and the judiciary, is similarly based on confidential opinions, including that of the Lord Chancellor, about a candidate's suitability. When the jobs all went to men, Josephine Hayes, a barrister who believed herself to be suitably qualified, brought an action under the Sex Discrimination Act 1975.[128] She subsequently withdrew her claim when the Attorney-General agreed that he would accept the jurisdiction of the employment tribunal in the event of future disputes and would not use secret soundings when selecting Treasury counsel in future. He also accepted that "informal consultation may have a tendency to result in the recommendation of people known personally to the consultees".[129] This, as Hayes suggests, would seem to "concede that secret soundings overlook qualified candidates and may cause indirect discrimination".

There were differences between this appointment to Treasury counsel and appointments to the judiciary, in that there were no advertisements and, therefore, no opportunities to apply, and the consultation was considerably less structured. Nevertheless, the use of confidential information gathering would still seem to be highly suspect on discrimination grounds. This was a concern, which would seem to have been shared by Lord Irvine, as it was shortly after the case that he announced the independent audit to be carried out by Sir Leonard Peach, former Commissioner for Public Appointments, the purpose of which was "to examine the selection procedures and whether safeguards against racial and sex discrimination are effective".[130]

Lord Irvine stated his belief that "the Macpherson Report on the inquiry into Stephen Lawrence's death and the forthcoming incorporation of the European Convention on Human Rights into the law underline the need for appointment procedures which guard against discrimination, however unconscious and unintended, and provide for equality of opportunity". He therefore asked Sir Leonard;

> to provide a report to the Lord Chancellor on the operation of the appointments procedures in relation to all judicial appointments and Queen's Counsel and in particular to advise on the appropriateness and effectiveness of a) the criteria and b) the proce-

---

[128] For full details, see Chapter Seven.
[129] J. Hayes, "The Plum Jobs all went to Men", *The Times*, 29 June 1999.
[130] LCD Press Notice, 203/99 (27 July 1999).

dures for selecting the best candidates; the extent to which candidates are assessed objectively against the criteria for appointment; the existence of safeguards in the procedures against discrimination on the grounds of race or gender; and to make recommendations, as appropriate, to the Lord Chancellor for further developments in the judicial appointments and Queen's Counsel selection procedures.

The audit was therefore concerned with "how appointments are made rather than by whom", a point that was confirmed by Lord Irvine's qualifying statement that "the Lord Chancellor will continue to involve serving members of the judiciary and senior members of the legal profession in the assessment of candidates and Civil Servants will still support him in his responsibilities for making appointments".[131] Lord Irvine denied that this limited Sir Leonard's inquiry, arguing that " the reality is that he is going to be looking at the whole machinery as a result of which particular appointments emerge . . . There is literally nothing which he is not going to be looking at".[132] This may have been the case, but his terms of reference, together with the Lord Chancellor's qualifying statement, made clear that it was beyond his brief to make recommendations on the part played by those involved in appointments.

Sir Leonard reported in December 1999 and, in the light of reforms to the process, sought to remove concerns about "secret soundings' or confidential consultations. Lord Irvine had announced in 1998 that while all candidates would remain subject to the usual consultation process, applicants for judicial appointment and for that of Queen's Counsel, would be allowed to "put forward the names of two members of the judiciary and/or the profession who they consider will be able to comment on their qualities and experience".[133] This at least ensured that their referees would be on the list of those consulted and, in this respect, brought the process into line with general application procedures. Peach found that the use of "nominated consultees" varied between categories of appointment[134] and recommended an across the board approach for all competitions, Moreover, he suggested that all candidates should be requested "to name not less than three, and not more than six, consultees", and that they should "automatically be contacted to provide information which will be requested on a form specifically geared to the criteria for appointment". These references "should be considered separately from the general consultation process and weighed accordingly".[135] Peach did not indicate what weight they should be given, but, at the very least, they would provide another factor to consider when making appointment decisions. Excellent references might therefore compensate for relatively sparse comments received from consultation.

---

[131] Sir Leonard Peach, *Report on the Scrutiny of Judicial Appointments* (1999).
[132] Home Affairs Committee, *The Work of the Lord Chancellor's Department* (1998–99) HC 882, Minutes of Evidence.
[133] LCD Press Notice, 43/98.
[134] e.g. It was not a requirement for circuit judges but was for assistant recorders.
[135] Sir Leonard Peach, *Report on the Scrutiny of Judicial Appointments* (1999).

Not surprisingly Peach found that the general opinion of the judges on consultation was that it was "the most important part of the selection process".[136] Given that a judge always sits on the selection panel, this suggests that at least one member of it is likely to accord the views of the consultees a greater weight than those of the referees and even than the performance of a candidate in interview. Moreover, in relation to those views, Peach was concerned that, despite the guidance given, those who were consulted did not always concentrate on the skills requirement of the post. In addition, he noted ; "It is also unclear whether the views contained in the submission are those of the individual consultee or whether others have contributed".[137] Clarity on this would seem to be fundamental if notions of the "club", operating to perpetuate itself are to be dispelled, and if suggestions that some of what is recorded is "hearsay" and impressionistic, rather than factual, are to be countered.

Despite his criticisms, Peach, nevertheless, concluded that "noting the amount of co-operation and support which at present exists from the contributors, as an experienced selector, my conclusion is that to abandon the consultation process would be a neglect of a valuable input into the assessment".[138] He did, however, make some recommendations, which included the redesign of the consultation form "to ensure that the comments invited are allied to the requirements of the post and not general" and the inclusion of a section, "which required the consultee to indicate the source of information contained within the entries, specifically whether it represents solely the consultee's views, those of others (how many and whom) and whether there were disagreements, reconciled or unreconciled",[139] a recommendation accepted and quickly put into practice by the LCD.

Moreover, in response to concerns that the consultation process results in there being more information on some candidates than on others, Peach saw "the onus" as being "on the shortlisting panel to ensure that it has evaluated all the information available in reaching its decision on which candidates are to be selected for interview, recognising that more material will be available on some candidates than others".[140] Thus candidates should not be disadvantaged if they are not so well known to those who are consulted. However, this in itself is not sufficient to prevent discrimination. As has already been noted, the criteria and qualities required may themselves be discriminatory and the way in which they are interpreted and judged by those consulted may further disadvantage candidates who are not in the mainstream. Valuing difference is one way of countering prejudice, but it is difficult to see how the system, as constituted, can take that philosophy forward.

---

[136] Sir Leonard Peach, *Report on the Scrutiny of Judicial Appointments* (1999).
[137] Ibid.
[138] Ibid.
[139] Ibid.
[140] Ibid.

The main concern expressed by Sir Leonard related to the appointment of Deputy High Court judges, of whom twenty were authorised to sit in 1998/99. These positions are not advertised; rather, after consultations have taken place, a direct invitation is made by the Lord Chancellor. Peach noted; "There does not appear to be a justification for not following the standard approach which is pursued for other part-time appointments". He therefore recommended that these posts should be filled "using the established appointments procedures"[141] and the Lord Chancellor subsequently confirmed that he would review the procedure for their appointment.

In relation to other aspects of the appointments system, Sir Leonard considered that the retention by the Lord Chancellor of the discretion to appoint those who had not applied was "acceptable", "providing that a common selection procedure is followed for all candidates and nominees for a similar post".[142] He compared the Lord Chancellor's discretion to the use of head-hunting in the private sector or for quango appointments. This would seem a dubious comparison, given the position of judges as public servants, their power and their tenure of office. Sir Leonard also equated the process that the Lord Chancellor followed in filling senior judicial appointments, whereby he regularly met senior judges[143] to review the needs of the High Court and Court of Appeal and to consider possible appointments to vacancies that would be occurring, with that used in large private sector companies "which set out to plan manpower". He therefore concluded that "the basis for a systematic process for succession planning . . . is already in existence". It simply required more formalisation. To this end he recommended the holding of formal meetings at least every six months to discuss candidates and draw up "succession lists", one of which should contain those candidates, who were agreed to be "immediately capable" of filling a position, and another which should contain those who within two or three years would be contenders.[144] He also proposed that the Lord Chancellor should only make recommendations from these lists, returning for further discussion if he wished to depart from them.

Sir Leonard was particularly impressed with the feedback system, introduced by Lord Ivine, commenting; "I am unaware of any other organisation or department which offers a facility of this kind and has a take up on such a large scale". However, he recommended that, in addition, the Lord Chancellor should create a commission for judicial appointments to provide an element of independent oversight. The commission, which Peach suggested should consist of a part-time chairman and around ten part-time commissioners,[145] "should be concerned

---

[141] LCD, *Judicial Appointments: Annual Report*, para. 3.13.

[142] Sir Leonard Peach, *Report on the Scrutiny of Judicial Appointments* (1999).

[143] Including the Lord Chief Justice, other Heads of Division, the Senior Presiding Judge, Vice President of the Queen's Bench Division and Vice President of the Court of Appeal.

[144] He recommended that at these meetings consideration should be given to lists of "the best available female and ethnic minority candidates, solicitors and barristers".

[145] No more than a third with a legal background (Ibid).

with the ongoing audit of the processes and policies for making and renewing judicial appointments, for handling grievances and appeals resulting from the application of those processes/policies and for recommending improvements and changes to the Lord Chancellor".[146] To this end the commissioners should sit on some selection panels and also act as "independents, monitoring the performance of the panel and any deficiencies in procedure and possible improvements".[147] Peach's model also involved grievances and complaints being handled by the chairman,[148] who could make recommendations to the Lord Chancellor and who, while having no power to take "unilateral action", would have the power to "amend or expunge parts of the records of any individual" and "to restore the complainant concerned, in the subsequent cycle of the appointment which he or she is seeking, to the point at which he or she was disadvantaged".[149] Peach saw the commission also being able to scrutinise any part of the judicial appointments procedure at the request of the Lord Chancellor and publishing an annual report, which would be included in the Lord Chancellor's report on Judicial Appointments to Parliament. Lord Irvine subsequently announced his intention of establishing such a commission.

Peach's overall impression of the way in which judicial appointments were processed by the LCD was "one of thoroughness, competence and professionalism". His assessment was "that the procedures and their execution are as good as any which I have seen in the Public Sector".[150] He did, however, recommend that the appointments process should be strengthened through the introduction of assessment centres. Such centres or courses form part of modern employment practices and are common within business, industry and parts of the public sector. They involve psychometric tests and inter-personal relations exercises to determine an applicant's suitability and in June 2000 Lord Irvine stated that such mechanisms would be used at the first level of appointment.

In defence of the appointments system Peach commented that "the size of the Department's operations seem to be little appreciated by its critics whose statistics concentrate on the top 150 appointments".[151] However, concentration on these appointments is not to neglect the others, but rather to recognise that these are the ones which have a high profile, are concerned with cases of a political nature, shape the law and which, with the increased importance of judicial review, have themselves become more important. Moreover, their importance will continue to increase with the Human Rights Act, the provisions of which extend judicial power further, and devolution legislation, which will require the most senior appointments to arbitrate between the Scottish, Welsh, Northern Ireland and Westminster Parliaments. It is therefore necessary to pay particular

---

[146] *Report on the Scrutiny of Judicial Appointments* (1999).
[147] Ibid.
[148] Individuals having been through the feedback system first.
[149] "This is subject to practicality, since there are one-off competitions in respect of a single post". (Ibid).
[150] Ibid.
[151] Letter to the Lord Chancellor, which accompanied the Report (3 December 1999).

attention to the way in which judges are appointed to these positions, first, to ensure that there are the necessary checks and balances in place by which the judges can be held to account for the power they wield and, secondly, to ensure their independence from the executive arm of government.[152] The appointments system has undergone considerable reform since the early 1990s and is much more transparent than previously. However, it is still based on "secret soundings" or "confidential consultations" which, despite Peach's reassurances, are seen by many as inherently discriminatory. In any case, these reforms have little relevance where the most senior judges are concerned and the system continues to be flawed by the fact that appointments lie in the gift of two politicians, the Lord Chancellor and the Prime Minister, with no external checks on the way in which it operates. Hence calls for the establishment of a judicial commission.

A JUDICIAL COMMISSION

In 1995, while in Opposition, the Labour Party produced a consultation paper, *Access to Justice*, which supported the establishment of a judicial commission. Similarly its policy statement on constitutional reform[153] spoke of the establishment of a judicial appointments and training commission. Labour therefore seemed committed to changing the system by which judges are appointed. Moreover, shortly after the party took office, *The Times* reported that the Lord Chancellor's officials were "drafting proposals to introduce public scrutiny and accountability into the way judges are chosen to redress the imbalance of a judiciary dominated by white, middle-class men" and to answer the criticisms that appointment is secret and via consultation with others in the legal profession. This was to be done by a judicial appointments commission.[154] This seemed confirmed by Lord Irvine who stated that the Government would be consulting on the matter.[155]

However, the issue "crept off" the agenda "almost as soon as it got there"[156] with the subsequent announcement by the Lord Chancellor that in view of the "other substantial priorities facing my Department, including a very heavy workload connected with legal aid and civil justice reforms, I have decided not to proceed with further work on a possible Commission but to concentrate on making those changes I regard as most urgent".[157] In December 1998 Lord Irvine seemed to waiver, saying he may consult on the setting up of a judicial appointments commission. This statement followed criticism of his appointment of two law lords, Lords Millet and Hobhouse, who were seen as shifting

[152] See Lord Patten, H. L. Debs., 1 March 1999, col. 1442.
[153] *A New Agenda for Democracy. Labour's Proposals on Constitutional Reform* (1997), p. 40.
[154] 27 May 1997.
[155] H. L. Debs., 23 June 1997, col. WA 145.
[156] G. Drewry, "Judicial Appointments", p. 2.
[157] LCD Press Notice, 220/97.

the balance of the House of Lords to the right and, given their background as commercial law judges, as being inappropriate at a time when the Human Rights Act was coming on stream.[158] However, no consultation document was forthcoming.

Lord Irvine therefore seems to be following the line of his predecessors in resisting the establishment of a judicial commission. Lord Mackay never faltered in his opposition. Despite pressure from organisations, such as JUSTICE, he held his line, arguing, first, that it was "not clear that any improvement in the quality of those appointed is likely to be achieved by any change which I have seen referred to";[159] secondly, that it would diminish the personal responsibility of the Lord Chancellor for appointments, as the advice of the Commission could be publicly relied upon;[160] and, thirdly, that it was "questionable" whether a judicial appointments commission would have available to it such a wide source of information on candidates.

Lord Taylor, when Lord Chief Justice, also indicated his opposition to a judicial appointments commission, arguing that a commission would bring politics into the process, as "[t]he Government of the day, the Lord Chancellor, the Prime Minister, whoever it may be, must be the person . . . who appoints the Commission that is going to do the appointing. So you have got room for a political element – or an accusation, at any rate, of a political element – whether valid or not".[161] Moreover, he noted that the need for the commission to be "balanced", would inevitably result in political allegiances being taken into account and in those on the commission "fighting the corner of those they represent", or appearing to do so.[162]

The concern that a judicial appointments commission would introduce politics into the process is also held by the Judges Council, which argued that those appointed to the commission would be subject to political scrutiny and there would be a danger of "extraneous or irrelevant criteria" being used in appointments and the requirements of openness would result in those being consulted being reluctant to give full and frank views.[163] However, such an argument fails to recognise that there is at present concern about whether the criteria used is always relevant and about the part played by "soundings". Moreover, if proper procedures for references were used, those giving them would be safeguarded. When the issue was discussed in 1996, the key concern of both the Judges Council and the Lord Chief Justice was that a judicial commission would result in the political scrutiny of judges in confirmation hearings in Parliament, similar to those in the United States. This was a fear that JUSTICE sought to allay on the basis that the lack of a Bill of Rights and the doctrine of parliamentary

---

[158] *The Times*, 14 December 1998.
[159] Home Affairs Committee, *Judicial Appointments Procedures*, HC 52-II, Q. 441.
[160] Ibid, Q. 445.
[161] Ibid, Q. 285.
[162] Ibid.
[163] Ibid, Appendix 16.

sovereignty meant that judges were not required to make political decisions to the same extent as in other countries.[164]

This statement shows how quickly things become outdated. Given the incorporation of the European Convention on Human Rights, there is a need for the public scrutiny of judges, as has been recognised in other countries which have adopted Bills of Rights. Thus South Africa has followed the United States system, with judges appointed to the Constitutional Court being brought before the legislature and cross-examined on their views, and Israel has also moved to this system, as the courts have become more involved in politics. Some involvement by Parliament is favoured by a number of groups, including, perhaps surprisingly, the Conservative shadow Lord Chancellor, Lord Kingsland. He has suggested that, when appointed, the law lords should appear before the House of Commons Public Administration Select Committee, which would have no veto but would be able to question the judges on their interests and attitudes, thereby ensuring that these were in the public domain. In the aftermath of Pinochet,[165] a Register of Judicial Interests may be a possibility. This could include commercial and non-commercial directorships, for "it is now in the public interest to know more about our judicial masters".[166] If such a register were adopted, this could form a basis for parliamentary questioning.

The testing of judicial attitudes on matters such as sexual and racial equality will also become increasingly important as the Human Rights Act brings judges more overtly into the political arena. Questions might include, as it does in the States, whether they are members of any segregated club or of a club that discriminates against women, the basis for the question being that "you cannot enforce a Bill of Rights if you belong to a club which does not allow women through the front door".[167] This raises questions about some golf and London clubs, as well, of course, about membership of a Masonic lodge, disclosure of which is now a requirement for those seeking judicial appointment, although voluntary for those already in office.

Membership of the Masons is generally discussed in terms of justice and issues of bias in relation to litigants and defendants. However, it is also relevant to judicial appointments; first, because the Masonic pledge to help other Masons may raise suspicions that Masonic members of the judiciary may be disposed to making positive comments about fellow members aspiring to judicial position, regardless of their merits; and, secondly, because Freemasonry discriminates against women candidates who are excluded from membership and

---

[164] Ibid, HC 52-I, para. 139.

[165] Where the decision of the House of Lords was vacated because Lord Hoffmann's chairmanship of the charitable arm of Amnesty International meant that he was disqualified from hearing the case and thus the panel was improperly constituted (see *R. v. Bow Street Metropolitan Stipendiary Magistrate and Others, ex parte Pinochet Ugarte* (No.2) [1999] 2 WLR 272.

[166] Lord Patten, H. L. Debs., 1 March 1999, col. 1442.

[167] R. Stevens, Ibid, Q. 538. Interestingly, the American Judiciary Committee and Senate requested the resignation of federal judges, who were members of the Athenaeum in London, on the grounds that it was a sexist club, which discriminated against women.

therefore do not have this opportunity of meeting judges socially and of informally enhancing their career prospects.

Models for a judicial appointments commission are varied but are supported in some form by many groups, including JUSTICE, the Law Society, NACRO and the Howard League for Penal Reform. A commission could be responsible for appointments at all levels, make appointments at lower levels and advise the Lord Chancellor on more senior appointments, simply advise the Lord Chancellor on appointments at circuit level and below, or just act to advise on appointing procedures. A full blown model would have responsibility for all appointments, oversee magistrates' advisory committees, be responsible for judicial training and career development and investigate complaints against individual judges. It would also appoint QCs. Alternatively, as David Pannick suggests, the Bar could be made responsible for its own promotions, on the basis that as "the bar values its independence, [i]t is . . . difficult to justify a system by which promotion to a senior status is dependent on the advice of civil servants and the decision of a politician, however wide the consultation. The Bar itself should decide the relevant policies, criteria and procedures, and should create an appointment panel consisting of eminent lawyers and distinguished non-lawyers to determine which applications should be approved".[168] In addition, a break should be made which connects the position historically with the Crown, and hence the Lord Chancellor, by renaming the position Senior Counsel.

The JUSTICE model, which initially sees the commission as advising the Lord Chancellor, suggests selection boards for lower judicial appointments which could be run on similar lines to those used by the Civil Service Commission, while for senior appointments the selection boards could be manned by the commission. In all cases, references would replace consultation and the Lord Chancellor would be required to give reasons for not accepting any particular candidate. Writing in 1987 David Pannick observed that regardless of how a judicial appointments commission "approach[ed] the task of helping the Lord Chancellor, it could hardly fail to improve on the unarticulated criteria, acts of God, and secret processes of nature which currently govern judicial appointments".[169] The criteria may now be articulated in most instances, but the secrecy remains and, despite Sir Leonard Peach's audit, continues to cast doubt over the process. Moreover, in the case of most senior judges, Pannick's observation remains true; nothing has changed.

As far as its composition is concerned, there is general support for a lay element. JUSTICE believes that this should form a majority, thereby preventing a majority of judges and lawyers tending "to appoint in their own image and kind" and thus perpetuating "the practice of appointing to the Bench white middle-class Oxbridge educated lawyers".[170] One of its concerns is "that we should

---

[168] *The Times*, 6 April 1999.
[169] D. Pannick, *The Judges*, p. 69.
[170] Aleksander, Home Affairs Committee, *Judicial Appointments Procedures*, HC 52-II, Q. 566.

not have a recruitment system that had within it a mirroring effect so that those making appointments appoint those in their image to take their place". It has therefore suggested that a commission could have seven lay persons, three barristers and three solicitors, with the judiciary having a small representation, and that groups such as JUSTICE, Liberty, Society of Public Teachers of Law, and Society of Black Lawyers should be represented. It considers that lay persons should be "functionally relevant", probably having experience in "selection, training, performance assessment and the management of change, preferably at a senior level"[171] and that, given the incorporation of the European Convention on Human Rights, it might be appropriate for members of the House of Commons to sit on the commission.[172]

The Law Society suggests there should be four main groups on the commission, none of which should dominate. These would be judges, legal academics and members of the professions, lay persons with expertise in recruitment and training at senior level, and lay people representing the community as a whole. Members might be nominated by the Lord Chancellor, after consultation, but it would be necessary to have all party consensus to reduce the risks of party political considerations influencing appointments. Once in place, there should be a statutory requirement that members of the commission should not be subject to ministerial direction or removal before the expiry of their term in office.[173] The commission would therefore be independent of the Government, a model favoured by Brazier, who calls for a statutory body, which is publicly accountable, with no minister being accountable to Parliament for it, and which "to a large degree" is independent of Parliament.[174] He argues that it should be "drawn predominately from representatives of the senior judiciary, and would also include the heads of divisions . . . Some lay members would be important, partly to help to offset professional insularity, and partly to ensure that the case was argued for widening the pool of potential judicial candidates".[175] He sees it as important that the lay membership should not be "just from the great and the good" but from those "who have certain expertise which is of critical importance, such as an understanding of selection and appointment procedures, so that the lawyers on the commission cannot hope to bamboozle the lay members".[176] In Brazier's model the commission would meet "in consultation with senior officials from the LCD" but have its own civil servants. It would consult on appointments, retaining appropriate confidentiality, and there would be a circuit judicial committee established for each of the six circuits to advise in the appointment of the lower judiciary.

---

[171] Ibid, HC 52-I, para. 133.
[172] R. Stevens, Ibid, HC 52-II, Q. 568.
[173] Ibid, HC 52-I, para. 134.
[174] Ibid, HC 52-II, Q. 562–3.
[175] Ibid, Appendix 26.
[176] Ibid, Q. 566.

The Home Affairs Committee, before which the idea of a commission was discussed in 1996 was not convinced by the arguments put forward. It considered that while a judicial appointments commission "might answer the criticism . . . that it was constitutionally unhealthy for Ministers to recommend candidates for judicial appointment", it might itself "be the scene of struggles (whether political or not)". Moreover, it was concerned that a commission "would dilute the direct responsibility for appointments currently vested in the Lord Chancellor" and that it "might reduce the dependence upon assessments of performance".[177] However, it saw the "key question" as being whether it would "improve the quality of appointments", concluding, that on this point, "we have not been persuaded".[178] The committee therefore rejected the idea of the commission.

CONCLUSION

The committee would seem to have addressed the wrong question, or, at least, been too narrow in its considerations. More relevant was whether, in order to sustain public confidence in the legal system, it was necessary for the appointing process to be more open and for the field of those involved in it to be widened. Since the committee examined the issue, the Human Rights Act and devolution legislation have made it increasingly important to distance judicial appointments from ministers and to ensure that there are external checks within the system. It is essential that judges are not only independent of the executive, but are seen to be so. The Human Rights Act makes this a legal requirement, through the incorporation of Article 6 of the ECHR, as became apparent in *Starrs* v. *Procurator Fiscal*,[179] a case concerning temporary sheriffs, which was heard in Scotland in 1999. The case has already been considered in Chapter Two but it is appropriate in the context of appointments briefly to restate the judgment of the court, which was that an appointment renewed on an annual basis by a member of the executive, for which there was no security of tenure, was contrary to the European Convention on Human Rights. This has implications for the appointment of assistant recorders and acting stipendiaries.

It is clearly advantageous that before a judge is appointed to a permanent position, his or her performance as a judge is assessed. The policy of the Lord Chancellor, which requires service in a part-time capacity to test competence and suitability, is therefore a sound one. The problem is that it is a policy operated by a government minister and therefore carries with it the danger of a judge "being influenced, consciously or unconsciously, by his hopes and fears about

---

[177] Aleksander, Home Affairs Committee, *Judicial Appointments Procedures*, HC 52-II, Q. 566, HC 52-I, para. 141.

[178] Ibid, para. 142.

[179] *Starrs* v. *Procurator Fiscal Linlithgow* [1999] *The Times*, 17 November.

his possible treatment by the executive".[180] The Lord Chancellor's responsibility for appointments therefore means that the legal requirements for judicial independence may not be met. More important, given the changes in the office of Lord Chancellor, it may undermine public confidence in the judiciary. This was the concern in February 2001 when it was revealed that Lord Irvine had suggested to lawyers, who had been invited to a fund raising dinner, that they should take the opportunity to make a 'significant contribution to party funds to ensure a second term [for Labour]'.[181] There was no suggestion that those seeking to become QCs or judges were being asked to buy favour, as had been the practice three centuries earlier, but there was concern that judicial advancement might be perceived to be influenced by the generosity of those who sought it. Such a perception would, no doubt, be wrong, but appearances matter, particularly given the new constitutional role of the courts, and as long as a politician is responsible for the appointment of judges, they leave much to be desired. The answer would seem to be the removal of the appointing function from the Lord Chancellor.

[180] Aleksander, para 142.
[181] *Sunday Times*, 18 February 2001.

7

The Accountability of the Lord Chancellor

INTRODUCTION

THE LORD CHANCELLOR, like all ministerial heads of departments, is accountable to Parliament through the convention of ministerial responsibility. Prior to the development of a resigning convention, the sanction imposed by Parliament upon a minister, who had committed serious errors, was impeachment and over the centuries several Lord Chancellors were impeached for activities seen as not befitting the office of Lord Chancellor, or indeed, any minister of the Crown. These included Sir Michael de la Pole in 1386, for using appropriated funds for purposes other than those specified,[1] Lord Bacon in 1620, for accepting bribes,[2] and the Earl of Macclesfield in 1725, for selling the offices of Masters in Chancery.[3] By the nineteenth century impeachment proceedings had been replaced by the requirement that a minister, who lost the support of Parliament, should resign,[4] and, in recognition of this requirement, in 1865 Lord Westbury relinquished office. His conduct had been censured in both Houses, the House of Commons resolving that there had been "a laxity of practice and want of caution with regard to the public interest on the part of the Lord Chancellor in sanctioning the grant of retiring pensions to public officers against whom grave charges were pending, which in the opinion of this House are calculated to discredit the administration of his great office".[5]

Westbury was the last Lord Chancellor to relinquish office in this way. Yet the sanction of resignation remains. Moreover, its importance was recognised by Lord Mackay who thought it "very helpful that there should be, at the head of the judiciary, someone who can be accountable to Parliament and can hold office in such a way that if Parliament is dissatisfied with the way in which its responsibilities are being discharged he could be relieved from his office without the necessity which protects all holders of permanent judicial office".[6] Thus, in

---

[1] S. Shetreet, *Judges on Trial*, p. 126.

[2] Ibid, p. 127.

[3] Ibid.

[4] On ministerial responsibility, see G. Marshall (ed.), *Ministerial Responsibility* (Oxford, Oxford University Press, 1989) and D. Woodhouse, *Ministers and Parliament; Accountability in Theory and Practice* (Oxford, Clarendon Press, 1994).

[5] 180 Parl. Deb., 3rd Ser., 1045 (1845) quoted in S. Shetreet, *Judges on Trial*, p. 147.

[6] Home Affairs Committee, The *Work of the Lord Chancellor's Department*, HC 214-i, Q. 1.

theory, the Lord Chancellor can be removed from office by politicians who are of the opinion that judges are being too lenient or too harsh, or even, too ready to find against the government of the day, for while the Lord Chancellor cannot interfere in the exercise of an individual judge's discretion, as head of the judiciary, he can exert influence over the direction taken by the courts and, according to Lord Mackay, is accountable to Parliament for that direction. He is also accountable to Parliament for the appointments he makes to the judiciary. Lord Mackay stated that as Lord Chancellor, he was "entirely open to receive questions" about individual appointments.[7] In practice, such questions have been infrequent, perhaps because Members of both Houses are entirely satisfied with all judicial appointments, or perhaps because they recognise that the confidentiality surrounding them means that there is little to be gained by asking questions.

During Lord Hailsham's time in office "no peer called [him] to account in these matters. There were no questions or debates in these matters. There were no questions or debate in that House about either the policy behind or the applications of his power to make judicial appointments, or his refusal to renew temporary judicial posts, or the removal of a circuit judge in 1983".[8] Similarly, Lord Mackay "could not in fact recall inquiries from a member of either House of Parliament about appointments that had been made".[9] The issue of judicial appointments became more contentious after Lord Irvine took office.[10] However, the focus was on the appointments system rather than individual appointments, and, in response to mounting pressure for information on it, in October 1997 the Lord Chancellor announced that he would present an annual report to Parliament. The first report was published two years later, and was heralded by Lord Irvine as a "tangible example" of his commitment to "the openness of, and [his] accountability for, the judicial appointments process".[11] It gave full details of appointments policies and procedures, changes to these that had been made during the year and full statistics on appointments. In so doing, the report clearly advanced the cause of accountability and its annual publication will continue to do so, particularly if, as some have requested, it contains additional information, such as, complaints against judges and how these were dealt with, details of judicial training, and a register of judicial interests.

The Lord Chancellor is not responsible for the individual decisions of judges or magistrates in particular cases; "These decisions are the responsibility of the judges or magistrates who take them . . . subject only to the disciplinary powers that the Lord Chancellor has in respect of certain levels of the judiciary and the powers of Parliament in respect of the higher judiciary".[12] Thus, according to

---

[7] Home Affairs Committee, *Judicial Appointments Procedures*, HC 52-I, para. 124.
[8] R. Brazier, "Government and the Law", p. 72.
[9] Home Affairs Committee, *Judicial Appointments Procedures*, HC 52-I, para. 124.
[10] See Chapter Six.
[11] LCD, *Judicial Appointments; Annual Report* (1998–99), Foreword.
[12] Lord Mackay, "The Lord Chancellor's Role within Government", p. 1652.

Lord Mackay, while the Lord Chancellor will give an account of the circumstances of a case, he will not give an opinion on the verdict. To do so would be an infringement of judicial independence. It is, however, the Lord Chancellor who initiates any action that Parliament might think appropriate and who deals with complaints about a judge, whether from MPs or members of the public. Indeed, like all ministers, he is required to deal with correspondence whether on this or other matters. As Lord Elwyn-Jones noted; "Another task with which my small but able staff had to cope was the considerable volume of complaints sent to me by Members of Parliament and the public".[13] The staff has increased in size since the time he was writing, but so too has the postbag. Lord Mackay recorded that he received 2,984 letters from peers and MPs in 1990, the answers to which were, in most instances, signed by him, and a total of 4,841 enquiries in 1994–5.[14] Lord Chancellors also see MPs, either alone or in deputation. However, none of this compensates for the fact that, unlike other ministers, the Lord Chancellor sits in the House of Lords, not in the House of Commons.

The traditional justification for the position of the Lord Chancellor in the House of Lords is that his responsibility for judicial independence makes it necessary for him to be insulated from party politics. Judicial independence has therefore been used to deflect criticism of the Lord Chancellor's lack of direct accountability to the elected chamber. Yet this absence of accountability presents problems. Lord Mackay noted that he was "responsible to Parliament for the delivery of a fair, effective and efficient overall system for the administration of justice within the constraints of the moneys voted to me for these purposes by the House of Commons"[15] and, that apart from judicial salaries, which are paid out of the Consolidated Fund, he was "answerable to Parliament for the stewardship of every penny of the very substantial remainder of my budget".[16] Yet the Lord Chancellor is answerable not in the House of Commons, which votes the money, but in the House of Lords, which has no constitutional responsibility to hold ministers to account for the way in which the money is spent. Given the current status of the LCD, as a large spending department, this is less than satisfactory, for it means the Lord Chancellor escapes the routine accountability, extracted from ministers in charge of departments, and the requirement that he appears before the House to answer for his department when things go wrong.

There are also problems concerning accountability for non-departmental public bodies, which come within his area of responsibility, including, for instance, the Legal Services Ombudsman, the Council on Tribunals, the Community Legal Service and the Law Commission. Such bodies operate at arm's length from ministers, who, as a consequence, are only indirectly accountable to Parliament for their operations. They may, therefore, confine themselves

---

[13] Lord Elwyn-Jones, *In My Time*, p. 283.
[14] Lord Mackay, "The Lord Chancellor in the 1990s", p. 257.
[15] Ibid, p. 244.
[16] Ibid, p. 246.

to repeating what they have been told by the chairman of the board, refusing to elaborate further. This indirect accountability can allow room for ministerial evasion and a confusion between "policy", which is the minister's direct responsibility, and "operations".[17] This problem is potentially more acute when the minister is the Lord Chancellor, for he is further distanced by his indirect accountability to the elected chamber. Nor is it just accountability for matters of policy which give rise to concern. Non-departmental public bodies and quangos within the remit of the Lord Chancellor provide him with considerable patronage. This was increased further during the 1990s with the appointment of lay interviewers and the establishment of the Civil Justice Council.[18] Yet he is accountable not in the House of Commons for such appointments but, as with the exercise of all his powers,[19] in the rarefied atmosphere of the House of Lords and while he may still be required to answer questions, these are less in number and veracity than those faced by his colleagues in the House of Commons.

As a consequence, even when confronted with a direct attack on his office, as when Lord Lester "rose to call attention to the arrangements for maintaining the separation of powers in the House of Lords between the judicial and executive branches of government; and to move papers",[20] the Lord Chancellor is unlikely to feel his position seriously threatened. His performance will seldom be subjected to the type of media scrutiny that his fellow ministers in the Commons frequently endure and he does not obviously need to carry his party with him. Even when Lord Mackay had to defend his position over the incident of Mr Justice Wood,[21] the debate was conducted with deference to Lord Mackay's office and integrity. Their lordships may have demonstrated their disquiet at what had happened, but they did so in measured tones. It may be that the more civilised debates in the House of Lords are to be preferred to the political point scoring and sound bites of the House of Commons, but this does not detract from the point that the Lord Chancellor is not accountable in the same way as other ministers and arguments, which suggest that he is "answerable to every Member of this House [of Commons]",[22] are flawed.

His accountability on the floor of the House of Commons operated through others. This means there are inevitable limitations. Prior to 1991, the Attorney or Solicitor-General spoke for the Lord Chancellor in the House. There was a short period in the 1960s when a Minister without Portfolio, Eric Fletcher, acted as a kind of third law officer responsible for judicial affairs,[23] but apart from

---

[17] On quangos, see A. Barker (ed.) *Quangos in Britain* (London, Macmillan Press, 1982); F. F. Ridley and D. Wilson (eds.), *The Quango Debate* (Oxford, OUP, 1995).

[18] Civil Procedure Act 1997, s. 6.

[19] His powers have also increased in recent years. See, for instance, the power provided by the Access to Justice Act 1999, which enables him "to determine the level of court which should hear appeal in different types of case".

[20] Lord Lester, H. L. Debs., 17 February 1999, cols. 710–39.

[21] H. L. Debs., 27 April 1994, col. 754 (and see Chapter Four).

[22] Sir Nicholas Lyell, H. C. Debs., 6 November 1997, col. 410.

[23] Lord Mackay, "The Lord Chancellor in the 1990s", p. 253.

this, the function fell to the law officers and, as Lord Silkin recognised, "they were no more than the mouthpiece for the Lord Chancellor . . ., declaring his policy and his decisions for which they had no greater responsibility than any other Minister, even if their legal training may enable them to understand and expound better".[24] It is therefore not surprising that the ministerial account-ability of the Lord Chancellor in the Commons was seen by many as less than satisfactory.[25]

Lord Mackay's appointment of a parliamentary secretary in 1991 to represent him in the lower chamber was an improvement to the accountability arrange-ments and an important concession. As such, it "will earn a footnote in future accounts of the long and often acrimonious debate – which can be traced back via the Haldane Report on the Machinery of Government in 1918, to Bentham and Brougham in the first half of the nineteenth century – about whether Britain should consign departmental responsibility for the justice-related function of the State to a minister of justice".[26] The recognition of the need to pay more than just lip service to accountability in the House of Commons was confirmed by Lord Irvine who, initially, appointed a parliamentary private secretary to assist the junior minister, and, subsequently, raised the number of junior minis-ters in the Commons to two.[27] Moreover, to ensure there would be no confusion about their accountability to the House, he stated that while David Lock would lead on House of Commons business, "ministerial statements, adjournment debates, written parliamentary questions and minister's cases" would follow the allocation of policy responsibilities.[28] Thus Mr Lock was responsible for legal aid and legal services, the Community Legal Service, civil justice and civil law development, the Northern Ireland Court Service, international policy, the Public Records Office, the Legal Services Ombudsman and the Statutory Publications Office, and had overall responsibility for IT issues. He also led on maintaining good working relationships with the professions. Ms Kennedy was responsible for the magistrates' courts, the Court Service, human rights, admin-istrative justice, devolution issues, the Public Trust Office, Land Registry, the Official Solicitor's department and the Council on Tribunals, as well as crimi-nal, family and immigration and asylum policy.

This formalised categorisation of responsibilities is a further indication that the Lord Chancellor's Department functions in the same way as all Whitehall departments. It has the equivalent of a secretary of state at its head and junior

[24] Lord Silkin, Attorney-General 1974–9, quoted by Lord Mackay (Ibid).

[25] e.g. R. Brazier, "Government and the Law" p. 68.

[26] G. Drewry, "Ministers, Politicians and the Courts" p. 50.

[27] David Lock was appointed as PPS to assist Geoff Hoon and when Hoon was elevated to the Foreign Office in 1999, Lock took his place as minister in the Commons, along with an additional parliamentary secretary, Jane Kennedy, who had the privilege of being the first non-lawyer and the first woman to be appointed to ministerial rank within the Department. In November 2000 another junior minister, Lord Bach, was appointed to take responsibility for common and leasehold reforms. However, he sits in the House of Lords not in the Commons.

[28] LCD website.

ministers with specific, but limited, responsibilities. Junior ministers in the LCD, as elsewhere, have no constitutional responsibility for actions within the department. These remain the responsibility of the Lord Chancellor. Whatever delegatory arrangements he might make with his junior ministers, he cannot devolve ministerial responsibility. As a consequence, except where their personal behaviour is concerned, they account to Parliament only on his behalf. The convention of ministerial responsibility therefore "both protects and enfeebles" junior ministers,[29] ensuring that when there are departmental failings, only the Lord Chancellor can answer for them, although, unlike the secretaries of state of other departments, he does so not in the House of Commons but in the House of Lords. Thus while the structure of the LCD may be the same as other departments, where accountability is concerned there is an important difference.

This raises the prospect of an unsatisfactory situation arising, whereby either the elected chamber will be unable to obtain the answers it requires, or a junior minister will be exposed to the needs of accountability, when, constitutionally, he should be protected by his minister. Such a situation unusually arose in 1983, not in connection with the LCD but the Foreign Office. When Argentina invaded the Falkland Islands, two junior ministers, Richard Luce and Humphrey Atkins, took the brunt of the Commons' anger, the Foreign Secretary, Lord Carrington, being unable to answer to the House because he sat in the Lords. Luce and Atkins resigned along with Lord Carrington, despite Carrington's insistence that it was inappropriate for a junior minister to accept departmental responsibility. Luce would probably have relinquished office anyway; he felt personally responsible because it was his section of the Foreign Office that was under attack. But the fact that he had to account to the House of Commons in Carrington's absence and bear the criticism of MPs no doubt confirmed his decision.[30]

For the head of a department of state, other than the Lord Chancellor, to sit in the House of Lords is, in modern times, a rarity, Lord Carrington and Lord Young, Secretary of State for the Department of Trade and Industry (1987–9) being notable exceptions. However, their situation was different from the Lord Chancellor, in that, although like him they were unelected members of the government, they were not confined to the House of Lords because of the office they held. The justification for the insulation of the Lord Chancellor from the party political rough and tumble of the House of Commons if once acceptable is now dubious. Given that his junior ministers are exposed to party political questioning about the administration of justice, there seems no reason why the Lord Chancellor should not likewise be exposed. If concerns for judicial independence stand in the way of accountability, the answer is the reallocation of the

---

[29] K. Theakston, *Junior Ministers in British Government* (Oxford, Blackwells, 1987) p. 68.
[30] For a detailed analysis of the Foreign Office resignations see D. Woodhouse, *Ministers and Parliament.*

Lord Chancellor's judicial and constitutional responsibilities so that he has only executive responsibilities for which to account.

ACCOUNTABILITY IN THE HOUSE OF COMMONS

Since the appointment of a junior minister to answer for the Lord Chancellor in the House of Commons,[31] accountability to the House has undoubtedly improved. This is evident from the number of questions asked, which doubled during the period 1991–8 to between six and seven hundred a year,[32] with a proportional rise in the number of oral questions.[33] Compared with other departments, the number of questions is still modest,[34] but, nevertheless, it represents a significant increase. This cannot necessarily be attributed to the presence of a junior minister in the Commons. There are other factors, notably the Lord Chancellor's assumption of responsibility for the magistrates' courts and the reformist programmes of Lords Mackay and Irvine, which, at times, have been politically contentious. The subject matter of the questions varies, of course, depending on whether there is legislation before the House or reforms in the offing. Thus questions on legal aid figured highly throughout the 1990s,[35] as did those on the magistrates' courts and judicial appointments and training. Questions relating to legal or law reform issues, including in 1997–8 the Family Law Act which was the responsibility of the Lord Chancellor, were also consistently high, as were those concerned with the administration of the LCD, these peaking in 1995–6 with the setting up of the Court Service Agency.[36] Otherwise, questions are wide ranging and include issues relating to the civil and Crown courts, immigration and asylum, the legal profession, the Lord Chancellor's role and responsibilities, probate and land registry, mediation, personal injury litigation and video links for child witnesses. Creeping onto the agenda in 1997–8 were questions on the constitution and, linked with the refurbishment of the Lord Chancellor's official residence, questions about Lord Irvine's accommodation.[37]

The range of questions reflects the spread of the Lord Chancellor's responsibilities. As with other departments, not all questions are answered, either

---

[31] Junior ministers at LCD between 1991–2000 were John Taylor (1991 to November 1995), Jonathan Evans (November 1995 to May 1996), Gary Streeter (June 1996 to May 1997), Geoff Hoon (May 1997 to 1999), David Lock and Jane Kennedy.

[32] In 1989/90 there were 363 questions.

[33] Seventy-one out of 717 in 1993/94; 106 out of 687 in 1995/96; 140 out of 607 in 1996/97; and 154 out of 812 in 1997/98.

[34] Most departments average between 1500–2500 questions. Only the Departments of Culture and International Development are lower than the LCD with approximately 700 and 400, respectively.

[35] Nearly 200 in 1992–3, of which forty were oral; 184 in 1994–5, of which thirty-eight were oral; 125 in 1997–8, of which thirty-seven were oral, together with forty-five questions on conditional fees.

[36] In 1994–5 there were ninety-eight written questions and a year later 136.

[37] Sixteen written and four oral questions.

because they are not within its responsibility, or because of disproportionate cost, or because the necessary information is not available.[38] Answers may also be refused on grounds of confidentiality, because it is inappropriate to answer,[39] or because the matter is sub judicae.[40] In addition, since 1995 all matters which come within the responsibility of the chief executive of the Court Service Agency are passed to him for a response.[41] His replies are recorded in *Hansard*, in a standard format, which states that this is "a matter which has been assigned to the Court Service under the terms of its framework document" and the minister has "therefore asked the Chief Executive to write to the honourable Member". The reply then follows, beginning with "The Parliamentary Secretary of the Lord Chancellor's Department has asked me to reply to your Question about . . ." The Chief Executive may likewise not answer on grounds of disproportionate cost or because the information is not available.

Some of the refusals in the House of Commons in the early 1990s were for information which it would seem reasonable to assume would be at hand; for instance, the number of judges with criminal convictions, how many statutory instruments had been laid before Parliament by the Lord Chancellor's Department, the number of complaints about the Solicitors Complaints Bureau (now the Office for the Supervision of Solicitors), which former MPs had been appointed to quangos by the Lord Chancellor since 1988, the waiting times in the courts, the number of barristers paid more than £200,000 from the legal aid fund, the number of complaints against the conduct of members of the judiciary, and details of the number of parliamentary questions.[42] Indeed, the LCD seemed not have acquired the habit of collecting and analysing statistics, no doubt not having felt the need previously to do so.

Since the Court Service Agency came into existence, much of the statistical information required forms the basis of standards and performance targets, and this has resulted in an improvement in the information available. Indeed, in the year 1996–7 the proportion of questions, which the minister declined to answer on grounds that the matter was not a responsibility of his department or was

---

[38] The figures for 1992–8 were as follows: 1992–3 fourteen disproportionate cost, twelve information not available, three were directed to the Home Office for answer; 1993–4 thirty-five disproportionate cost, eleven information not available; 1994–95 forty-two disproportionate cost (plus eight similarly classified by chief executive of CSA), sixteen information not available, one not the Lord Chancellor's responsibility; 1995–6 twenty-eight disproportionate cost (plus fifteen from CSA), five information not available; 1996–7 twenty-three disproportionate cost (plus seventeen from CSA), thirteen information not available; 1997–8 thirty-nine disproportionate cost, ten information not available.

[39] Two in 1992–3, two in 1994–5, six in 1995–6, one 1997–8.

[40] One in 1992–3.

[41] In 1994–5 fifty-three questions were answered by the Chief Executive, in 1995–6 103 and in 1996–7 eighty-two. NB. Recent Annual Reports of the Court Service Agency (e.g. (1998–9) HC 706), which are structured around performance indicators, do not give this information, as there is no PI for answering parliamentary questions.

[42] All the examples were from the period 1992–5 and the refusal was in all cases, except one, on grounds of disproportionate cost.

confidential, was lower than any other department.[43] These "blocking answers", which are recorded by the Table Office, prevent the same question being asked again for three months, unless there is a change in circumstances. The LCD therefore blocked fewer questions than most. It also performed comparatively well in fulfilling the requirement, which took effect from 1996, that any information withheld on grounds of confidentiality or responsibility should make reference to the relevant exemption of the Code of Practice on Access to Government Information 1994, which was intended to create a common set of standards for the disclosure of information. This has not always happened. Indeed, the Public Administration Committee noted in November 1999 that it continued "to be disappointed by this failure by many departments".[44]

As far as the Lord Chancellor's Department was concerned, there were only six questions during 1996–7, listed by the committee as "blocking questions", about which the Public Administration Committee sought explanation. They covered four topics. The first concerned military law and related to disciplinary proceedings being taken against an officer. Information had been denied on the basis of confidentiality,[45] but no code exemption was given at the time, although the LCD subsequently categorised the proceedings as being quasi-legal and so falling within Exemption 4, which concerns law enforcement and legal proceedings.[46] The second was a question concerning the tax treatment of members of the legal profession. This drew the response that it was "not appropriate to comment on any discussion that may have taken place within Government",[47] but again no reference was made to the Code. The LCD later justified the withholding of information with reference to Exemption 2, internal discussion and advice, and Exemption 6, effective management of the economy and collection of tax. On both occasions, the withholding of information would seem to have been justified and it seems that the failure to quote code exemptions was either an oversight or, more seriously, a lack of respect for Parliament – in this the LCD is no different from other departments.

The remaining two topics related to the closure of magistrates' courts, where two questions had not been answered on the grounds that "in the absence of appeal (against closure) the Lord Chancellor has no locus" and the "future of any magistrates' court is for the relevant Magistrates' Courts Committee to determine",[48] and the refurbishment of the Lord Chancellor's accommodation,

[43] In 1996–7 it was only 1.12 per cent compared with Environment and Transport nearly eight per cent, Department of Culture, Media and Sport nearly twenty per cent and Department of Trade and Industry nearly thirty per cent. (Figures from Public Administration Committee, Fourth Report, *Ministerial Accountability and Parliamentary Questions* (1997–98) HC 820.)

[44] Public Administration Committee, *Ministerial Accountability and Parliamentary Questions* (1998–99), HC 821, para. 10.

[45] H.C. Debs., 4 December 1997, col. 331 (Q. 19220).

[46] In Part II of the Code (Public Administration Committee, *Ministerial Accountability and Parliamentary Questions*, HC 821, Memorandum 11).

[47] H. C. Debs., 17 February 1998, col. 594 (Q. 28099).

[48] H. C. Debs., 17 June 1997, col. 111 (Q. 3725); H. C. Debs, 10 November 1997, col. 428 (Q. 14041).

where answers had been refused on the basis that this was a matter for "the Lords authorities especially the House of Lords' Offices Committee and sub-committees on Administration and Works and on Finance and Staff".[49] The Lord Chancellor's Department refused to accept that these were "blocking answers", noting in both cases that "there was no refusal to answer, and no withholding of information". In the case of the magistrates' courts the answers were a statement of the factual position. Where the Lord Chancellor's accommodation was concerned, they stated "correctly, that the responsibility for supplying the information requested lay elsewhere".[50]

However, the refusal to accept responsibility meant that further questions on a subject, about which many government backbenchers were concerned, were blocked and Members were unable to hold the Lord Chancellor to account, even through his junior minister. Moreover, while technically "correct", in that, as the Lord Chancellor's residence is in the House of Lords, its committees have to agree to work done on them, the Lord Chancellor had taken an active role in determining how the refurbishment should be carried out and the minutes of the Select Committee of the House of Lords' Offices recorded the expenditure as approved, "outside the current estimate".[51] In addition, although the decision was taken by the committee, it was on proposals put by Black Rod on behalf of the Lord Chancellor. Thus, while refurbishment may have been part of an ongoing programme, the detail of how it was to be done lay with Lord Irvine, as did the decision on the extent to which the public would have access to his residence to view the restoration. Lord Irvine's handling of the issue, through his junior minister, was therefore hardly a model of accountability[52] and the inability of elected Members to question the Lord Chancellor on this issue on the floor of the House increased antagonism towards him. He was seen by many Labour backbenchers to lack political judgment and to be damaging the Government.

There was also "a sense of unease that this is a very powerful public figure who is not elected".[53] As a result, a Commons Resolution was tabled by fifty Labour MPs, which called for the abolition of the office of Lord Chancellor and the establishment of a Justice Department under an elected Cabinet minister accountable to the Commons.[54] The early day motion, although eventually being signed by one hundred MPs, was unsuccessful but the hostility of government backbenchers towards the Lord Chancellor was such that the chairman of the Parliamentary Labour Party saw fit to invite Lord Irvine to its weekly meet-

---

[49] H. C. Debs., 19 February 1998, col. 850 (Question numbers 30232 and Q. 30460).

[50] Public Administration Committee, *Ministerial Accountability and Parliamentary Questions*, HC 821, Memorandum 11.

[51] July 22 1997.

[52] Moreover, while he was questioned in the House of Lords, the emphasis was different and there was general support for restoring his rooms to their former glory, thereby demonstrating the contrast between accountability to the House of Commons and to the Lords (see H. L. Debs., 22 July 1997).

[53] Robert Marshall Andrews QC, MP, *The Independent*, 12 March 1998.

[54] H. C. Debs., 11 March 1998, Early day motion 961.

ing in an attempt to repair the damage. Only a handful of peers usually attend and it is unusual for a peer to address the meeting and exceptional for a Lord Chancellor to do so.[55] Lord Irvine's decision to speak was therefore a recognition of a potentially serious situation and it is ironic that the Lord Chancellor, who justifies his position in the House of Lords on the basis of the need to be insulated from the political fray in the Commons, felt the need to appear before a party meeting. Such an appearance represented a limited accountability. However, accountability in private to the party in Parliament is no substitute for public accountability to the full House.

It is not only on matters concerning the Lord Chancellor's conduct that the House of Commons may be frustrated by his not being in the Chamber. Bills introduced there, rather than in the House of Lords, where the Lord Chancellor can be questioned in person, may likewise create problems for accountability. This was evident when the Supreme Court (Offices) Bill was introduced in the House of Commons, rather than in the Lords, "as one might have expected – if only because the political and legal head of the department concerned is the Lord Chancellor".[56] The Bill removed the requirement that the permanent secretary at the LCD should be either a barrister or solicitor of at least ten years' standing or have had at least five years in the LCD and was "the Lord Chancellor's cookie". Not unreasonably, therefore, MPs would "have liked to hear his explanations at the outset".[57] Instead, the dialogue was with the minister, Geoff Hoon. Moreover, the Bill was rushed through with all stages being taken in the same session on the basis that it was "a modest" Bill and merely "a technical adjustment to the machinery of government".[58] In fact, it needed to make quick progress so that the position of permanent secretary could be advertised forthwith.[59] This led to the comment; "It is a pernicious development when it is assumed that a Bill can be rubber-stamped by this House without a proper debate".[60] However, rubber-stamped it was, despite reservations from some MPs, one of whom expressed the hope that when "those in another place . . . read the report of this debate, [t]hey may well conclude that the Bill deserves more scrutiny and answers to the questions that were not answered in this House. Given that it is the Lord Chancellor's business, they may well take that opportunity. I hope that they do".[61] In the event they did, present and retired law lords, in particular, expressing concern about the constitutional

---

[55] Lord Carrington spoke to the Conservative Party group after the invasion of the Falklands but was unsuccessful in dispelling the anger of those present. Lord Irvine therefore followed in his steps, although, unlike Carrington, he continued in office, but then matters relating to a Lord Chancellor's accommodation are not in the same league as those concerned with the loss of territory.

[56] Grieve, MP, H. C. Debs., 6 November 1997, col. 424.

[57] Ibid.

[58] Hoon, col. 407.

[59] It is acceptable practice in such instances to advertise once a measure has been passed by the House of Commons.

[60] Grieve, col. 424.

[61] Forth, MP, col. 453.

implications of the measure.[62] But the arguments and concerns put forward, and the Lord Chancellor's explanations, could not inform the House of Commons debate, which had been undertaken in a vacuum.

APPEARANCES BEFORE SELECT COMMITTEES

One area where there has been considerable improvement in accountability is before parliamentary select committees. The LCD, like all government departments, has been accountable to the Public Accounts Committee (PAC) since the nineteenth century. The inquiries of the PAC, before whom the permanent secretary appears as Accounting Officer, are informed by the reports of the Comptroller and Auditor General and the National Audit Office, who conduct routine and "economy, effectiveness and efficiency" audits on all government departments.[63] Throughout the 1990s these reports were critical of the LCD's financial control over legal aid spending. Indeed, in 1999 for the ninth consecutive year, the National Audit Office failed to approve the accounts of the Department,[64] a failure for which the permanent secretary was required to account to the PAC.

Until 1991 the PAC was the only committee with jurisdiction to look at the operations of the LCD, Lord Hailsham having secured an exemption for his department, when the select committee system was reformed in 1979. Committees were established to shadow all government departments, except the LCD and the law officers, Lord Hailsham arguing that investigations into matters relating to the judiciary and the relationship between the judges and the Lord Chancellor would be a threat to judicial independence.[65] In 1991 on a recommendation from the Liaison Committee, the House of Commons passed a motion that the Home Affairs Committee's terms of reference should be extended to enable it to inquire into "the policy, administration and expenditure of the Lord Chancellor's department"[66] or, as Sir John Wheeler, chair of the committee stated; "to look at policy and the expenditure and quality of the service which flows from the various responsibilities [of the] Lord Chancellor".[67] However, given that the select committee also undertakes inquiries into the many responsibilities of the Home Office, it is not surprising if its scrutiny of the LCD is patchy and, according to its chairman in 1997, inadequate.[68] There is

---

[62] See Chapter Three.

[63] National Audit Act 1983.

[64] National Audit Office, *Appropriation Accounts* (1998–9) Vol. 8: Class VIII, "Lord Chancellor's and Law Officers' Departments", HC 11.

[65] See H. C. Debs., 25 June 1979, col. 35 and Lord St John of Fawsey in evidence to Select Committee on Procedure, *The Working of the Select Committee System* (1989–90), HC 19-II, para. 742.

[66] 18 July 1991. Its terms of reference were also extended to include the law officers.

[67] Home Affairs Committee, *The Work of the Lord Chancellor's Department*, HC 214, Chairman's opening address.

[68] Liaison Committee, *The Work of Select Committees* (1996–97) HC 323-I, p. 46.

also a potential problem in that the Lord Chancellor, as a member of the House of Lords, only appears before a Commons committee as a favour. Should he refuse to attend, the committee cannot seek a resolution of Parliament ordering him to do so, as this would be a breach of the privileges of the House of Lords. Such a situation has not arisen, and may not do so. Nevertheless, it again emphasises the insulation of the Lord Chancellor from the accountability process.

The first formal session with a Lord Chancellor, which related to his responsibilities, was held by the Home Affairs Select Committee in 1992, not long after Lord Mackay's appointment of a junior minister to represent him in the House of Commons.[69] Concern that the committee, whose members included two JPs (Wheeler and Woodcock) and two practising members of the Bar (Ashby and Bermingham), might be deferential and concerned to protect the sensitivities of their witness was largely ill-founded. Indeed, Lord Mackay was chided by the chairman, Sir John Wheeler, for not having statistics available on the frequency with which the courts exercise their discretion to allow small companies to represent themselves. He noted; "This serves to illustrate one point; the appointment of a Minister in the Commons will give rise to frequent questions which seek factual information of this kind. I am sure your Department would be well advised to provide the detail of the information which is likely to flow both from the appointment of a Minister and also the work of this Committee on issues of this kind".[70]

Lord Irvine's first appearance before a select committee was less than auspicious. He was requested to appear before the Public Administration Committee, during its 1997–8 session, to give evidence on the Government's constitutional reform programme. However, the session coincided with news of the refurbishment of his apartment and MPs used the opportunity to question him on this matter. His response, which included ill-conceived remarks about the quality of wallpaper sold by DIY stores, did little to endear him to members of the committee[71] and provided the press with considerable ammunition . However, he seemed to learn some important lessons, because when he subsequently appeared before the Home Affairs Select Committee, he gave "an accomplished performance", in which he "fielded questions comfortably, defused potential conflict by admitting to changes in heart, and mastered even the odd 'googly' – his word – with ease".[72]

---

[69] Lord Chancellors had given evidence to select committees before e.g. Lord Hailsham gave evidence to the Home Affairs Committee's inquiry into the Prison Service (Fourth Report, *The Prison Service* (1980–81) HC 412-II) and to the Committee on the Parliamentary Commissioner for Administration (*Report of the Parliamentary Commissioner for Administration* (1986–87) HC 284-ii). Lord Mackay also gave evidence to the Committee on the PCA (*Report of the Parliamentary Commissioner for Administration* (1988–89) HC 159-ii).

[70] Home Affairs Committee, *The Work of the Lord Chancellor's Department*, HC 214-II, Q. 50.

[71] Public Administration Committee, *Your Right to Know: The Government's Proposals for a Freedom of Information Act* (1997–8) HC 398–v.

[72] *The Times*, 9 November 1998.

Nevertheless, he had to be reminded that it was not for him to determine the limits of the committee's inquiry, when, in response to a question about a particular judge, he replied; "I really have to put on the record . . . that the remit of the Home Affairs Committee does exclude from it consideration of individual cases".[73] The question concerned a judge whose removal from a case after allegations of bias or the appearance of bias had been at the instigation of the prosecuting authority and Lord Irvine went on to confirm that any application for the removal of a judge should be in open court or before a judge in chambers. However, this did not prevent the point being made by the committee that while "broadly speaking" individual cases were excluded, "that does not alter the fact that if we believe it necessary to pursue a particular matter arising from a complaint, it is up to the Committee. We are our own master fortunately in how we go about our business, subject only to the Chamber of the House of Commons".[74] The problem for the committee is that it has no power to insist on answers to its questions from the Lord Chancellor, not even if it has the support of the full House.

In fact, while a Lord Chancellor's appearances before a select committee may make the headlines, it is the routine accountability of his Department, which is most significant. Under the Courts and Legal Services Act 1990, the Court Service is required to provide an annual report to be "laid before Parliament by the Lord High Chancellor pursuant to Section 1(12)". This, along with the LCD's Annual Report and Strategic Plan, forms part of the agenda for the accountability of the LCD to the Home Affairs Committee. However, the Committee has not always been successful in extracting the information it required. In the early days of accountability to the committee, this was largely because of a failure of the Department to collect and collate the necessary statistics. For instance, when asked about the cost and impact upon the courts of the failure of Group 4 to properly carry out their contract, with "prisoners escaping and vans arriving late",[75] an official from the Court Service did not know; there was no mechanism for judges to report back or for the collection and collation of information. All he could say was that "if the courts were seriously disrupted we would hear".[76] Similarly, when the permanent secretary, Sir Thomas Legg, was questioned on whether the LCD had received direct representations from magistrates dissatisfied with some of the provisions within the Criminal Justice Act, he responded "No, not I think in that sense, representations, no. I cannot say that we have received none. If we had, I have to say, we would have passed them to the Home Office".[77] He added that he was aware of dissatisfaction through the press and informal contacts but as there had not

[73] Home Affairs Committee, *The Work of the Lord Chancellor's Department* (1998–99) HC 882, Q. 95.
[74] Ibid, Q. 96.
[75] Home Affairs Committee, *Lord Chancellor's Department: Annual Report* (1992–3) HC 655-I, Q. 14.
[76] Q.16.
[77] Ibid, Q. 50.

been an "unusually large" number of resignations, it was not worth finding out if these were because of the Act or for other reasons. His response led to the accusation that he had a "laid-back" attitude to "something about which Members of Parliament . . ., on both sides of the House, feel very strongly".[78] His answers were also criticised for showing "a certain degree of complacency",[79] given that the Magistrates' Association had identified at least thirty resignations.

The committee was not only frustrated by the lack of information on this issue but also by the permanent secretary adhering strictly to the rules relating to ministerial responsibility. Thus when first asked about the resignation of magistrates, Sir Thomas replied; "I do not at all wish to pass the buck or try to wriggle off the hook . . .but the Criminal Justice Act is very much within the sphere of responsibility of the Home Secretary".[80] This was correct but the Lord Chancellor is answerable for the appointment of magistrates and their departure from office. Subsequently, when asked if the Lord Chancellor, through his Department, had made representations to the Home Office on the issues upsetting magistrates, Sir Thomas' response was likewise couched in terms of ministerial responsibility and the Osmotherly Rules, which restrict what officials can say.[81] He replied; "I do not in the least wish to seem unhelpful, but the way you frame your questions puts me in a slight difficulty . . . The Criminal Justice Act is the responsibility not of the Lord Chancellor but of the Home Secretary on this matter. As I am sure the Committee is well aware, it is difficult for me or for any official to say more on a subject such as the one you have raised than that consultation between Departments runs throughout the whole fabric of Government and that we do it all the time".[82] Moreover, the "slight difficulty" became a "real difficulty" when he was asked "not . . . what the Home Office is going to do" but "what you have done".[83] No reply was forthcoming.

The Home Office was also cited as the responsible department with regard to Group Four contracts[84] and other agencies were also used to disclaim responsibility. Thus issues concerning fraud trials were for the Serious Fraud Office and those concerning witnesses were for the police, although the length of time witnesses have to spend waiting in court seems likely to be affected by the listing of

---

[78] Barbara Roche, MP, Ibid., Q. 51.

[79] Mike O'Brien MP, Ibid, Q. 55.

[80] Ibid, Q. 48.

[81] These are issued by the Cabinet Office and since 1997 have officially been entitled, *Departmental Evidence and Response to Select Committees.* Prior to that they were entitled, *A Memorandum of Guidance for Officials appearing before Select Committees* and the title "Osmotherly Rules" came from the official who issued the 1980 edition. The Rules direct civil servants to be as forthcoming and helpful as possible to select committees but also list the categories of questions they should not answer. These include advice given to ministers and consultation and discussion within government. They are also told "to avoid being drawn into discussion of the merits of alternative policies where this is politically contentious".

[82] Home Affairs Committee, *Lord Chancellor's Department; Annual Report* (1992–3), HC 655-i, Q. 55.

[83] Ibid, Q. 56.

[84] Ibid, Q. 14.

cases, a responsibility of the Court Service, and the conditions in which they are required to wait is totally within its remit. Information was further restricted on the grounds of commercial confidentiality. When asked about savings made by market testing, an official stated; "the early indications from bids that I have seen, but would prefer not to discuss because there is commercial confidentiality here and we have not yet had the board, indicate that the savings could be quite substantial".[85] There was also some stonewalling by Sir Thomas Legg when the award of contracts for court shorthand writers was raised. This had resulted in an application in the High Court for judicial review (the details of which are discussed later in the chapter) and Lord Justice Rose, although refusing the application, had described the process by which the contracts had been awarded as unfair. He asked; "Is one not entitled to expect a higher standard of conduct from a Government Department than from a second-hand car salesman?".[86] When questioned on the matter, Sir Thomas stated that the Department would "examine the procedure which we adopted and . . . if we find that there is any way in which the procedure was unfair and should be changed, we will change it for future occasions".[87] However, he did not accept that it was unfair. Nor would he answer directly questions about the effectiveness of the contracts, which were awarded, stating that he did not have their detailed history at the moment.[88]

During the Home Affairs Committee's inquiry into judicial appointments, Sir Thomas also had difficulties with some of the questions, notably those relating to the role of the Prime Minister in appointments. When asked whether the Prime Minister has a veto over senior judicial appointments, whether he is given a list and invited to choose, and whether the Lord Chancellor makes his preference clear, he replied; "I feel in difficulty as a civil servant about answering a question about the procedure which operates between two Ministers . . . on matters which really are their responsibility".[89] As is the case generally with officials appearing before select committees, civil servants from the LCD have been concerned not to step over the boundary between administration and policy. This was evident in the context of questions on legal aid when they were asked about the "ill-advised" proposal that even those on social security would be expected to make a contribution to legal aid,[90] an official from the LCD responding, "I think we are shading into an area of policy making rather than mere administration".[91] In this instance he, nevertheless, addressed the question.

---

[85] Home Affairs Committee, *Lord Chancellor's Department; Annual Report* (1992–3), HC 655-i, Q. 25.
[86] Ibid, Q. 26.
[87] Ibid.
[88] Ibid, Qs 27 and 28.
[89] Home Affairs Committee, *Judicial Appointments Procedures*, HC 52-II, Q. 67.
[90] Home Affairs Committee, *Lord Chancellor's Department; Annual Report* (1995–6) HC 596-I, Q. 94.
[91] Ibid, Q. 95.

More recent reports do not demonstrate the same tension between the LCD and the select committee, evident in the inquiries cited above. The LCD has no doubt become more familiar with the process and with the expectations of the committee, and the changed culture within the Department makes the giving of information more routine than previously. However, perhaps the most important development has been the move to a more structured accountability process across government which, where routine select committee inquiries are concerned, centres on departmental strategic and business plans and annual reports. The LCD, in common with all government departments, therefore has considerable control over the accountability agenda, which tends to sideline delicate issues of policy and policy choices and concentrates on monitoring operational progress against targets.

THE COURT SERVICE AGENCY

The accountability of the LCD changed with the creation of Court Service Agency on 3 April 1995. The Framework Document, which set up the agency, is couched in the same terms as other such documents. It therefore asserts that the Lord Chancellor remains accountable to Parliament for the Court Service and that the chief executive has delegated responsibility for its day to day management. Moreover, although the Lord Chancellor expects "to be consulted by the chief executive on the handling of operational matters, which could give rise to substantial public, Parliamentary or judicial concern", he "will not normally intervene" in the Agency, the Chief Executive being directly accountable to him for its "effective, efficient and economic management". As is the case with all agencies, MPs are encouraged to write to the chief executive about matters concerning the operation of the agency[92] and Parliamentary questions are also redirected to him, where appropriate (see above). In addition, the chief executive is designated agency accounting officer and is "responsible for ensuring that proper procedures are followed to ensure the propriety and regularity of expenditure of the Court Service. He must ensure that funds for which he is responsible are properly managed". Both the permanent secretary and the chief executive may be summoned to appear before the Public Accounts Committee, concerning their respective accounting officer responsibilities. However, "it will be for the Lord Chancellor to decide who should appear before hearings of the Home Affairs Select Committee", although "where the subject of the hearing is the day to day operation of the Court Service, he will normally invite the Chief Executive to attend".

In theory, therefore, the Lord Chancellor could refuse to allow the chief executive to give evidence. Moreover, despite attempts by select committees to

---

[92] In 1996–7 the chief executive dealt with 1,156 letters from MPs, compared with 1,337 in 1995–6.

secure a change in the rules,[93] the position remains, as with all agencies, that the chief executive does not speak on his own behalf but on behalf of the minister. Thus a chief executive, under fire from a committee, may be unable to defend himself adequately. He would not be able to blame bad policy or constant policy changes for operational failings nor draw attention to extensive ministerial interference within the agency. He could therefore be held responsible for errors or misjudgments, which more appropriately lay with the minister.[94] There is no evidence so far to suggest that this has inhibited the accountability of the Court Service Agency to the select committee, nor has the fear of critics that the move to agency status would distance the LCD from parliamentary scrutiny been realised.[95] Both LCD and Court Service Agency would seem to be more accountable to Parliament through the select committee than previously. However, this does not alter the fact that the chief executive, as well as departmental officials, is constrained in what he can say and that accountability could be frustrated by ministerial instructions not to answer specific questions. Nor does it remove the possibility that, should the agency become the subject of political controversy, the Lord Chancellor would insist that the fault was operational and thus the responsibility of the chief executive, rather than related to policy and, as a consequence, a matter for him.[96]

Where agencies are concerned, there is also a tendency for the Government to define accountability in terms of its management objectives. In the 1995 Framework Document of the Court Service Agency, Lord Mackay stated; "I shall continue to set challenging targets for the Court Service. These will be published in the agency's annual Business Plan. The Court Service will continue to report each year to Parliament and the public on its performance against those targets". This process has continued and annual reports centre on progress against quantifiable performance targets and strategic tasks, set out in the three year Court Service Plan. One such strategic task is "to strengthen consultation and co-operation with other criminal justice agencies and the judiciary". This includes developing "IT multilaterally with other criminal justice agencies", and the actions related to that for 1998–9 were to "ensure that the needs of other agencies are considered in developing new IT systems" and "through Co-ordination of Computerisation in the Criminal Justice System [to] increase the

[93] e.g. Public Service Committee, Second Report, *Ministerial Accountability and Responsibility* (1995–6) HC 313.

[94] As Derek Lewis, Chief Executive of the Prison Service, was. Lewis was dismissed from his position after a number of breaches in prison security on the basis that the errors were operational. Lewis, however, maintained that the Home Secretary, Michael Howard, had constantly interfered in the operation of the agency and thus could not distance himself from responsibility. (See D. Lewis, *Hidden Agendas* (London, Hamish Hamilton, 1996).

[95] See (1997) 139 *Solicitors' Journal* 13, p. 307.

[96] Some agencies, such as the Prison Service Agency, are always likely to be in the political spotlight. However, even agencies concerned with routine administrative matters may become politically controversial, as the Passport Agency discovered in the summer of 1999, when public confidence was lost in its ability to cope with a backlog of passport applications. (See Home Affairs Committee, *Home Office Annual Report 1998–99* (1999–2000) HC 653).

number of electronic links for transfer of information".[97] However, if the select committee accepts the Government's agenda for accountability and confines itself to questioning the Court Service on progress against its targets, it does little more than act as a mechanism for managerial accountability with broader questions about whether these are the right targets being ignored. Thus while transparency has undoubtedly improved, constitutional accountability may have been sidelined, the Home Affairs Committee lacking the time, and possibly the inclination, to undertake investigations into particular aspects of the Court Service's work, thereby confining itself to monitoring performance.

AN UNCERTAIN DIVISION OF RESPONSIBILITIES

A further problem for accountability is the sometime uncertain division and overlap of responsibilities between the Home Office and the LCD. This ensures that there is always friction between the Home Secretary and the Lord Chancellor. Even "Lord Mackay, who was the sweetest of men, had some serious run-ins with Michael Howard"[98] and the relationship between Irvine and Straw is known to have been difficult. As far as the LCD is concerned; "It's a difficult split of responsibilities . . . The same problem always came up: it was the Lord Chancellor's Department that took the rap for things going wrong in the justice system, because, inevitably, the buck stopped with the judge appointed by the Lord Chancellor, sitting in a court administered by the Lord Chancellor, funded very often by legal aid administered by the Lord Chancellor".[99] The other side of the coin is, of course, that the Home Secretary's policies can, at times, be frustrated by failures within the court system and by the judges themselves. It is inevitable, therefore, that there is a degree of shifting the blame between the two departments, which can create problems for accountability. Prior to 1993, this was exacerbated by the split in ministerial responsibility for magistrates, by which the Lord Chancellor was responsible for their appointment and the Home Office for the running of the magistrates' courts. This produced uncertainties and was a particularly unsatisfactory situation, given that the Lord Chancellor was responsible for the rest of the court system. It was resolved when Lord Mackay assumed total ministerial responsibility for magistrates. Yet problems may still arise over the split in responsibilities between the Lord Chancellor and the local magistrates' committees.

Law reform is another area where responsibilities are theoretically divided, the Lord Chancellor being responsible for the reform of the civil law and the Home Secretary for criminal law reform. But, as Lord Gardiner observed; "The line is not clear". He noted; "when as a Junior Counsel at the Bar I found some

[97] The Court Service Plan 1998–2001.
[98] Sheila Thompson, ex Information Officer at the LCD, quoted in D. Egan, *Irvine: Politically Correct?*, p. 135.
[99] Ibid.

obvious defective criminal law, I wrote to the Lord Chancellor about it and he said it was a matter for the Home Secretary. I wrote to the Home Secretary and he said it was a matter for the Lord Chancellor . . . Somewhere between the Lord Chancellor's Office and the Home Office is a large hole where projects for the reform of our criminal law lie deeply rooted".[100] His experience as Lord Chancellor did little to alter his view.

Lord Hailsham, similarly, saw "the fragmentation of policy within government",[101] as an obstacle to law reform. It meant that responsibility for the reform of the criminal law was uncertain. He believed that the initiative for all law reform should lie with the Lord Chancellor but was unsuccessful in consolidating responsibility within his office. He subsequently blamed the Home Office for the non-implementation of the first part of a criminal code produced by the Law Commission in 1985 and, by so doing, demonstrated the underlying problem when the Law Commission, which is accountable to the Lord Chancellor and, in theory, is confined to civil law matters, extends its remit to aspects of criminal law. Thus the Lord Chancellor finds himself having to push for criminal law reform when this should be the responsibility of the Home Secretary. In addition, to confuse matters further, individual departments are responsible for the reform of the law within the areas of their responsibility. It therefore becomes difficult to determine who should be held to account for inadequacies in the law.

The effect of this opaque division of responsibilities is that it may not be easy for select committees and others to know where to direct their questions and to secure the information they require. This was evident when the chairman of the Home Affairs Select Committee sought to find out if any work had been done to determine the cost savings, which might be made by codifying the criminal law. The permanent secretary, Sir Thomas Legg, replied; "this subject is one in which the responsibility lies with the Home Secretary and not with the Lord Chancellor, because the Home Secretary is responsible for the criminal law".[102] He did, however, state that he believed that the LCD was planning to do some joint work with the Home Office. A further problem, which arises from the Lord Chancellor having responsibility for law reform, is that "any pressure which there might be in the House of Commons for law reform cannot be brought to bear on a minister with overall responsibility for it . . . the Lord Chancellor is beyond the influence of MPs".[103] This may be less true today, when the Lord Chancellor has a junior minister in the lower chamber, but he is, nevertheless, personally removed from such pressures and while junior ministers may inform him of the issues and advise him on a course of action, they have no authority to do more.

---

[100] M. Box, *Rebel Advocate; a Biography of Gerald Gardiner*, p. 174.
[101] G. Lewis, *Lord Hailsham*, p. 305.
[102] Home Affairs Committee, *Lord Chancellor's Department: Annual Report* (1994–95) HC 399.
[103] R. Brazier, "Government and the Law", p. 70.

Not all problems of uncertain responsibility have related to law reform. In the final years of the twentieth century they also arose over constitutional reform. This was apparent from Lord Irvine's evidence in 1998 to the Committee on Public Administration, in which he noted that while he chaired the Cabinet committees on Devolution, Freedom of Information and the Human Rights Bill, he did not have ministerial responsibility for the reforms. Thus although he took the Human Rights Bill through its House of Lords stages, he was "not the minister responsible for the Bill or for the development of policy". Indeed, he pointed out that "the team of civil servants who worked with me in connection with the taking of that Bill through the House of Lords stages were Home Office civil servants".[104] As a result, the questions he was prepared to answer were limited. He was "very, very happy to give . . . as much assistance as [he could], but arising exclusively out of [his] Chairmanship of Cabinet Committees", where his "responsibility was to get basic policy to bed through the Committees" and "without Ministerial responsibility".[105] While this openness relating to Cabinet responsibilities was refreshing, it could have led to lines being artificially drawn to avoid awkward questions. There was no indication of Lord Irvine seeking to do so. He was, for instance, unable to answer why it was that, under Clause 79 of the Government of Wales Bill, Members of the Assembly in Wales had been made subject to the Official Secrets Act but undertook to write to the committee on the matter. He subsequently wrote; "In the case of Clause 79 of the Government of Wales Bill the responsibility rests with Ron Davies, the Secretary of State for Wales. None-the-less I would be happy to have written to you but, having spoken to Ron Davies, I think it would be better for an explanation on this subject to come from him".[106] He noted that he was sending a copy of his letter to Ron Davies.

As far as the White Paper on the Freedom of Information Bill was concerned, Lord Irvine refused to take total credit for its proposals, which suggested a more liberal Bill than had been expected.[107] Being perhaps uncharacteristically modest, he stated; "I would not take away credit from the Chancellor of the Duchy of Lancaster. There is no doubt that as the Minister responsible he has at least an equal entitlement to the credit for it and really more as the responsible Minister".[108] However, he refused to be drawn on Home Office opposition, commenting; "The position is that many Cabinet Ministers were represented on this Committee and what emerged is the view of us all and you cannot expect me to discuss the give and take of discussion within a Cabinet Committee".[109]

---

[104] Public Administration Committee, *Your Right to Know: The Government's Proposals for a Freedom of Information Act*, HC 398–v, Q. 290.

[105] Ibid, Q. 292.

[106] Ibid, Appendix 3.

[107] The Government subsequently retreated from the liberal approach of the White Paper.

[108] Public Administration Committee, *Your Right to Know: The Government's Proposals for a Freedom of Information Act*, HC 398-v, Q. 386.

[109] Ibid, Q. 287.

The traditional position, inherent in the convention of collective responsibility, was therefore maintained.

Similarly, when questioned about whether the committee had started examining House of Lords reform, beyond the abolition of hereditary peers, he replied; "Obviously I shall not tell you about Cabinet papers, but of course we are looking not merely at the issue of the removal of the rights of hereditaries but we are also looking at all issues which are relevant to a reformed and more representative upper house".[110] Lord Irvine was pressed about consultation with the other political parties over the reform of the House of Lords and while saying, "we do not exclude discussions with the other parties at an appropriate time",[111] he gave the impression that no such consultations had taken place. Indeed he told the committee "I think there is unanimity in the country that the rights of hereditaries must go. That is the position of my Party, . . . the Liberal Democrats and, as I read the puffs of smoke emerging from the Conservative Party, they have given up as a lost cause the defence of the rights of hereditaries so I have the impression that there is no subject there to consult anybody about because everybody agrees that the hereditaries" rights are bizarre and have to go".[112] He was subsequently accused of misleading the committee over consultation, when it emerged the following day that Lord Richard, Leader of the Lords, and Lord Carter, Chief Whip, had held two meetings with their counterparts, Viscount Cranborne and Lord Strathclyde. The chairman of the Public Administration Committee, Rhodri Morgan, stated that it was "not satisfactory if he is telling us one thing when something else is happening" and he therefore wrote to Lord Irvine to "seek clarification".[113]

The accountability of the Lord Chancellor is therefore limited by collective responsibility, with its emphasis on confidentiality or secrecy, and by political and pragmatic considerations. In this it is no different from the accountability of other ministers. The limitations which arise as a consequence of an uncertain division of responsibilities are, however, specific to the Lord Chancellor and in a system which centres on political accountability, are less than satisfactory.

ACCOUNTABILITY TO THE COURTS

While accountability to Parliament, through the convention of ministerial responsibility, dominates, the Lord Chancellor is also accountable to the courts. Moreover, his responsibility for the courts means that actions in negligence are brought against him, "as the sole judge appointed *durante bene placito*".[114] In exceptional circumstances it is the Lord Chancellor who would have to resign. On

---

[110] Ibid, Q. 425.
[111] Ibid, Q. 435.
[112] Ibid, Q. 426.
[113] *The Times*, 21 March 1998.
[114] Lord Hailsham, "The Office of Lord Chancellor and the Separation of Powers", p. 315.

occasions he may have to bear the brunt of a dissatisfied litigant, who seeks to find someone to blame for his or her legal failure. Such was the case in 1999 when a tenant, unhappy with the way in which a dispute between himself and his landlady had been resolved by the courts, sued the Lord Chancellor, the Master of the Rolls and others for wrongs, including lying and dishonesty, committed against him while they were carrying out their official duties. The action was unsuccessful.[115]

However, the main form of accountability to the courts is through judicial review. The Lord Chancellor, like all judges, is subject to judicial review of decisions made in his judicial capacity. One of the most famous cases, concerning a Lord Chancellor, was the nineteenth century case of *Dimes* v. *Grand Union Canal*,[116] where Lord Cottenham had sat as judge in a case in which one of the parties was the Grand Union Canal, a company in which he had shares. His decision was quashed by the House of Lords for bias and the case remains a precedent for automatic disqualification on grounds of pecuniary interest. The Lord Chancellor is also subject to judicial review for the exercise of his powers relating to the regulation and disposal of judges. Once more a case from the mid-nineteenth century provides a precedent, Chief Justice Campbell holding in 1852 that the Lord Chancellor's power to remove a county court judge was "subject to the control of this Court" and that relief would be given if he had acted outside his powers or contrary to the rules of natural justice. This meant that an applicant might have redress if he had received no notice of the charges against him, had been given no opportunity to be heard, there was no evidence to support the charges, or if the complaints against him were not for "inability or misbehaviour in his office, and were of such a nature that, if proved or admitted, they could not disqualify him for his office, or amount to inability or misbehaviour, within the meaning of the Act of Parliament".[117]

A century later the control of the court over dismissal decisions was tested when for the first time a magistrate sought judicial review of the Lord Chancellor's decision to dismiss her from the Bench for "inability or misbehaviour". The magistrate, a member of CND, had taken part in a demonstration outside the court, in which she sat, and she refused to promise not to do so again. The Magistrates' Advisory Committee found that her conduct had caused damage to the integrity and impartiality of the magistracy and referred the decision to the Lord Chancellor, who dismissed her. Her application for leave was refused on the grounds that there had been evidence to dismiss her, the Lord Chancellor had considered the relevant factors and the rules of natural justice had not been infringed.[118]

In *ex parte Stockler*[119] the decision the applicant sought to challenge related to the Lord Chancellor's authorisation of a retired High Court judge to continue

---

[115] *Krasucki* v. *Lord Chancellor* CA (26 March 1999, unreported).

[116] (1852) 3 HL Cases 759.

[117] *ex parte Ramshay* 18 QB 173, 189–90 (1852) in D. Pannick, *The Judges*, pp. 91–2 and S. Shetreet, *Judges on Trial*, p. 88.

[118] *R* v. *Lord Chancellor, ex parte Cripps* (24 September 1985, unreported).

[119] *R* v. *Lord Chancellor, ex parte Stockler* [1996] *The Times*, 7 May.

sitting in a case beyond his seventy-fifth birthday. There was no question about the authorisation given to the judge, Sir Mervyn Davies, at the start of the case in January 1995. At that time the Supreme Court Act 1981, section 9, made provision for High Court judges to sit after the age of seventy-five, when they were requested to do so by the Lord Chancellor or an official delegated with that power. However, on 31 March, before the case was finished, the Judicial Pensions and Retirement Act 1993 came into effect, which amended section 9, removing the power of authorisation and prohibiting a judge from sitting beyond his seventy-fifth birthday. To prevent uncertainty about Sir Mervyn's position, if he was still hearing the case when the Act took effect, he had received a further letter on 28 March, which had invited him to sit "until such time as you conclude the two current part heard cases . . . [including] any period on which you return to deliver any reserved judgment". Stockler argued that this authority had no lawful basis and, as a consequence, the decision of the judge was void for lack of jurisdiction. However, the Court of Appeal, which saw the case as having a "startling lack of merit", dismissed this argument on the grounds that there was provision within the Act[120] for a judge to continue sitting in such circumstances.

The Lord Chancellor's decision on the disposal of judicial manpower was also challenged when a High Court judge, who had been promoted to the Court of Appeal, refused to deal with further charges against a defendant on the grounds that he had no jurisdiction to do so. The judge had been appointed to preside over a complex fraud trial in the Crown Court, and, at a preparatory hearing, had ordered that the counts in the indictment should be severed, with only two of the ten charges being heard initially. The defendants were acquitted on these two counts, whereupon the prosecution stated its intention of proceeding with the trial on the remaining counts. The judge, who, after his promotion to the Court of Appeal, had been requested to continue with the first trial by the Lord Chancellor,[121] received no further request and the defendants applied for judicial review of the Lord Chancellor's decision not to request him to continue sitting, on the grounds, *inter alia*, that it was irrational.

The application was dismissed, the court holding that when "considering whether to request the judge to deal with the remaining counts in the indictment the Lord Chancellor had to decide on the best disposal of judicial manpower for the proper administration of justice and had to balance the contribution the judge could make in the trial of those counts against his broader contribution in the Court of Appeal and the wider interests in having a Court of Appeal up to full strength at a critical time. That balance, and the weight to be given to various aspects of the process, were matters for the Lord Chancellor and not the court. Since the Lord Chancellor had approached the matter correctly and reached a decision within the discretion accorded to him, the contention that his

---

[120] Section 27(1).
[121] Power under s. 9(1) Supreme Court Act 1981.

decision was irrational was unsustainable". Moreover, while the court accepted that in theory the Lord Chancellor's discretion in such matters was open to challenge by way of judicial review, it noted that "realistically most such challenges were doomed to failure" and, as a consequence, "should be discouraged and so critically examined at the leave stage".[122]

Indeed, it seems unlikely that any challenge of the Lord Chancellor's powers, which relate to the appointment, disciplining or disposition of judges, will succeed, unless he has acted outside the terms of a relevant statute or infringed the rules of natural justice. However, two Roman Catholic barristers in Northern Ireland were successful in their challenge of the Lord Chancellor's decision that they must declare that they would "well and truly serve Queen Elizabeth II" before they could become QCs. The High Court in Belfast ruled that his decision was based on a mistaken belief that Northern Ireland judges were in favour of keeping the declaration. In fact, they had not expressed a view on a Bar report, which recommended the dropping of the reference to the Queen.[123]

The Lord Chancellor is, of course, subject to judicial review of all his statutory powers, including his powers of regulation of the legal profession, the granting of rights of audience, and his power to determine fees for legal aid work. It was the exercise of this last power, which was challenged by the Bar Council in 1986. Under the Legal Aid Act 1974, the Lord Chancellor had made regulations, which set the scale of fees for legally aided defence work. The Act required him to have regard for the principle of allowing "fair remuneration for work actually and reasonably done". There was no provision which required him to have regard for the size of the public purse, but there was a practical limitation, imposed by the Treasury, on any increase in the scale of fees imposed by the Treasury. The Lord Chancellor, Lord Hailsham, therefore found himself unable to increase the fees in line with the recommendations made by management consultants, employed to conduct a review of payment for legally aided defence work, or even to use the recommendations as a starting point for negotiations, as the Bar believed he had promised to do. He was only able to offer a five per cent rise, which was in line with inflation and which barristers considered totally inadequate.

As a consequence, the Bar sought an application for judicial review of the Lord Chancellor's decision on the grounds that he had made no attempt to provide "fair remuneration for work actually and reasonably done", as the Act required, and that he had created a legitimate expectation of proper negotiations, which he had failed to fulfil. It soon became apparent that, if the case continued, the court would find the Lord Chancellor had acted unlawfully and Lord Lane, who was hearing the case with two other judges, "gave a broad hint that the litigants should sit down together outside Court and agree a timetable for further discussions. The hint was taken, a timetable was agreed and the case

[122] R v. *Lord Chancellor, ex parte Maxwell* [1996] 4 All ER 751; [1997] 1 WLR 104.
[123] *The Times*, 5 May 2000.

brought to an end".[124] However, an order for costs was made against the Lord Chancellor and, at a time when judicial review applications against government ministers were rare, he had to endure headlines, which read; "The Lord Chancellor in the Dock", together with the judgment that his "handling of the affair had done his reputation for ministerial competence harm that will not easily be mended".[125] Shortly after this incident, the Legal Aid Act 1988 altered the provisions for the remuneration of legal aid work to include the requirement that regard must be had to the cost to public funds and that regulations must be subject to the consent of the Treasury.[126]

In 1993 a different Lord Chancellor, Lord Mackay, also faced a challenge related to legal aid, this time by the Law Society. The Law Society claimed, *inter alia*, that the regulations made by the Lord Chancellor under the Legal Aid Act 1988 were, first, unlawful, in that they frustrated rather than promoted the purposes of the Act, secondly, unreasonable, and, thirdly, that they had been made without proper consultation with the Law Society, which had a right, or at least a legitimate expectation, to be consulted. The Law Society was less successful than the Bar had been, the court accepting that it had a legitimate expectation but, nevertheless, refusing to give relief.[127] It similarly dismissed an application, which sought to use remarks made by the Lord Chancellor in the House of Lords to challenge the proposals on grounds of unreasonableness or irrationality,[128] and a subsequent challenge of Lord Irvine's legal aid policy, as being contrary to the European Convention on Human Rights, was likewise unsuccessful.[129]

One of the few successful legal actions against a Lord Chancellor concerned Lord Mackay's policy on court fees. In 1996 in pursuit of the Government's aim of making the civil court system pay for itself, he made an order, which not only increased court fees, but removed the exemption from such charges for those on income support. As a result, Mr Witham was unable to bring an action in defamation against an insurance company and in the subsequent judicial review action brought by him, Mr Justice Laws considered this to be a denial of justice and the removal of a constitutional right of such importance that it could only be achieved through primary legislation. Section 130 of the Supreme Court Act, under which the regulations were made, contained "nothing to alert the reader to any possibility that fees might be imposed in circumstances such as to deny absolutely the citizen's right of access to the Queen's courts" and the High Court therefore held the order to be unlawful.[130]

---

[124] G. Lewis, *Lord Hailsham*, p. 301.

[125] *The Times*, 27 March 1986.

[126] Legal Aid Act 1988, s.34.

[127] *R v.Lord Chancellor, ex parte the Law Society* [1993] *The Independent*, 22 June; [1993] *The Times*, 25 June.

[128] *R v. Lord Chancellor, ex parte Edey*, CA (2 July 1993, unreported).

[129] February 2000.

[130] *R v. Lord Chancellor, ex parte Witham* [1998] QB 575; [1997] 2 All ER 779; [1998] 2 WLR 849.

After the judgment, Lord Mackay expressed his concern "about the potential injustice where litigants in person, who are exempted or remitted from court fees, bring unjustified actions against defendants who must then pay to defend themselves with no prospect of recovering their costs". However, he did not ask leave of the Court of Appeal to appeal and pledged to reimburse the cost of the court fees to anyone who could show that they would have qualified for exemption under the rules previously. *Witham* looked as if it might open the floodgates to a range of challenges of court fees. This has not been the case and a subsequent challenge of the requirement that a fee be paid on presentation of a bankruptcy petition was rejected by the Court of Appeal as neither infringing the constitutional right of access to a court nor Article 6 of the European Convention on Human Rights.[131]

Successful challenges of ministerial policies, whether those of the Lord Chancellor or of another minister, are rare, even when they arise from secondary legislation. For although the courts have become more liberal in considering applications for judicial review, they remain concerned not to encroach on parliamentary or executive territory. More likely to succeed are applications which are based on fairness or a breach of natural justice. Such an application was made in 1992 against the Lord Chancellor's decision to award the contract for the court reporting service for the Chelmsford group of courts to a particular firm. The Lord Chancellor's Department had invited tenders for a three-year period for twenty-two groups of courts throughout England and Wales. Hibbit and Sanders, who were providing shorthand writers to the Chelmsford group of courts, submitted their tender which, in line with the tendering requirements, was a "firm price tender" and included, as required, details of the staff employed and their training and skills. However, the stipulation that staff be named was contested by many of those tendering, on the basis that they could not recruit until they knew they had the contract, and, unknown to Hibbit and Sanders, the requirement was dropped. In addition, others of those seeking contracts were given the opportunity to resubmit and lower their estimate of costs, particularly those relating to staff. This opportunity was not given to Hibbit and Sanders and when they were not awarded the contract, they sought judicial review on the grounds that the process had been unfair. The High Court accepted that they had been unfairly treated and that this had been to their prejudice. However, it rejected the application for judicial review, since the matter was purely commercial.[132]

As well as legal actions being brought against the Lord Chancellor, they are also brought against the LCD. These have included challenges of its decision to limit consultation on the consultation paper, "Access to Justice",[133] the

---

[131] R. v. LC, *ex parte Lightfoot* [1999] *The Times*, 18 August.

[132] R v *Lord Chancellor, ex parte Hibbit and Sanders* [1993] COD 326; [1993] *The Independent*, 16 March 1993; see D. Oliver [1993] *Public Law* 214.

[133] R v LCD, *ex parte Thompson* (7 July 1998, unreported).

rejection of a plea for the remission for court fees,[134] and the preparation by the Civil Appeals Office of the summary of a case for an appeal in the Court of Appeal,[135] all of which were unsuccessful. Also unsuccessful was an action for damages for personal injuries sustained in an accident at the Royal Courts of Justice by a security officer, employed by the LCD[136] and a number of actions, claiming unfair dismissal or discrimination, which reached the Employment Appeals Tribunal.[137] While employment and discrimination cases are usually brought against the Department, in 1999 such an action was brought against the Lord Chancellor himself. Rather than being concerned with the employment policies and practices of the LCD, it was Lord Irvine's own appointment practices that were challenged. The action was brought by two women, Jane Coker, an immigration lawyer, and Martha Osamor, a legal adviser, on the grounds that the Lord Chancellor's appointment of his friend, Gary Hart, as special adviser, was contrary to equal opportunities. They claimed that because they were given no opportunity to apply for the position, which was not advertised, they had suffered racial and sexual discrimination. Lord Irvine had not looked beyond his circle of white male contacts and had therefore excluded women and black people from the process.

At a preliminary hearing the tribunal required the Lord Chancellor to provide the applicants with all the documents they had requested and it was initially reported that Lord Irvine would give evidence in person to the tribunal. In fact, he did not do so. The employment tribunal found no case of direct or indirect discrimination against Ms Osamor, who did not have the necessary qualifications for the job, nor of direct discrimination against Ms Coker. However, it did find that Lord Irvine and his Department had indirectly discriminated against Coker, on the grounds of gender. It recognised that there is no legal requirement for the position of special adviser to be advertised, but considered that; "Any minister who chooses to take advantage of the discretion given to him . . . needs to take account of the imbalance of gender or race that might exist from the circle from which he is minded to select a special adviser". The chairman of the tribunal also noted; "The further the departmental staff went in showing how good their [recruitment] procedures were, the more it put into sharp relief the inadequacy of the Lord Chancellor's personal way of proceeding in employing a person as his special adviser. It should have been apparent to the Lord Chancellor and all ministers that open recruitment enhances the prospect of obtaining a person of

---

[134] *Roach v. LCD*, CA (19 February 1998, unreported); *R v. LCD, ex parte Low* (7 March 1996, unreported).

[135] *R v. LCD, ex parte Kalibala* (25 August 1992, unreported).

[136] *Wite v. LCD* (9 October 1997, unreported).

[137] e.g. *Bennett v. LCD*, CA (20 June 1997, unreported) an unfair dismissal claim; *Osigbesan v. LCD* [1996] EAT 26, racial discrimination; *Elkins v. LCD* [1996] EAT 24, constructive dismissal and sex discrimination; *Prabhu v. LCD* [1988] EAT 14, racial discrimination; in R v. *LCD, ex parte Nangle* [1992] 1 All ER 897 complaints that the applicant had been unfairly treated were recognised but no relief give as there was not a sufficient public law element. The case should have gone to the Employment Tribunal.

the highest ability".[138] However, in January 2001 the tribunal's decision was overturned by the EAT, which held that special advisers are not subject to the same general rules as civil servants and that, in any case the appointment process had not discriminated against women more than men.

The Lord Chancellor was also required to take notice of an action brought against the Attorney-General. The applicant, Josephine Hayes, a woman barrister, claimed that the process of appointing First Treasury Juniors, which had resulted in the appointment of a member of Lord Irvine's former chambers whose expertise lay in commercial rather than administrative law, was in breach of the Sex Discrimination Act 1975. The process involved taking secret soundings and Hayes maintained that she was ruled out because those consulted, who included the Lord Chancellor and the Lord Chief Justice but were otherwise unknown, had not heard of her. The tribunal ruled that the Attorney-General must give Hayes' lawyers details of these soundings. Ms Hayes in fact withdrew her action before it was heard, after the Attorney-General agreed, first, that in any future dispute over the appointment of First Treasury Juniors, he would accept the jurisdiction of an employment tribunal, or for other counsel, the county court; second, that he would abandon the use of secret soundings, which had, in any case, been undermined by the tribunal's ruling and meant that the details of them could not be guaranteed to be confidential; and, third, that "the system of appointment used until July 1998 'may have contributed to the under-representation of women on the main panels' of barristers used for government civil work' ".[139]

The Human Rights Act 1998 provides another ground for challenging the actions and decisions of the Lord Chancellor. The problem of him sitting as judge has been discussed in Chapter Five and the position of assistant recorders, which may be susceptible to challenge and require the Lord Chancellor to rethink his policy in relation to their appointment and security of tenure,[140] has been considered in Chapter Six. But the Lord Chancellor, like all ministers, is also vulnerable in the exercise of his executive powers. Article 6, the right to a fair trial, which is concerned with procedural fairness in both civil and criminal litigation, before ordinary courts and administrative and disciplinary tribunals, has particular relevance where the Lord Chancellor is concerned. It provides[141] for the right of access to a court and is therefore relevant to the *Witham* situation,[142] but it also has implications for other aspects of the Lord Chancellor's legal aid reforms. A right of access has been construed by the ECHR to mean a right of effective access and this could require the provision of civil legal aid in certain cases. While the Convention makes no specific mention of this,[143] in

---

[138] *The Times*, 27 March 1999.
[139] Josephine Hayes, "The plum jobs all went to men", *The Times*, 29 June 1999.
[140] See *Starrs v. Procurator Fiscal Linlithgow* [1997] *The Times*, 17 November .
[141] Article 6(1).
[142] See above; [1997]2 All ER 779.
[143] There is a provision for criminal legal aid – Article 6(3)c).

Airey v. *Ireland*[144] it was held to be unrealistic for an applicant, seeking an order for judicial separation from her husband, to effectively conduct her own case, which potentially raised complex points of law. Ireland had therefore infringed Article 6(1) by refusing her legal aid. Potentially problematic for the Lord Chancellor is the non-availability of legal aid for actions before industrial tribunals, which has already been challenged in Scotland as contrary to the HRA.[145] Similarly, provisions of the Access to Justice Bill on legal aid were questioned by the Law Society, when the Bill was in its final stages, on the grounds that, under the proposed legislation, tenants, who sought to use the courts to force landlords to undertake repairs to their properties, would be denied effective access. Legal aid is not available for these cases and the Bill removed conditional fee arrangements for housing repairs.

Legal accountability is likely to increase in importance. Until the year 2000 legal challenges of the Lord Chancellor were still relatively small in number and the success rate was even lower. Nevertheless, the trend was upwards and this trend is likely to accelerate with the Human Rights Act.

ACCOUNTABILITY TO THE PUBLIC

Parliament and the courts are the traditional locations for holding ministers to account. However, as far as the public is concerned the accountability they provide is limited. In the case of Parliament it is indirect and while the courts provide direct accountability to the individuals concerned, the process is expensive and the chances of success small. In the closing decades of the twentieth century, there was a move to supplement, and to an extent replace, accountability to Parliament with direct accountability to the users of public services. The LCD was late in entering the user culture but change has been rapid. It is no longer an aloof department, which sees its mission to serve the interests of judges rather than of court users. Indeed, with the establishment of the Court Service Agency, users have become paramount. In the civil context they increasingly fund the court system, while in the criminal context the need to cut costs by achieving a quicker throughput has focused attention on those involved in the process, whether witnesses, victims or defendants. The Courts' Charter, which provides accountability to the users of the service, was first published in November 1992 and covers not only areas of the Court Service's responsibilities (and thus the Lord Chancellor's) but also those of the Crown Prosecution Service (the Attorney-General's responsibility) and Home Office, where they affect the court. It "sets out the standards of service, which the courts are obliged to pro-

---

[144] (1979) 2 EHRR 305.
[145] An action against the LCD and the Legal Aid Board was started in 1998 by an applicant in a complex sexual harassment case. She sought judicial review of the non-availability of legal aid, but dropped the case when she received funding from the EOC.

vide"[146] and the Court Service is held accountable by the Home Affairs Committee for fulfilling this obligation.

In the early days of the Courts' Charter, the LCD was criticised for its failure to reflect notions of quality of service within the charter and for failing to monitor its effectiveness. Indeed, in the LCD's annual report of 1992/3 "quality of service" was all but ignored, "the Courts' Charter merit[ing] one descriptive paragraph of about half a dozen sentences, [which said] nothing at all about whether you are going to look at whether anything had been achieved within its terms".[147] Indeed, the Courts' Charter was subject to the same criticisms as the Citizen's Charter in general, namely, that it moved towards a quasi-contractual accountability which focused on quantifiable standards, which did not, necessarily, produce a better service, and were not subjected to independent checks on whether they were met.[148] In addition, there was concern that, like all charters, "the stress on customers might lead to a lack of appreciation of the extent to which public services . . . [were] concerned with more than the service to individual customers".[149] There was also the problem of determining who was the "customer" in the criminal justice context and thus at whom the charter should be aimed.

By the end of the 1990s, the same criticisms could not be made. In 1998 after extensive consultation with consumer groups and court users a new charter was produced.[150] This was developed under the "Service First" initiative, which aims to make public services more responsive to their users and, instead of comprising one large document, it consists of fifteen separate leaflets, targeted at users of particular courts, such as the county courts, Royal Courts of Justice, Immigration Appellate Authorities and the Land Tribunal, and at different groups of court users, such as witnesses, jurors, defendants. The individual courts are required to display their performance against charter targets, for instance, the actual time spent waiting for a case to be called against the target waiting time. Accountability to the public thus goes hand in hand with management accountability and efficiency. As Lord Irvine indicated; "By making courts more accountable and easier to understand, the Charter complements our reforms to make courts quicker, cheaper and easier to use".[151]

An important element of charters is the provision of information about how to complain. In the case of the Courts' Charter, users are told they can complain about "any aspect of the handling of your case by court staff", the performance

---

[146] Lord Chancellor's Department *Court Service Annual Report* (1992–93) HC 808, para. 4.3.

[147] Home Affairs Committee, *Lord Chancellor's Department; Annual Report* (1992–93) HC 655-I, Q. 2.

[148] Only four out of fifteen charters in existence in early 1994 were subject to independent checking regarding the meeting of targets (*Financial Times*, 14 March 1994).

[149] Treasury and Civil Service Committee, *The Role of the Civil Service: Interim Report* (1992–93) HC 390, para. 14.3.

[150] In addition, the magistrates' courts were required to bring charters up to the standard of the model charter, produced by the LCD, by 1April 1999.

[151] LCD, Press Notice 295/98 (28 September 1998).

of other agencies, such as the Crown Prosecution Service, the police and members of the legal profession, and the treatment received from a judge. In addition, during 1996–7, the Court Service produced a comprehensive guide on complaints handling and the Customer Service Unit implemented a computerised complaints logging and tracking system and a monitoring system for complaints to see if improvements could be made.[152] Also during that year, the LCD reported that it had paid out over six hundred thousand pounds by way of ex gratia payments for administrative errors and delays,[153] although, in accordance with Treasury guidelines, compensation was only offered where administrative error had resulted in direct financial loss.[154]

Like all charters, the standards contained in the Charter for Court Users are, in the main, ones that can easily be assessed, such as the provision of information, the availability of certain facilities and time stipulations. However, also included are requirements of politeness and, particularly important given the context in which the code operates, those of fairness and equal treatment, "irrespective of race, ethnic origin, disability, gender, sexual orientation or religious beliefs". The charter therefore offers accountability to individual users of the Court Service, which is based on certain principles, although these omit any reference to the public interest. It remains pseudo-contractual by nature and, while not providing the remedies available at private law, it provides a minimal facility for redress. However, its main concern is to impose targets against which the agency's performance can be measured, both by the users of the service and its managers.

THE PARLIAMENTARY OMBUDSMAN (PCA)

An additional avenue through which court users can complain about the administration of the court service is through their MP to the Parliamentary Ombudsman (Parliamentary Commissioner for Administration (PCA)).[155] This route was not always available. The Parliamentary Commissioner for Administration Act 1967 gave the PCA jurisdiction over government departments and offices,[156] including the Lord Chancellor's Department. However, the Act also listed matters that were excluded and thus not subject to investigation by the PCA. Legal proceedings were, not surprisingly, excluded but another exclusion was "action taken by the administrative staff of a court or tribunal on the direction or on the authority, express or implied, of a judge or a member of

---

[152] Lord Chancellor's Department, *Annual Report* (1997–98) HC 73.
[153] Actual total £608,094.67 in a total of sixty-one claims. One individual payment was over £100,000 (Ibid).
[154] Ibid.
[155] For discussion of the role of the Parliamentary Ombudsman see, A. Bradley, "The Parliamentary Ombudsman Again" [1995] *Public Law* 345; C. Harlow and R. Rawlings, *Law and Administration* (2nd edn., Weidenfeld and Nicolson,1997).
[156] Section 4 and Schedule 2, now replaced by Act of 1987.

the tribunal".[157] This raised questions about whether court staff were in any way subject to the PCA's jurisdiction, particularly as the courts had not been included in the jurisdictional list. The matter was tested when a court user, who claimed to be the victim of maladministration within the Court of Appeal (Criminal Division), requested the PCA to assert his jurisdiction. The Lord Chief Justice stated that on a true construction of the Parliamentary Commissioner for Administration Act 1967, the matter was not administrative but judicial and therefore outside the ombudsman's jurisdiction. The ombudsman appealed to the PCA Committee who took evidence from the Lord Chancellor, Lord Hailsham, who provided legal opinion to back the view of the Lord Chief Justice.

For Lord Hailsham his role in the dispute illustrated "in an unusual way the value of the Lord Chancellor's Office, which is directly responsible to Parliament and therefore its holder legitimately amenable to the jurisdiction of the Committee to deal with a matter which otherwise might have lead to a *Stockdale* v. *Hansard* situation between the Commons and the Lord Chief Justice".[158] Less dramatically, his role ensured the exemption of court staff until 1990 when the Courts and Legal Services Act 1990 (section 110) brought court and tribunal staff within the jurisdiction of the PCA. This opened the way for complaints on grounds of maladministration against them.

The number of referrals to the Parliamentary Ombudsman of claims of maladministration in the LCD, which includes the Court Service Agency, is high compared with other public bodies. In 1998–9 eighty-five new complaints were made and only the Department of Social Security, the Department of Environment, Transport and the Regions, the Inland Revenue and the Legal Aid Board, which, of course, also comes within the responsibility of the Lord Chancellor, had more.[159] More than half of the complaints were rejected[160] and of the eight investigated, five were found to be justified and three partly so, which placed the LCD sixth out of fifty-seven in the ombudsman's league table.[161] Its high place can probably be accounted for by the fact that the Court Service, along with the agencies and departments above it, is in the front line of service delivery. Moreover, where the Court Service is concerned, maladministration may result in the complainant having suffered financially. As the PCA stated; "Those involved in legal proceedings must expect to incur costs as a result. But, even if they win, maladministration by official bodies can sometimes

---

[157] Section 5 and 3rd Schedule.

[158] Lord Hailsham, "The Office of Lord Chancellor and the Separation of Powers", p. 316.

[159] Department of Social Services, 647; Department of Environment, ninety-four; Inland Revenue, ninety-three; Legal Aid Board, ninety-one. (Statistics from Parliamentary Commissioner for Administration, *Seventh Report* (1998–9) HC 572).

[160] The total of cases before the PCA concerning the LCD was ninety-seven in 1998/99, which includes twelve carried over from the previous year. Of these, fifty-eight were rejected; thirty-one were carried over into the next year.

[161] The five public bodies above the LCD were those listed above, plus the Department of Education, which had less referrals during 1998/99 but more cases accepted than the LCD.

cause those costs to be higher than they should have been or even to be wasted altogether".[162]

This was evident in the failure of the Court Service to supply notes of county court proceedings, the result of which was a delay in the case proceeding and, subsequently, in the complainant being unable to secure the full amount of costs awarded against her opponent, the judge attributing part of the costs to maladministration by the Court Service. Moreover, the initial failure of the Court Service was compounded by its refusal to reimburse the complainant for the shortfall in costs. This led the ombudsman to find there had been a "catalogue of maladministration over a prolonged period". His finding resulted in an apology from the chief executive, reassurances of improvement in the future and an agreement to an ex gratia payment for the complainant.[163] Similarly, apologies were forthcoming, reassurances given and payments made when, through the fault of court staff, a court hearing had to be adjourned[164] and "persistent mishandling of a case at two county courts" caused unnecessary expenditure and prevented the claimant from enforcing payment of a debt owed to him by a company, while it was still trading.[165]

While the Courts and Legal Services Act removed the exemption for court officials, "to maintain the separation of functions" the exemption of legal proceedings was maintained.[166] Thus while the accountability of court staff has increased, both through changes to the jurisdiction of the PCA and the Courts' Charter, judges remain largely insulated from accountability. Complaints about the personal conduct of a judge can be made to the Lord Chancellor. In 1998 a unit was set up to deal specifically with them and between August 1998 and December 1999 it handled 3,903 complaints, of which three hundred and sixty-seven were about personal conduct. In two hundred and eighty-two cases the Lord Chancellor sought a response from the judge concerned and on thirteen occasions, "saw fit to take further action, either by writing to the judge or arranging for him or her to be seen by officials".[167] However, making a complaint seldom produces a satisfactory remedy, for what is said to a judge is not communicated to the complainant and thus it is "unlikely to remove his sense of grievance".[168] This is a problem particularly when comments made by the judge are damaging to an individual's reputation, as in the High Court and above they are covered by absolute, and in the inferior courts by qualified, privilege. One solution could be the establishment of a judicial ombudsman or a

---

[162] PCA, *Seventh Report* (1998–99) HC 572.

[163] This was composed of £1,606.72, the amount deducted by the judge, interest of £189.83, and £300 in recognition of extra expenses incurred and the "exceptional aggravation" the complainant had experienced. (Parliamentary Commissioner for Administration, *Sixth Report* (1998–99) HC 571, Case No. 197/98).

[164] £2,123.77 for wasted costs (PCA, *Seventh Report* (1998–99) HC 572, Case No. 1151/97).

[165] £845.38 (Ibid; Case No. 686/99).

[166] Home Affairs Committee, *The Work of the Lord Chancellor's Department*, HC 214-i.

[167] *LCD Annual Report, 2000*, para. 25.

[168] D. Pannick, *The Judges*, p. 93.

judicial performance commission who investigates complaints and reports his findings to the Lord Chancellor. He would have no power to impose a sanction but "the publication of a report would in most cases be sufficient to remedy and deter injudicious conduct".[169] Such an office would not only provide the public with a better mechanism for holding judges to account, it could also act to protect the interests of judges facing disciplinary action by the Lord Chancellor because of complaints about their behaviour out of court. The Lord Chancellor could be obliged to refer such complaints to the ombudsman for investigation before making a decision to dismiss the judge concerned, thereby ensuring that the judge had a fair hearing and that the facts were in the open, rather than, as at present, disciplinary action taking place behind the closed doors of the LCD.[170]

The process would therefore be more transparent and while transparency should not be confused with accountability, it is an important aid in holding those responsible to account – whether this is a judge, for his behaviour, or the Lord Chancellor, for the exercise of his powers of regulation. Transparency, and hence accountability, has already been achieved through the requirement that from 1998 a newly appointed judge or magistrate must declare if he is a member of a Masonic lodge. The making of such a declaration is now a condition of appointment. More significant will be the requirements imposed by the Freedom of Information Act, although the exemptions contained within it will limit its effect on some of the Lord Chancellor's responsibilities, particularly as they relate to judges. The Code of Practice on Access to Government Information has, since 1994, provided a limited mechanism for securing information, from which the LCD has not been immune. It has not been inundated with requests, during 1997 receiving twenty-five requests under the Code.[171] Of these only four were refused, although given the small numbers, this represents a sixteen per cent refusal rate and thus suggests that the move towards greater transparency is tempered by caution.

Transparency is also more in evidence in the exercise of the Lord Chancellor's powers of patronage. In 1998 Lord Irvine announced that he was "ensuring that the process for appointing chairmen and members of [Magistrates] Advisory Committees and Sub-Committees is now more open".[172] In addition, the appointment to quango positions within his remit are required to follow the appointment procedures recommended by the Committee on Standards in Public Life [173] and are therefore also more open. All those occupying such

---

[169] Ibid, p. 101.
[170] Ibid.
[171] Twenty-one of which were completed within twenty working days.
[172] LCD Press notice, 251/98 (3 August 1998).
[173] *Nolan Report* (1995). Since 1995 quango appointments have been overseen by an independent Commissioner for Public Appointments and required to comply with the *Code of Practice for Public Appointments Procedures*. This sets out the principles which should govern such appointments. They include selection on merit, independent scrutiny of the appointments process, openness and transparency in appointment and procedures.

positions are now made public on the Internet as well as in documentary form. Indeed, the amount of information on the LCD's website and in hard copy about this and many other matters is impressive.[174]

CONCLUSION

The developments over the last decade have lessened the criticisms about the accountability of the Lord Chancellor. There are now ministers who account on his behalf in the House of Commons, both Lords Mackay and Irvine have appeared before select committees, and officials appear regularly to answer for the annual reports of the LCD and the Court Service. The establishment of the Court Service Agency has also improved accountability, both to Parliament and to the public, and court officials now come within the jurisdiction of the PCA. In addition, the willingness of judges to be more interventionist, evident in applications for judicial review, has resulted in some increase in accountability to the courts. There has also been a dramatic "opening up" of government, to which the LCD has been no exception, as its website testifies.

Yet the Lord Chancellor remains a problem. In part this is because one of his most important responsibilities, the appointment and regulation of the judiciary, while much more open than previously, remains largely secret. In the past, Lord Chancellors argued that they were accountable for the quality of appointments to the legal profession through membership of their Inn, Lord Jowitt observing; "How should I have felt if I had made a lot of unworthy appointments, when I noticed the cold looks that I should have received when next I went to lunch at the Inn".[175] Accountability of this nature may have been satisfactory half a century ago but has little to recommend it today. More important, however, is the nature of the office of Lord Chancellor itself, which confuses judicial, executive and legislative functions and locates its holder in the upper chamber of Parliament, insulated from the processes of accountability required in a modern democracy. Lord Mackay argued that it was wrong to suggest that the Lord Chancellor was not accountable, as he was directly accountable to the Prime Minister, who can dismiss him at any time.[176] Likewise, Sir Nichoas Lyell, an ex Attorney-General, stated that the Lord Chancellor was responsible to his government and his government was responsible for his integrity.[177] However, such accountability has more to do with the Prime Minister's powers

---

[174] In 1999 the LCD published a free booklet, *Working for Justice; A Guide to the Lord Chancellor's Department*. Seventy thousand copies were printed and made available to the public in the courts. "Written in clear English and attractively designed and illustrated, it explains the role and the functions of the department, as well as tracing the history of the office of Lord Chancellor". (Geoff Hoon, H. C. Debs., 16 February 1999, col. 725).

[175] Quoted in S. Shetreet, *Judges on Trial*, p. 52.

[176] In C. Anderson, *Unreliable Evidence*.

[177] Interview with J. Rozenburg, Radio 4, 18 December 1998.

of patronage than with democratic accountability. It is therefore perhaps not unexpected that in recent times the press has taken particular interest in the office of Lord Chancellor. As it has become more important in the spending stakes and thus a bigger political player, the gap in accountability has become increasingly evident. This is even more the case when the Lord Chancellor has a powerful position at the centre of government.

Moreover, while the LCD has undoubtedly become more transparent than previously, there is a danger of confusing transparency with accountability. Transparent government does not necessarily produce accountable government. It makes it easier to hold it to account but if the person responsible does not account to the democratically elected assembly, then much of the advantage is lost. In any case, while the developments in the latter part of the twentieth century had the effect of strengthening the mechanisms for the accountability of officials, both in the LCD and the Court Service, they did little to improve the Lord Chancellor's political accountability. The type of accountability on offer is managerial accountability, that is accountability for performance against targets set by the Government, not accountability for policy choices or even policy success or failure. The measurement of success and failure is confined to the management of policies, what used to be called implementation. Joined-up government initiatives also tend to focus on official responsibilities and accountability rather than the accountability of ministers for aspects of the projects. Such a slant on accountability is common across the whole of government, and not specific to the Lord Chancellor. However, the fact that his democratic accountability is already so limited, makes the contrast between managerial and political accountability more stark. It also makes it difficult to hold him to account.

Writing in 1989 Rodney Brazier noted that because of historic evolution "ministerial responsibility for the law in England and Wales has developed in ways which would not be acceptable in other states. No modern state which wished to establish ministerial responsibility for such things as the administration of justice, public order, the treatment of offenders, law reform, and the appointment of the judiciary would allocate those and related matters almost haphazardly between two ministers. Nor would that state place each of those ministers in different chambers of the legislatures, one minister having no junior minister to represent him in the other House (and for good measure having non-ministerial duties as well)".[178] Things have changed since then. The Lord Chancellor now has two junior ministers representing him in the House of Commons and he and officials from his Department regularly give evidence to select committees. In addition, the ombudsman and the courts extract accountability from him and his Department. Yet the situation remains unsatisfactory. A minister who heads a large spending department with such important responsibilities should not be located in the rarefied atmosphere of the House of Lords

---

[178] R. Brazier", Government and the Law" p. 67.

but should be a member of the elected chamber. Indeed, rather than a creature of prime ministerial patronage, he should be subject to the democratic process and to the accountability requirements which go with it. These may not always be adequate but they provide a better check than exists at present.

8

The Reform of the Office of Lord Chancellor

INTRODUCTION

T HE PRECEDING CHAPTERS have analysed the constitutional, executive and judicial roles of the Lord Chancellor and considered the developments in the twentieth century which have affected the balance between them and changed the nature of the office of Lord Chancellor. The conclusion must be that it is no longer sustainable for the Lord Chancellor to retain his multiple functions. The question is whether he should maintain a role at all or whether the office should be abolished.

The fusing of executive and judicial functions in the office of Lord Chancellor has been challenged on a number of occasions during the last one hundred and fifty years. Proposals for reform have usually centred on him relinquishing his executive role and these have formed the basis for calls for a ministry of justice. However, at the beginning of the twenty-first century, the call has been for him to abandon his judicial function. This poses a greater threat to the office of Lord Chancellor than suggestions that he should give up his executive responsibilities, because, relatively small though it is, his judicial role is the one which makes the Lord Chancellor different from other ministers. Without it, there is no rationale for an unelected minister sitting in Cabinet and commanding a modern government department.

THE LORD CHANCELLOR'S JUDICIAL ROLE

There has been a tendency to play down the role of the Lord Chancellor as judge, as if it were inconsequential. At the beginning of the twenty-first century, this is far from being the case. The Lord Chancellor may not sit often, but he continues to sit and his judicial involvement is contentious. The increased involvement of the Appellate Committee of the House of Lords in high profile judicial review cases, the incorporation of the European Convention on Human Rights, and the role given to the Judicial Committee of the Privy Council to determine *vires* disputes mean that, even if he is selective in the cases he hears, it is no longer acceptable for a government minister to preside over the final court of appeal, which is, in effect, a constitutional court. Lord Irvine, while refusing to accept a classification of "constitutional" cases, has reaffirmed that Lord Chancellors should not sit on cases in which the Government has a direct interest. This must include human rights and *vires* cases. However, such reassurance is insufficient. The reforms undertaken by the Blair Government, in which, ironically, the Lord Chancellor played a leading part, require a total separation between the executive and the judiciary to ensure that judges are not only independent but are seen to be so. The Lord Chancellor sitting as judge in any case is in danger of undermining this independence and, following *McGonnell*,[1] may be in breach of the European Convention on Human Rights. He should therefore relinquish his role as judge.

JUDICIAL APPOINTMENTS

Logic suggests that a Lord Chancellor, who no longer sits as a judge, should also not be responsible for judicial appointments. One of the justifications, made by Lord Chancellors for retaining their judicial role, is that it enables them to keep in touch with the profession and, by so doing, aids them in their task of selecting the best judges. This link will be broken if the Lord Chancellor no longer sits as judge and the only rationale for him retaining his appointing role will therefore be an historic one. But logic aside – and Britain's constitutional arrangements can hardly be said to be based on logic – there are more fundamental reasons why the method by which judges are appointed should change. These again relate to the need to make a more obvious separation between the judiciary and the executive and, in addition, to the requirement that senior judges, who with the Human Rights Act will be involved in making political decisions, should be accountable.

Weiler[2] suggests two models of judicial selection. The first, which assumes that judging is not "political" but adjudicatory, insulates candidates from partisan politics by a selection process, which is structured so as to preserve the notion of judges as independent arbitrators, whose prerequisites for holding office centre on their legal training and skills and their moral character. The second assumes that the courts are concerned with policy making and are therefore "political". Thus, in line with the requirements of a liberal democracy, they should be accountable for the political power they exercise. Such accountability may be achieved by the election of judges, who stand on a platform which emphasises their political programmes rather than their legal experience, or by a process of selection, in which different groups have a formal and legitimised role.

The appointment of judges in the UK is reflected in the first model, although how well judges are insulated from partisan politics, when, in the case of senior judges, the Lord Chancellor and the Prime Minister do the appointing, has long

---

[1] *McGonnell* v. *United Kingdom* No. 28488/95 (8/02/00) ECHR (see Chapter Five).
[2] P. Weiler, "Two Models of Judicial Decision-Making" (1968) 46 *Canadian Bar Review* 406.

been a matter of some concern, as has the partiality of the process and the secrecy surrounding it. Changes to the appointments system, during the final years of the twentieth century, have made it more open and transparent. Yet, despite the reassurances given in the Peach report,[3] concerns about the process have not been dispelled. Moreover, if the requirement is for appointments to be, and appear to be, insulated from party politics, questions remain about the role of the Lord Chancellor and Prime Minister. However, more fundamental, is whether a model of appointing, based on the premise that judges simply exercise an adjudicatory function, is still appropriate, if it ever was. Constitutional change, which gives the courts a constitutional role through the interpretation of the Human Rights Act and the settling of devolution disputes, makes it inevitable that judicial decisions will have an effect on public policy. This makes the rationale for excluding political considerations from the selection process much weaker and suggests that Weiler's second model, in which the political nature of the judicial process is recognised, is more appropriate. Indeed, failure to change the selection process carries the danger that judges will continue to be appointed as if their role were adjudicatory, but that, behind the scenes and thus beyond public scrutiny, "political" factors will be considered in making these appointments. In addition, the overt involvement of the judges in public policy-making will result in their being seen as political players but, under the current appointments system, as lacking the "democratic legitimacy"[4] required of political actors. Such legitimacy can only be achieved through a change in the process by which judges are appointed and by the Lord Chancellor, who lacks any democratic mandate, relinquishing his responsibility for it.

Recognition of the political role of the judges, which stops short of judges being elected, is evident in many appointments systems. The way in which Supreme Court judges are appointed in the United States provides an obvious example of partisan politics entering the appointments process. The confirmation hearings, which form part of the process, are, at times, controversial. Nevertheless, in recognition of the need for democratic scrutiny of judges, whose role is political, similar hearings have been adopted in South Africa and Israel. The appointment of judges to the West German Constitutional Court is likewise entrusted to elected representatives, half being selected by the Bundesrat, the upper chamber of the legislature,[5] from an "eligible judges list" drawn up by the Ministry of Justice, and the other half by a representative committee[6] of the Bundestag, the directly elected lower chamber. The involvement of the legislature in the above examples "maintains . . . a mediated chain of democratic legitimation"[7] and thus provides the judges with the legitimacy

---

[3] Sir Leonard Peach, *Report on the Scrutiny of Judicial Appointments* (1999) (see Chapter Six).

[4] Lord Steyn, reported in *The Times* (4 July 2000).

[5] Which contains representatives from the Lander.

[6] The committee consists of twelve members, selected in line with party representation in the House and while politics may be the main consideration, it is evident that legal and other abilities are also considered.

[7] J. Bell, *Policy Arguments in Judicial Decisions*, p. 259.

required. An alternative to the direct involvement of legislatures is the use of appointing bodies, of which there are many examples, with varying powers and constitutions. A number of US states have a nominating commission, chaired by a judge with representatives appointed by the governor and by the Bar in equal proportions, which nominates three candidates to fill a vacancy, one of which is chosen by the governor. In Canada a Judicial Appointments Committee, consisting of judges, representatives of the legal profession and lay members, makes recommendations to the Attorney-General, who then appoints. While in Italy, the Superior Magisterial Council, on which the President of the Republic, the President and Procurator General and thirty elected members sit,[8] makes appointments itself.[9]

The idea of a UK judicial appointments commission, which represents a variety of interests, both lay and legal, is supported by a growing number of groups and organisations. Moreover, it was given added impetus by the announcement that, following a ruling that the appointment of temporary sheriffs by a member of the executive was contrary to the European Convention,[10] such a body was to be established in Scotland. Modest proposals for England and Wales advocate a commission making recommendations to the Lord Chancellor. However, these assume that this office has a place in a modern constitution, which would seem doubtful. Others see a commission making recommendations to an elected minister or making appointments itself and being directly accountable to a select committee of Parliament. Given the constitutional developments of the late 1990s, it is the more far-reaching proposals, which remove the Lord Chancellor from the process, which would seem most appropriate.

THE LORD CHANCELLOR'S CONSTITUTIONAL ROLE

If the Lord Chancellor were to lose his judicial and appointing roles, logic and constitutional propriety dictate that he should also give up his position as head of the judiciary, a position he came to occupy because of these roles. The head of the judiciary can hardly be someone who is not a judge, nor should he be a government minister. The Lord Chancellor's role as guardian of judicial independence has always been difficult to justify because of its infringement of the separation of powers and, at the beginning of the twenty-first century, the nature and extent of his executive responsibilities make justification impossible. Not only do these responsibilities make the inappropriateness of him holding this role more evident, they also raise questions about the extent to which he is able effectively to protect what judges consider to be their interests. The evidence of the 1990s suggests that, when faced with a conflict between the inter-

---

[8] Twenty are elected by the magistracy from its own ranks and ten are elected by Parliament from university law professors and lawyers of at least fifteen years' standing.

[9] It also has disciplinary and regulatory functions.

[10] *Starrs* v. *Procurator Fiscal Linlithgow* [1999] *The Times*, 17 November.

ests of the Government and those of the judges, the Lord Chancellor's position as Cabinet minister assumes precedence over his role as head of the judiciary. It is therefore not surprising that judicial confidence in the Lord Chancellor has diminished. The position of head of the judiciary should, as a consequence, pass to the Lord Chief Justice.

THE LORD CHANCELLOR'S EXECUTIVE ROLE

The main reason for discomfort over the Lord Chancellor's judicial and constitutional roles is the domination of his executive responsibilities. In the twenty-first century the Lord Chancellor is first and foremost a government minister and his role, as such, accords, in most respects, with the role of other Cabinet ministers. He, like them, is responsible for a large department, for implementing policies, which contribute to the government's programme, and for securing the necessary funds from the Treasury and there is little justification for these responsibilities being carried out by an unelected minister who is accountable only in the upper chamber. This lends support to the notion of a ministry of justice or department of Legal Affairs to carry out these responsibilities, with a Secretary of State accountable in the House of Commons. References to a "Ministry of Justice" are evident throughout the last one hundred and fifty years or so, but there has "never in fact been a real consensus about what a "Ministry of Justice" really means".[11] The term has meant different things to different people at different times, there having been no "single coherent 'debate' on the subject, just a disjointed series of mini-debates".[12] However, most proposals assume a separation of judicial and executive functions.

Suggestions that the executive and judicial functions of the Lord Chancellor should be separated surfaced in the nineteenth century, largely in response to public concern about the running of the Court of Chancery. This was the responsibility of the Lord Chancellor and there was a view that "the accumulation of political and ministerial functions which had gradually arisen round that officer was the root of the abuses in the Court of Chancery".[13] Lord Chancellor Cottenham proposed that he should lose his authority over Chancery but otherwise retain his powers. But this was opposed in the House of Lords on the grounds that the plan "suffered from the cardinal mischief of failing to separate entirely the judicial and ministerial functions of the Chancellor".[14] A counter proposal was that the Lord Chancellor should remain in charge of Chancery but that "the political functions of the Chancellor should be discharged by a Keeper of the Great Seal, who was to hold no judicial office, but was to act as a

---

[11] G. Drewry; "The Debate about a Ministry of Justice – a Joad's-eye view" [1987]*Public Law* 502 at 503.
[12] Ibid.
[13] J. B. Atlay, "The Victorian Chancellors", p. 395.
[14] Ibid.

minister of law and justice; and that the appellate efficiency of the House of Lords should be secured by the presence of a permanent judge".[15]

This idea of a minister for justice to undertake the administrative and political functions of the Lord Chancellor "won small favour", but the separation of his functions remained on the agenda, largely because of his continued heavy workload in Chancery. Indeed, a few years later, it was proposed that the presidency of the Chancery courts and "the ecclesiastical and legal patronage hitherto attached to the Great Seal" would be removed from the Lord Chancellor's responsibility.[16] Instead, two Lord Justices were authorised to exercise the same judicial power in Chancery as the Lord Chancellor, and he "was set free to attend to his duties in the House of Lords, and as a minister of State". The subsequent restructuring of the English legal system resulted again in suggestions that there should be a minister for justice responsible for its administration, "the Utilitarians almost persuad[ing] the Judicature Commission (1867) to institute such a Minister within the Home Office".[17] The judges, however, won the day, and the Lord Chancellor assumed that function, thus confirming his position as judge/minister.

However, the concept of a ministry of justice, which had at least some of the administrative functions of the Lord Chancellor did not die and in 1918 Haldane recommended the appointment of a "Minister responsible for the subject of Justice".[18] He believed that the Lord Chancellor's responsibilities should centre on judicial appointments,[19] although he would also remain keeper of the Great Seal, advise the Cabinet on legal and constitutional matters and have a duty to "watch and master all questions relating to legislation".[20] Otherwise, his duties of Speaker would be removed, his judicial function would be reduced to hearing appeals from the Dominions on constitutional issues, and all other functions concerned with the administration of justice would transfer to the Home Secretary, who would become a minister for justice.

His recommendations were strongly opposed by Lord Birkenhead and his permanent secretary, Sir Claud Schuster, and came to nothing. Nevertheless, suggestions for a Ministry of Justice resurfaced from time to time throughout the twentieth century[21] and in 1987 became part of the political agenda. The manifesto of the SDP/Liberal Alliance for the 1987 general election included a commitment to setting up a ministry of justice,[22] which would be responsible for

---

[15]   J. B. Atlay, "The Victorian Chancellors", p. 397.

[16]   Ibid, p. 450.

[17]   R. Stevens, *The Independence of the Judiciary*, p. 8.

[18]   Cd. 9230 (1918), Chap. X, p. 63, para. 1.

[19]   Subject to consultation with the PM, the minister for justice (i.e. the old Home Secretary) previous Lord Chancellors and the Lord Chief Justice.

[20]   Cd. 9230, p. 74, paras. 37 and 38.

[21]   For instance, after the Second World War by the Haldane Club and during 1950s and 1960s in publications such as G. Williams (ed.), *The Reform of the Law* (1951) and G. Gardiner and A. Martin, *Law Reform NOW* (1963).

[22]   *Government, Law and Justice: the case for a Ministry of Justice* (Alliance Papers No. 1 (1985).

law reform, the appointment of judges through a judicial services commission, legal aid, prosecutions and some of the other functions exercised by the Attorney-General. It would be headed by the Lord Chancellor, who, with some of his "irrelevant" functions removed, should preferably sit in the House of Commons. The Social and Liberal Democratic Party also subsequently advocated a ministry of justice.[23]

For its part, the Labour Party voted at its conference in 1987 to abolish the Home Office and LCD and set up a ministry of justice. Labour's 1992 manifesto declared; "We will appoint from the House of Commons a Minister for Legal Administration, who will initially be part of the Lord Chancellor's Department. We will go on to create a Department of Legal Administration headed by a Minister in the Commons who will be responsible for all the courts and tribunals in England and Wales". In June 1994 the commitment was still evident with Paul Boateng, Labour's legal affairs spokesman, stating; "Labour will take executive functions away from the Lord Chancellor and give them to a Minister of Justice, headed by an MP".[24] But less than a year later he was saying, "We are not really going to get hung up on the issue of the Lord Chancellor, whether or not he should be in the Cabinet or anything like that".[25] By then, of course, a Labour victory at the next election was looking likely.

Calls for a ministry of justice have been consistently opposed by judges and Lord Chancellors on the grounds that it is "at best, an eccentric irrelevance and, at worst, a threat to judicial independence and the rule of law".[26] However, part of the concern is undoubtedly territorial, judges being concerned that in any formal division between "administration" and "judicial" responsibilities they will be the losers and Lord Chancellors being reluctant to relinquish power. Opposition has also been founded on the concern that "the minister who appoints judges or justices [would] be subject to day-to-day pressures in the House of Commons"[27] and more convincingly on arguments against the Home Secretary or a minister in the Home Office assuming the role of minster for justice, if the Home Office retained responsibility for the police and prisons and, as in some proposals, also took on responsibility for prosecutions. As Lord Mackay noted, there is an "important distinction between the role of the prosecutor and the role of the judge, the role of the court" and "the Home Office with its responsibility for prisons, for the police and other agencies associated with the criminal justice system, falls to be distinguished from the courts on the one hand and the prosecution on the other hand".[28]

One of the problems has been that details of the responsibilities a ministry of justice would assume and how it would relate to other ministries have seldom

---

[23] "The Rights and Liberties of the Citizen" (Federal Green Paper No. 1 (1988)).
[24] *The Independent*, 22 March 1995.
[25] Ibid.
[26] G. Drewry, "Lord Haldane's Ministry of Justice – Stillborn or Strangled at Birth?" p. 411.
[27] Lord Hailsham, "Problems of a Lord Chancellor".
[28] Home Affairs Committee, *The Work of the Lord Chancellor's Department*, HC 214-ii, Q. 2.

been articulated. For some a ministry of justice is simply an extended, renamed Home Office. For others, it is a replacement for the LCD, and yet others see it as an addition, with responsibility for "the general work of judicial administration in connection with justice, the courts buildings and staff, legal aid, tribunals, prisoners' complaints, land registration and public records",[29] the Home Office concentrating on law and order and the LCD on judicial appointments.

Arguments for a ministry of justice have centred on "the untidy arbitrariness" of the distribution of functions between the Home Office, the Law Officers' Department and the LCD[30] and the fact that the Lord Chancellor sits in the House of Lords, thereby "denying the House of Commons access to the Cabinet ministerial responsibility for an important and increasingly expensive service".[31] The transfer of the magistrates' courts from the Home Office to the LCD and the appointment by the Lord Chancellor of a junior minister to sit in the House of Commons, both of which happened in the early 1990s, may have lessened the strength of this argument. However, the increase in the executive functions of the Lord Chancellor, together with their political nature, have given it added vibrancy. Moreover, claims that the Lord Chancellor is, "in effect", a minister of justice[32] poses the question why, if this is the case, should not he, or someone else, assume the role, in practice. The truth is that while the Lord Chancellor may carry out the functions of such a minister, his other responsibilities mask his ministerial role, at times detracting from it and preventing the accountability constitutionally required. In addition, the undefined nature of his office means that he can wield considerable influence and power across government, in a way in which regular ministers are seldom able to do, and, because he is unelected, escape accountability on the floor of the House of Commons. This hardly accords with the principles of a modern democracy or of modern government.

On 1 April 1998 Mr Austin Mitchell presented a Bill in the House of Commons, which would have effectively abolished the office of Lord Chancellor, an office which, he described as, "in a sense a medieval relic, ripe for the modernisation that the Labour Party is undertaking in so many other sectors of government". He noted of the Lord Chancellor; "His three-in-one role could perhaps be performed by the Almighty, but it is something of a difficult role for a mere mortal, which I understand that the Lord Chancellor is"[33] and therefore proposed removing judicial appointments from the remit of the Lord Chancellor through the establishment of a judicial appointments and training commission, and setting up a ministry of justice.[34]

---

[29] A. Samuels, "Do we need a Ministry of Justice?" (1971) *New Law Journal*, 11 February, 111 at 112.
[30] G. Drewry, "Ministers, Parliament and the Courts", p. 50.
[31] Ibid.
[32] See, for example, LCD website and Lord Hailsham, Home Affairs Committee, *The Prison Service* (1980–81), HC 412-ii, Q. 995.
[33] H.C. Debs., 1 April 1998, col. 1263.
[34] Ibid, col. 1262.

His rationale for a ministry of justice was that there needed to be a minister accountable to the House of Commons because "Here is where the problems and grievances of the people are raised and where complaints about the adequacy of structures and their operation need to be addressed. The minister for justice would also be answerable to a select committee of the House of Commons for performing the brief of modernising the whole system and ensuring that it serves the purposes of the people".[35] Such a proposal would seem to give effect to the new user or customer orientation of the LCD and accord with its mission statement of putting the users of its services first. The logic of accepting it is thus hard to resist.

Lord Lester likewise calls for a minister for justice, whose role would be similar to that of the Attorney-General in Ireland but who "we can call Lord Chancellor". He would be elected and sit in the House of Commons and would combine responsibility for criminal and civil justice, human rights, the functioning of the courts and the giving of legal advice to the Government.[36] Brazier has similarly recommended that reform should not just be limited to the redistribution of functions between the existing departments, that is between the Lord Chancellor's Department, Home Office and Law Officers, but should involve the abolition of the office of Lord Chancellor. His detailed and well thought out model sees judicial service matters, that is appointment, promotion and discipline, being transferred to a body independent of government, the quasi-judicial functions of the Law Officers, in relation to law enforcement, being handed to an independent officer and a department of legal affairs being created, the functions of which would include establishing and maintaining comprehensive legal services, maintaining relations with the legal professions, overseeing the administration of the courts and being responsible for determining judicial salaries and the resources of the Crown Prosecution Service. The department would also be responsible for both criminal and civil law reform, civil rights, that is immigration law, passports, extradition, refugees and censorship, and recommendations regarding the prerogative of mercy and the release of prisoners on parole and licence, as well as having general oversight over government legislation and a duty to ensure that UK law complies with EC law and with Britain's international obligations. Among its miscellaneous responsibilities would be the Great Seal and letters patent, the Land Registry, the Public Records Office and the Official Solicitor. The Home Office would remain responsible for law and order and prisons.[37]

Whatever responsibilities are given to a ministry of justice or department of legal affairs, the creation of such a ministry would provide the opportunity to consider all the responsibilities of the LCD, the Home Office and Law Officers in total and to make a division which is logical and coherent, avoids any conflict of interest within a department, separates the judicial and executive arms of

---

[35] Ibid, col. 1263.
[36] In C. Anderson, *Unreliable Evidence.*
[37] R. Brazier, "Government and the Law", p. 74.

government, and aids the accountability process. It is unlikely that the LCD would figure in any new arrangements.

CONCLUSION

Developments such as the Human Rights Act and devolution make it unacceptable for the Lord Chancellor to sit as a judge. Once he ceases to sit, he will no longer have personal experience of those who seek judicial appointment and there will therefore be no reason for him to retain his responsibility for the system through which such appointments are made. In any case, questions must be asked about a minister appointing judges who will hear cases against the Government. Once he stops sitting as judge and appointing other judges, then he can no longer be head of the judiciary, as this role flows from the other two. Moreover, the incorporation of the European Convention on Human Rights raises questions about the constitutional validity of his remaining as head of a judiciary, which is concerned with upholding rights against a government of which he is a member.

This leaves him with the roles of member of the Cabinet, with responsibility for the administration of justice, and Speaker in the House of Lords. His executive responsibilities should transfer to a minister for justice, who is elected and responsible to the House of Commons. As far as his role as Speaker is concerned, this may cease if the House of Lords is reformed in line with the Wakeham report, for although this was not a recommendation of the Commission, a part-elected chamber may prefer to elect its own Speaker, particularly if the changed nature of the House means that he, or she, requires greater regulatory powers than those possessed by the Lord Chancellor. Alternatively, the Lord Chancellor may continue to hold the position of Speaker, as his sole responsibility, the Lord Chancellor therefore becoming an honorary post, a relic of constitutional history which is concerned with pomp and ceremony, silk stockings and wigs, but not with the exercise of executive or judicial power.

The office of Lord Chancellor has long been controversial. During the closing decades of the twentieth century, the nature and extent of the Lord Chancellor's executive responsibilities, his role at the centre of government and the constitutional reforms of the Labour Government, in which he played a major part, have made his position unsustainable. He "cannot radically change everything around him and remain untouched himself".[38] It is time for him to make one further reform, which will consign the office of Lord Chancellor to history.

---

[38] M. Berlins, *A Man for All Roles*.

Bibliography

Articles and Books

Abel, R., "Between Market and state: The Legal Profession in Turmoil" 1989 52 *Modern Law Review* 285.

Abel-Smith, B. and Stevens, R., *Lawyers and the Courts* (London, Heineman, 1967).

—— —— *In Search of Justice* (London, Allen Lane, the Penguin Press, 1968).

Ackner, Lord, "More Power to the Executive?" (1998) 148 *New Law Journal* 1512.

Alsop, F. H., "A Ministry of Justice" (1975) *Law Society Gazette*, 29 January.

Anson, Sir William, *The Law and Custom of the Constitution*, Vol. II (4th edn., Oxford, Clarendon Press, 1935).

Atlay, J. B., *The Victorian Chancellors*, Vol. 1 (London, Smith, Elder & Co., 1906).

Bagehot, W., *The English Constitution* (London, Fontana Press, 1963).

Bailey, S. H. and Gunn, M. J., *Smith and Bailey on the Modern English Legal System* (2nd edn., London, Sweet & Maxwell, 1991).

Baker, R. J. S., "The New Courts Administration: A Case for a Systems Theory Approach" (1974) 52 *Public Administration* 285–302.

Barker, A. (ed.), *Quangos in Britain* (London, Macmillan Press, 1982).

Bell, J., *Policy Arguments in Judicial Decisions* (Oxford, Clarendon Press, 1983).

Bellamy, R. and Greenaway, J., "New Right Conception of Citizenship" (1995) 30 *Government and Opposition* 4 at 483.

Benn, T., *Out of the Wilderness: Diaries 1963–67* (London, Arrow Books, 1988).

Birkenhead, Viscount, *Points of View* (London, 1922).

Blom-Cooper, L. and Drewry, G., *Final Appeal: A Study of the House of Lords* (Oxford, Clarendon Press, 1972).

Box, M., *Rebel Advocate; a Biography of Gerald Gardiner* (London, Victor Gollancz, 1983).

Bradley, A., "The Parliamentary Ombudsman Again" [1995] *Public Law* 345.

Bradley, A. W., "Judges and the Media – the Kilmuir Rules" [1986] *Public Law* 384.

—— and Ewing, K. D., *Constitutional and Administrative Law* (11th edn., London, Longman, 1993).

Bradney, A., "The Judicial Activity of the Lord Chancellor 1946–87: A Pellet" (1989) 16 *Journal of Law and Society* 360.

Brazier, R., "Government and the Law" [1989] *Public Law* 64.

—— *Constitutional Practice* (Oxford, Clarendon Press, 1990).

Browne-Wilkinson, Sir Nicolas, "The Independence of the Judiciary in the 1980s" [1988] *Public Law* 44–57.

Campbell, John Lord, *Lives of the Lord Chancellors* (5th edn., Oxford, 1868).

Crossman, R., *The Diaries of a Cabinet Minister*, Vol. 1 (London, Hamish Hamilton, 1975).

Denning, Lord, *The Road to Justice* (London, Butterworths, 1955).

—— *The Due Process of Law* (London, Butterworths, 1980).

Drewry, G., *Law, Justice and Politics* (2nd edn., Essex, Longman, 1981).
—— *The Lord Chancellor as Judge* (London, Macmillan, 1982).
—— "Lord Haldane"s Ministry of Justice; Stillborn or Strangled at Birth?" (1983) 61 *Public Administration* 396–414.
—— "The Debate about a Ministry of Justice – a Joad's-eye view" [1987] *Public Law* 502.
—— "Judicial Independence in Britain; Challenges Real and Threats Imagined" in P. Norton (ed.), *New Directions in British Politics* (Aldershot, Edwin Elgar, 1991).
—— "Justice and Public Administration; Some Constitutional Tensions" (1992) 42 *Current Legal Problems* 2, 187–212.
—— "Ministers, Parliament and the Courts" (1992) 142 *New Law Journal* 6535, p. 50.
—— "Judicial Independence in Britain; Challenges Real and Threats Imagined" in R. Blackburn (ed.), *Constitutional Studies* (London, Mansell, 1992).
—— "Judicial Appointments" [1998] *Public Law* 1–7.
Egan, D., *Irvine: Politically Correct?* (Edinburgh, Mainstream Publishing, 1999).
Elwyn-Jones, Lord, *In My Time; an Autobiography* (London, Futura, 1988).
Griffith, J. A. G., *The Politics of the Judiciary* (4th edn., London, Fontana Press, 1991).
Hailsham, Lord, "Problems of a Lord Chancellor" (Holdsworth Lecture 1972) in B. Harvey (ed.), *The Lawyer and Justice* (London, Sweet & Maxwell, 1978).
—— "The Office of Lord Chancellor and the Separation of Powers" (1989) *Civil Justice Quarterly* 308–18.
—— *The Door Wherein I Went*, (London, Collins, 1975).
—— *A Sparrow's Flight* (London, Collins, 1990).
Hailsham, Viscount, "The Duties of a Lord Chancellor" (Holdsworth Lecture 1936) in B. Harvey (ed.), *The Lawyer and Justice* (London, Sweet & Maxwell, 1978).
Haldane, R. B., An Autobiography in S. H. Bailey and M. J. Gunn, *Smith and Bailey on the Modern English Legal System*.
Harlow, C. and Rawlings, R., *Law and Administration* (2nd edn., London, Weidenfeld and Nicolson,1997).
Hayes, J., "The plum jobs all went to men" (1999) *The Times*, 29 June.
Heuston, R. F. V., *Lives of the Lord Chancellors 1885–1940* (Oxford, Clarendon Press, 1964).
—— "The Office of Lord Chancellor" (1970) 86 *Law Quarterly Review* 33.
—— *Lives of the Lord Chancellors 1940–1970* (Oxford, Clarendon Press, 1987).
Hewart, Lord, *The New Despotism* (New York, Cosmopolitan Book Corp., 1929).
Hood Phillips, O., "A Constitutional Myth; Separation of Powers" (1977) 93 *Law Quarterly Review* 11.
Irvine, Lord, "Judges and Decision Makers: the Theory and Practice of *Wednesbury* Review" [1996] *Public Law* 59.
—— *Speech to the Lord Mayor's Dinner for Her Majesty's Judges* (Mansion House, London, July 1997).
—— *Speech to the Lord Mayor's Dinner for Her Majesty's Judges* (Mansion House, London, July 2000).
Jackson, R. M., *The Machinery of Justice in England* (7th edn., Cambridge, Cambridge University Press, 1977).
Jenkins, R., *Gladstone* (London, Macmillan, 1995).
Jowell, J. and Oliver, D. (eds.),*The Changing Constitution* (3rd edn., Oxford, Clarendon Press, 1994).

Kilmuir, Lord, "Office of the Lord Chancellor" (1956) 9 *Parliamentary Affairs* 132.

Kilmuir, Earl of, *Memoirs: Political Adventure* (London, Weidenfeld and Nicolson, 1962).

—— *In My Life* (London, Allen Lane, 1968).

Laski, H. J., "The Techniques of Judicial Appointments" in *Studies in Law and Politics* (1932).

Lawson, *The View from No. 11 – Memoirs of a Tory Radical* (London, Corgi, 1993).

Lee, S., *Judging the Judges* (London, Faber and Faber, 1988).

Lewis, D., *Hidden Agendas* (London, Hamish Hamilton, 1996).

Lewis, G., *Lord Hailsham: A Life* (London, Pimlico, 1998).

Mackay, Lord, "The Lord Chancellor in the 1990s" (1991) 44 *Current Legal Problems* 241–59.

—— *The Administration of Justice* (Hamlyn Lecture, 1994).

—— "The Lord Chancellor's Role within Government" (1995) 145 *New Law Journal* 6719, pp. 1650–53.

Macmillan, H., *Riding the Storm 1956–59*, (London, Macmillan, 1971).

—— *At the End of the Day* (London, Macmillan, 1973).

Maitland, F. W., *The Constitutional History of England* (Cambridge, Cambridge University Press, 1965).

Marshall, G. (ed.), *Ministerial Responsibility* (Oxford, Oxford University Press, 1989).

Mitchell, R. C., *Chronicle of English Judges, Chancellors, Attorneys General and Solicitors General* (Oswego, N.Y., W. P. Mitchell, 1937).

Morrison, F., *Courts and the Political Process in England* (London, Sage, 1973).

Oliver, D., "Politicians and the Courts" (1988) 41 *Parliamentary Affairs* 1.

—— "Pepper v. Hart; a suitable case for reference to Hansard?" [1993] *Public Law* 5.

—— "The Lord Chancellor's Department" [1994] *Public Law* 163.

Pannick, D., *The Judges* (Oxford, Oxford University Press, 1988).

Paterson, A., *The Law Lords* (London, Macmillan, 1982).

Paterson, A. and Bates, St. John, *The Legal System in Scotland* (2nd edn., Edinburgh, Green, 1986).

Patterson, C. P., *The Administration of Justice in Great Britain* (Austin, Texas, University of Texas, 1936).

Philipsborn, C., "Closed Whitehall cynicism must shift" (1996) 10 *The Lawyer* 18, p. 9.

Polden, P., *Guide to the Records of the Lord Chancellor's Department* (London, HMSO, 1988).

Purchas, Sir Francis, "The Constitution in the Market Place" (1993) 143 *New Law Journal* 6624, pp. 1604–9.

—— "Lord Mackay and the Judiciary" (1994) 144 *New Law Journal* 6644, pp. 527–30.

—— "What is Happening to Judicial Independence?" (1994) 144 *New Law Journal* 6665, pp. 1306–10.

Ridley, F. F., and Wilson, D. (eds.), *The Quango Debate* (Oxford, OUP, 1995).

Robson, W. A., *Justice and Administrative Law* (3rd edn., London, Stevens, 1951).

Rozenberg, J., *The Search for Justice* (London, Sceptre, 1994).

Samuels, A., "Do we need a Ministry of Justice?" (1971) *New Law Journal*, 11 February, p. 111.

Samuels, A., "Appointing the Judges" (1984) 134 *New Law Journal* 6139.

Scott, I. R., "The Council of Judges in the Supreme Court of England and Wales" [1989] *Public Law* 379–88.

Sedley, Sir Stephen, "The Sound of Silence: Constitutional Law without a Constitution" (1994) 110 *Law Quarterly Review* 270–91.

Shetreet, S., *Judges on Trial; A Study on the Appointment and Accountability of the English Judiciary* (Amsterdam, North Holland Publishing, 1976).

Shuster, Lord, "The Office of Lord Chancellor" [1949] *CLJ* 175 at 177.

Smith, R., "Strategy, Management and Politics" (1994) 144 *New Law Journal* 6648, p. 670.

—— "The Lord Chancellor under the Spotlight" (1998) 148 *New Law Jounral* 6822.

Stevens, R., *Law and Politics: The House of Lords as a Judicial Body 1800–1976* (London, Chapel Hill, 1983).

—— *The Independence of the Judiciary; the View from the Lord Chancellor's Office* (Oxford, Clarendon Press, 1997).

—— "Judges, Politicians and the Confusing Role of the Judiciary" in K. Hawkins (ed.), *The Human Face of Law* (Oxford, Clarendon Press, 1997).

Steyn, Lord, "The Weakest and Least Dangerous Department of Government" [1997] *Public Law* 84–95.

Thatcher, M., *The Downing Street Years* (London, Harper Collins, 1993).

Theakston, *Junior Ministers in British Government*, (Oxford, Blackwells, 1987).

Turpin, C., *British Government and the Constitution* (3rd edn., London, Butterworths, 1999).

Underhill, N., *The Lord Chancellor* (Lavenham, Suffolk, Terence Dalton, 1978).

Vile, M. J. C., *Constitutionalism and Separation of Powers* (Oxford, Oxford University Press, 1967).

Wade, H. W. R., and Forsyth, C. F., *Administrative Law* (7th edn., Oxford, Clarendon Press, 1994).

Weiler, P., "Two Models of Judicial Decision-Making" (1968) 46 *Canadian Bar Review* 406.

Wilson, H., "The County Courts in Limbo" (1994) 144 *New Law Journal* 1453.

Woodhouse, D., *Ministers and Parliament; Accountability in Theory and Practice* (Oxford, Clarendon Press, 1994).

—— "Politicians and the Judges; a Conflict of Interest" (1996) 49 *Parliamentary Affairs* 3.

Woodhouse, D., *In Pursuit of Good Administration; Ministers, Civil Servants and Judges* (Oxford, Clarendon Press, 1997).

Young, H., *One of Us* (London, Macmillan, 1990).

Radio Programmes

C. Anderson, *Unreliable Evidence* BBC Radio 4, 6 April 1999.

M. Berlins, *A Man for All Roles*, BBC Radio 4, 9 April 1998.

Official Publications

Cabinet Office, *A Memorandum of Guidance for Officials appearing before Select Committees* (1979) ("The Osmotherly Rules").

Cabinet Office, *Departmental Evidence and Response to Select Committees* (1997).

Committee on the Parliamentary Commissioner for Administration, *Report of the Parliamentary Commissioner for Administration* (1988–89) HC 159.

Committee on Standards in Public Life, *First Report* (1995) Cm. 2850

Court Service, *Framework Document* (1995).

—— *Annual Report* (1995–96) HC 492.

—— *Annual Report* (1996–97) HC 73.

—— *Three Year Plan* (1998–01).

Delegated Powers and Deregulation Committee, *Fifth Report*, (1998–99) HL 17.

Efficiency Unit, *Improving Management in Government; The Next Steps* (Report to the Prime Minister) (London, HMSO, 1988).

Home Affairs Committee, *The Prison Service* (1980–81) HC 412.

—— *The Work of the Lord Chancellor's Department* (1991–92) HC 214.

—— *Lord Chancellor's Department: Annual Report* (1992–93) HC 655.

—— *Lord Chancellor's Department: Annual Report* (1994–95) HC 399.

—— *Judicial Appointments Procedures* (1995–96) HC 52.

—— *Lord Chancellor's Department: Annual Report* (1995–96) HC 596.

—— *Home Office Annual Report* (1998–99) HC 653.

—— *The Work of the Lord Chancellor's Department* (1998–99) HC 882.

—— *Lord Chancellor's Department, Crown Prosecution Service, Home Office: Criminal Justice; Working Together* (1999–00) HC 29;

Liaison Committee, *The Work of Select Committees* (1996–97) HC 323.

Lord Chancellor's Department, *Judicial Appointments: the Lord Chancellor's Policies and Procedures* (May 1986; revised edn. 1995).

—— *Court Service Annual Report* (1992–93) HC 808.

—— *Strategic Plan 1994/95–1996/97* (1994).

—— *Court Service Annual Report* (1994–95) HC 579.

—— *StrategicPlan1996/97–1998/99* (1996).

—— *Business Plan 1996/97* (1996).

—— *Annual Report* (1997–98) HC 315.

—— *Judicial Appointments: Annual Report* (1998–99).

—— *Annual Report* (2000–2002).

National Audit Office, *Appropriation Accounts* (1998–9) Vol. 8: Class VIII, "Lord Chancellor's and Law Officers' Departments", HC 11.

Parliamentary Commissioner for Administration, *Sixth Report* (1998–99) HC 571.

—— *Seventh Report* (1998–99) HC 572.

Peach, Sir Leonard, *Report on the Scrutiny of Judicial Appointments and Queen's Counsel Selection Procedures* (1999).

Procedure Committee, *The Working of the Select Committee System* (1989–90) HC 19.

Public Administration Committee, Fourth Report, *Ministerial Accountability and Parliamentary Questions* (1997–98) HC 820.

—— Third Report, *Your Right to Know: The Government's Proposals for a Freedom of Information Act* (1997–98) HC 398.

—— Fourth Report, *Ministerial Accountability and Parliamentary Questions,* (1998–99) HC 821.

Public Service Committee, Second Report, *Ministerial Accountability and Responsibility* (1995–96) HC 313.

Treasury and Civil Service Committee, *The Civil Service Management Reforms: The Next Steps* (1988–89) HC 494.

—— *Developments in the Next Steps Programme* (1988–89) HC 348.
—— *Progress in the Next Steps Initiative* (1989–90) HC 481.
—— *The Role of the Civil Service: Interim Report* (1992–93) HC 390.
—— *The Role of the Civil Service* (1993–94) HC 27.
Scott, Sir Richard, *Report of the Inquiry into the Export of Defence Equipment and Dual-Use Goods to Iraq and Related Prosecutions* (1995–96) HC 115.
Wakeham, Lord, *Report of the Royal Commission on the Reform of the House of Lords: A House for the Future* (2000) Cm. 4534.

Additional Command Papers

The Work and Organisation of the Legal Profession (1989) Cm. 570.
Contingency Fees (1989) Cm. 571.
Conveyancing by Authorised Practitioners (1989) Cm. 572.
Legal Aid; Targeting Need (1995) Cm. 2854.
Striking the Balance: The Future of Legal Aid in England and Wales (1996) Cm. 3305.

Index